MAKING IT
in high heels
3

Innovators and Trailblazers

Edited by Sheyla Abdic

Published by BurmanBooks Inc.
260 Queens Quay West
Suite 1102
Toronto, Ontario
Canada M5J 2N3

Cover design: Eric Zerkel
Interior design: Jack Steiner
Editing: Sheyla Abdic
Proofreader: T. U. Dawood

Distribution:
TruMedia Group LLC
575 Prospect Street, Suite 301
Lakewood, NJ 08701

Printed and bound in The United States of America.

ISBN 978-1-927005-32-3

Dedication

To all the women trying their best to make it in this world,
don't give up.
Everyone in this book participated because
they want you to succeed.

Please visit

www.makingitinhighheels.com

Table of Contents

1

Zulekha Nathoo

I had never carried a suitcase that heavy before. If only it was just full of clothes and shoes. Not even close. Dried pasta, bags of rice, soup cans, a flashlight—anything my mom could shove in, convinced I would find myself in some sort of emergency in Nairobi. I barely managed to lift the tattered thing before I let it drop on the scale at the airport. Please, don't be overweight. I'd be lucky if the old black bag, which had way too many threads hanging loose to be used in public at all, made it all the way to Africa. I pictured, instead, the zipper breaking half way through the trip and all of my underwear mixed with leaking chicken noodle soup whirring around a baggage carousel when I arrived. Unfortunately, there would be no denying it was mine; my mom had also attached several handwritten pieces of paper with my name written in large, dark letters in case someone tried to steal it.

As we walked toward the gate, my parents kept reminding me not to drink the water; to wash every single piece of fruit with soap and to clutch my purse tightly, especially if I was walking alone. But hah! That was a trick statement, because really, I shouldn't be walking anywhere alone at all, they insisted. It was just too dangerous! And no matter how delicious it smells, don't eat the food from street vendors! Unless I wanted to risk an E-coli infection, or salmonella, or worse!

She held me tighter than usual as we said goodbye. My dad kissed me on both cheeks, said a prayer over my forehead and reluctantly, let me go.

I was going to the one country my parents had vowed never to return to.

The place they fled thirty years before, because politics and independence had plunged Kenya into chaos, unraveling the health and education systems, as well as the economy.

They left behind a successful business, friends and family, and all their happy memories, so their two daughters would live a better life in North America.

And now, one of their daughters was going back, leaving them to wonder why they made all those sacrifices.

And me, desperately hoping my gut was right on this one.

My decision at the age of 28 to move to Nairobi, Kenya, a city labeled one of the most dangerous in the world for its poverty, crime and corruption, is not even close to the beginning of my story. But it's a good place to start. It tells you a lot about me and what I believe has helped me get to where I am today. Namely, that learning to trust my instincts has been the hardest work with the biggest reward; that there are people who helped me climb to remarkable places of growth and opportunity, simply because I let them; and that at the end of the day, the only person ever standing in my way, is myself.

I wasn't trying to rebel against my parents or do something risky just for the sake of it. That's not why I uprooted my whole life to live on another continent for a year. I went, because a little voice inside me insisted I didn't know enough about where my family was from; or enough about the world I was reporting on every day as a journalist. A voice that had been there for years, but had stopped whispering and instead, started using a bullhorn to get the message across.

Let me go back a little, so you get a better idea of what led me to this point in my life.

I grew up in Calgary, Alberta, Canada, in a suburb that today we might call "racially homogenous", but back then, we just called *very white*.

I was one of five visible minorities in my elementary school.

On the first day, we all had to identify where our parents were from so our teacher could put a little pin on a map, which would stay up for the rest of the school year. The map was only of Europe, which worked fine for most of the class. But when my turn came, the teacher was so stumped as to where East Africa was, that she simply grabbed a marker and put a little star on the top right corner of the map, which, by now, was full of colorful tacks. It was as isolated as I felt. Incidentally, it was also in the opposite direction of Africa.

My teachers all pronounced my name Zoo-LEEK-ah, and I never corrected them, because I convinced myself they knew better what my name was than I did, which meant I spent the next six years answering to the wrong name.

And at least once a month, a fellow student, sometimes even younger than me, would shove past and yell "Paki" at the top of his or her lungs.

At that age, I thought all my problems would be solved if only I looked the same as everyone else.

If only my parents were from Britain or Ireland, rather than countries like Kenya and Tanzania, which no one had ever heard of and could barely pronounce.

But there's a point when you have to stop wanting to be someone else, and start accepting who you are.

For me, that didn't come until high school.

I had a lot of friends, but won't even try to pretend I had grown into a tall, pretty, exotic teenager.

I was 5 foot 3, but only when I stood with my back completely straight. I lost all my height genes to my older sister, who is a statuesque 5'10".

I was not considered the pretty one in my clique. My thick hair took the form of a perfect pyramid, ending squarely at my chin. Even today, I'm embarrassed to admit that style was courtesy of my dad, who insisted he could cut it "just like in a salon." Sadly, I believed him.

I was also unaware that I needed a good eyebrow tweezing, if only so I could finally have two.

I was never allowed to wear makeup. My mom was a big proponent of inner beauty, as mothers should be. But in order to sell the idea to her daughters eager to look more grown up, she managed to convince us from a young age that putting on lipstick would permanently discolor and shrivel up our lips beyond recognition and that the rest of the public just didn't know it yet. Of all the fallacies I challenged as a kid that, surprisingly, was not one of them.

But since I never relied on my looks to make friends or win over boys, I was instead the smart one and funny one, who could tell a great story.

I was in the debating club, drama club and speech club.

Any group that let me spend hours talking, arguing and entertaining was perfect for me.

I volunteered at shelters, concerts and even sports camps.

I worked at the Gap for a little extra pocket money. And to this day, I still fold my shirts into a perfect square.

I liked anything that got me involved with different people, different perspectives and new ideas.

I had a big voice with even bigger opinions. And it eventually got the attention of someone who gave me my first gig.

The Calgary newspaper was starting a teenager section, and wanted me to write for them.

I could write about anything that I wanted to.

And so, I wrote about what most 16-year-old girls might: fashion.

Despite my lack of personal grooming, fashion had become a passion of mine.

So I interviewed fashion designers, talked to store owners and read magazines.

Every week, I faxed in a story to the newsroom. Yes, that's right—faxed. It was the 1990s.

And seeing my name in print—what I would only later find out was actually called a "byline"—got me hooked.

Journalism with its questions, writing, and final presentation, combined everything I was interested in, and good at.

I was doing it for free as a kid, but it's also how I decided I wanted to make my living as an adult.

You might find it a little odd then, that when it came time for University acceptances and I found out I got into journalism school, I turned it down. I decided instead to study History. I told myself having a foundation of world understanding was essential to accurate reporting. And in hindsight, I truly believe that. But I'd be dishonest if I didn't share the real reason I said no to journalism school and why I didn't even bother to join the University newspaper or campus radio station.

It's not because I didn't want the experience or a taste of what my future might hold.

In fact, that's exactly why I didn't join.

I was *petrified* I'd fail at it.

What would happen if I wasn't any good at the one thing I wanted to do with my life?

What if my writing sucked in the real world, outside the safety of high school, and nobody cared about what I had to say?

What if other people, who didn't even want it as badly, were better at the job than me?

I'd be mortified.

It was much easier to SAY I wanted to be a journalist when people asked, knowing full well I would end up in a much simpler, more comfortable job.

I mean, how many people actually end up doing exactly what they wanted to do growing up?

Not many. It was time for me to forget those pipe dreams and move on to a more realistic career.

And so, self-doubt engulfed me and I stayed away from writing anything other than University papers, tests, and journal entries.

As my University years went by, I seemed to forget what made me so happy in high school, and the self-assurance I once felt was slowly dwindling. I convinced myself I had just changed my mind, and that very few people succeed in the newspaper business, let alone in broadcast anyway.

I graduated from History with Honours and got a job as a social auditor with Correctional Services Canada.

I went to different prisons across the country, to check whether the staff was following the rules; making sure inmates got their showers, their exercise and education.

A typical government job with a good pay cheque and lots of chances to travel across the country.

Along the way, I had a first-hand look at the files of some of the worst criminals in Canada.

But also, of people who had made one mistake. One mistake that changed the entire course of their lives and landed them in jail for months, or years.

It was flipping through those files one day, on an audit, that I started to realize how many of the men and women I was reading about were in their twenties. Some, in their late teens even. They were close to the same age as me.

Some of them, from the same sleepy town as me, where crime seemed to be non-existent.

One turning point had changed their lives completely. But I wondered if another turning point could change their lives once more, and possibly for the better.

Not everyone gets a second-chance, and not everyone deserves one. But if they did, maybe some of these inmates could surprise themselves and succeed at things they never thought possible.

And that's how being inside a prison helped me break free of one I had created for myself.

The following day, I began filling out an application to get into Journalism school.

New fears quickly arose the minute I started filling out the forms. I had no samples of any journalism work. No resume-builders like internships or a good reference from someone in the business. Essentially, I was screwed. I was applying to a masters-level program that accepted forty people from the entire country. And all I had to show for it were a couple of articles written in the Calgary newspaper when I was 16 years old.

I hoped that my entrance essay, which re-visited the dreams I held as a young child, would somehow win them over.

But I wasn't holding my breath.

I promised myself after I sent the application that if I got in, I would use it as a constant reminder that destiny is a force not to be messed with. That it has the best intentions for us, but sometimes that means getting out of its way so it can do its own work. When I got the call that I had been accepted to one of the best schools in the country, and told that it was my unique specialty in history and even more unique job in prisons that won them over, I reminded myself that the universe really does work in mysterious ways. And that I am the only person standing in the way of what I want to achieve. Moving aside was the best thing I had done in a long time.

As it turns out, only a handful of the people who graduated from the Journalism program with me went on to become working journalists. A few went into newspapers, and as far as I can see, maybe two or three are successfully working in broadcast. Most went into Public Relations almost immediately, seen as the "dark side" for journalists, but really, it's often the smarter choice: easier work, better hours, and definitely better pay. But I wasn't about to fall back into old patterns and choose the more comfortable route. Which is how I found myself once again, living in a small town. But this time, it wasn't nearly as big as my hometown, which now seemed gargantuan in comparison. Bathurst, New Brunswick was less than half the population of my previous University campus.

Looking back, I believe the ones who made it had a few things in common. We were willing to endure long hours at the bottom of the ladder if it meant we would be anywhere close to a newsroom. We also saw the pathetic comedy of *being* at the bottom of the ladder even after getting a Masters degree. And we knew that if we were going to get any credibility, we had to start in a small market and pay our dues.

Bathurst is a tiny coastal city in eastern Canada where moose roam the backroads, people's homes are either "up river" or down river", and if you had a bad breakup, stay away from the one nightclub in town on Friday nights, because that's where every person under the age of 50 goes to dance and flirt. "Give 'er" is the most popular saying there, referring to everything from drinking whiskey to revving an engine to trying to squeeze into a tight pair of jeans. I believe I was one of about three people who weren't white in that town. And while I stuck out like a sore thumb everywhere I walked, I also made it my mission over the two years I lived there to blend in and make a life for myself. I had no family. No friends. And no idea how I was going to survive in my new job: to shoot, report and edit my own stories for television every night. I applied for the job to get my foot in the door to the largest news outlet in Canada, thinking I had no chance of getting it. And now, I was moving to the other side of the country AND into a job I had never done before. I was so far out of my comfort zone that I wasn't sure I could do it at all.

But those are often the times you realize just what you're made of—and quickly. Within a matter of months, I adjusted to the icy driving conditions.

I got used to the busy grind of working alone to produce a news story every night for the evening newscast. And the painful realization that clothes shopping was no longer going to happen unless I was prepared to build a wardrobe from items sold at SAAN and that, I was not.

I also knew that if I was going to stick to my two-year commitment in this place, I needed to make some friends. And fast. I was lucky enough that while I was there, an entire cohort of people my age were also living there, most originally from the city, but who had left for work or school until they ran out of money and were now trying to figure out what to do with their lives. Their post-schooling crises became my gain. I instantly made friends with an entire core group of twentysomethings. Dawn, the travelling hippie, who had worked her way to each corner of the world and was using her parents' home in Bathurst as a pit-stop in between travels. Travis, the University grad, who was trying to save enough to work abroad by waiting tables at the Marina bar. Robert, the graphic designer, who taught me how to snowboard, how to make sushi, and how to ride a scooter. And Renee, the well-connected, perfectly bilingual civil servant, who had a sharp sense of humor and a heart of gold. I had hoped to make some pals who might help pass the time, but I ended up with life-long friendships that eventually made my departure two years later much harder than I expected.

Still, when a reporter job opened up in Calgary, I couldn't ignore the opportunity or the signs. In the last two years of working in the Maritimes, I had gained a new identity. I had developed a confidence in my writing and on-air presentation. I had found a group of friends that filled my weekends with entertainment and a healthy amount of trouble-making. And reading by the bay on a summer day had become my ideal way to spend an afternoon. You might say, it was the place I found *myself.* I was ready for a change, but not so sure I wanted the big-city lifestyle I had once coveted.

Moving home after I got the job was not as easy as I thought it would be. I had been away from home for nearly 10 years. And returning back to the city where I was born and raised made me feel like I never left. I ran into friends on the street, who had stayed after high school, and I had nothing in common with them anymore. Many had settled into a life working as accountants, actuaries or engineers. Married. Ready to have kids. A perfectly normal and suitable life choice. But worlds apart from the one I wanted for myself.

And so, I threw myself into my work once again. Anytime a big story broke—murders, car crashes, gang shootings—I volunteered to cover the story. I worked overtime and weekends to prove I could handle the job.

I started filling in as an anchor for the evening news. And when I wasn't at work, I was partying with the friends I had managed to get along with. Boyfriends came and went. And in my down time, I was travelling abroad. It wasn't a bad life, living in my newly-purchased downtown condo, being in close proximity to my aging parents when they needed anything, and working in a market that was growing tremendously. I was, for all intents and purposes, living the dream I had set out to achieve back in high school.

But a funny thing happens when you catch yourself attaining a goal, perhaps earlier than anticipated. Rather than patting myself on the back, I started to wonder if I had set the bar too low for myself. I began to wonder if, after all this time, I was capable of so much more than I was allowing myself to pursue.

I thought Calgary was going to be the end of a long road. But I was starting to realize, it was only the beginning.

And that's how I ended up at the airport, on the way to Nairobi, Kenya.

I came across a fellowship that was offering a one year position to report overseas in East Africa. At first, it sounded crazy. I couldn't leave my steady pay cheque, my mortgage, my job, my LIFE to leave the country at the age of twenty-eight, when I was already starting to feel the social pressures of 'settling down'!

Still, I found myself thinking about the opportunity every night before I went to sleep. And every morning. Maybe I could try to rent out my place? Maybe I could take an unpaid leave from my job? After all, reporting abroad would only make me a better journalist when I came back. The more I rationalized the decision in my head, the more I realized I had made up my mind for real. I was ready to test my survival skills in another country. And I wanted to see the place my family was from. I applied for the position a day before the deadline, and told myself if everything fell into place, it was meant to be. I wouldn't try to force it, but I wouldn't stand in the way of making it work. And when I, once again, made the decision to get out of my *own* way, every piece fell into place. My workplace granted me a leave of absence, so I could come back to my job after a year. I found a tenant which made it easy to cover my mortgage costs. And after a long battle with my parents, who could not understand for the life of them why I wanted to go to the country they had tried to save me from when they immigrated to Canada, I set off on one of the wildest and most fulfilling journeys of my life.

Nairobi is a city of contrasts. Everybody walks in completely non-linear directions on the sidewalk, and yet, nobody ever bumps into each other. Yet, if you walk in a perfectly straight line on one side of the road, you'll likely get in everyone's way. Pedestrian crossings are clearly marked. But cars speed up, rather than slow down, when they see people walking. I'm convinced it's for the sheer pleasure of watching people bolt out of the way in record time. And even though temperatures hover near 22 degrees Celsius every day of the year, on the few days they drop by a few degrees, you'll see people sporting big jackets and boots at the same time that I'm wearing a T-shirt.

The good thing about being a foreigner is that your eyes see things locals have simply become immune to. And that becomes a lifeline when trying to find good stories as a journalist.

I was able to spot ideas simply because I was looking at everything with a fresher and more critical eye. But when you're in a country that's not your own, you also have to be careful not to impose your own standards and values on the people you're working with. Cultural sensitivity becomes extremely important.

I learned that on my first day, when, after a news conference was held by a Minister, every journalist in the room was given cash by his staff. "It's for tea", was what I was told by a colleague. In reality, it was a bribe. And I had to get used to being the only reporter in the room, who would say no each time they were handed out.

Still, I learned to love the work itself. Stories on corruption, environment and mass killings were almost an everyday occurrence. And unlike in Canada, where a slow news day consisted of being stuck on a weather story or the latest pothole in your community, a slow news day in Nairobi didn't exist. There was too much crime, not enough police and on the brighter side, a lot of people trying to make a difference.

I did exposés on poor health conditions, on women's rights, meeting a young girl who was able to escape an arranged marriage to an 81 year old man, and even climbed one of the biggest mountains in Africa to help raise money for famine relief.

I learned to accept the stares each time I took public transit with everyone else, rather than a taxi, as foreigners typically do.

I became proficient at bargaining in Swahili so I wouldn't get swindled at the markets.

And whenever the car horns, loud music and petty crime became too much to handle, I could get away pretty easily, since Nairobi is a major hub for travel.

From Kampala to Cairo, Capetown to Zanzibar, I saw all the places my parents had spoken of for years. I met family I had never known before, who became my guides to the past, showing me my family's old house and roots. I couldn't wait for our weekly phone calls to share what I was learning. Every day, I would open my bedroom curtains and look out at the palm trees illuminated by a glorious sun that rose and set at the same time each day.

I was living a life that certainly wasn't for everyone. But for me, it was a dream come true. And for the first time in my life, I wasn't worried about reaching another goal. I was savoring every moment for what it was.

The people I worked with were my best guides to good stories, good food, and good nightlife. I never expected to make the friendships I did while there, but you might notice a pattern by now. Each time I was convinced I had little in common with the people I was going to encounter, I ended up sharing so much more with them than I ever expected.

The day I landed back in Calgary, I saw my parents very differently. They weren't just the rule-makers anymore. In fact, quite the opposite. They broke all the rules of their own life to make a better one for my sister and me. I saw what they had left behind and what they gave up. I saw their favorite streets and restaurants. The place they first met and where they got married. Their serene weekend getaway and the lush trees and flowers that fill the air with sweet aromas. The hospital where my older sister was born and the gardens she played in. Not long after, our family dinner conversations grew richer. I started to ask more questions, and they shared more personal stories about their previous life. And as hard as it was for them to let me go there, they knew I had come back understanding them—and myself—so much better. Most of all, I learned that I wasn't the only one who had broken free from comfort zones. My parents had done the exact same thing a generation ago. And every opportunity I have had since was a direct result of that big decision they made.

Now, it was time to make my own. I could go back to my hometown and my job, satisfied that I had explored my roots and pushed my limits as a journalist. Or I could take what I learned, and at great risk to my comfortable self, try to achieve a new set of goals—unsure whether it would work out.

I knew which road was easier.

And I also knew which road I was meant to take.

Moving to Toronto—Canada's biggest city—was one of those turning points that even today, when I think back, changed my direction in life. And only now can I say with certainty it was for the better.

It was a calculated risk.

I left behind my friends, my cushy lifestyle and my familiar job.

I was also taking a leap of faith. After years of heartache and bad relationships, I had met my match. I had met the person with whom I wanted to spend the rest of my life—and he was based in Toronto.

When I moved, I banked on the fact that I could rely on my professional track record, a positive spirit and a little bit of luck to get my foot into the country's largest media market.

All of the major networks are based in Toronto so it's your best shot at climbing beyond local, and into national news.

But it's also much easier to get pushed aside, because there are about ten other people willing to take your place if you make a mistake.

I thought my previous experience would be recognized right away.

What I didn't realize is that the moment you hit a market as big as this one, it doesn't matter how much experience you have. Most of the time, you're starting from scratch.

I was a small-town fish in a very big pond, and it was sink or swim.

And so I became relentless.

I had meetings and coffee dates to make sure every manager I knew was aware I had moved and need a job.

I took every shift I could, at times working 15 hour days, very early mornings, and overnight.

I went through weeks where the only time I came home was to sleep and change clothes before starting again.

I was exhausted, discouraged, and left to question whether I had made the right decision. Maybe I wasn't cut out for this life after all.

What had I done?

But soon, things started to change.

I started reporting on the streets every day, and eventually, on some of the biggest stories in the country.

My years on the East coast and West side of the country helped me become a geographical go-to person when it came to national breaking news.

And the confidence you can get only through years of hard work in the field, shined through each time I was assigned a big story.

I had arrived. And even though I felt like I had to start from the bottom all over again, there was something I didn't realize had happened.

All the years I had spent honing my journalistic talent had culminated to where I was today.

It was in those years that I learned how to handle any curveball, tell any story, and ask any question to get the answers I needed.

Each city had taught me something new—about work and about myself.

So by the time I got to the big pond, I might have still been a small-town fish. But I was the fastest swimmer I could be, and knew what it took to stay afloat.

Eventually, talent will always be recognized, but the first step is recognizing it in yourself. And that's often the hardest part.

Zulekha Nathoo now works as a national arts and entertainment reporter for CBC-TV. After years of moving around and putting her career first, she is now also learning the importance of balance in life. Zulekha recently got engaged to the love of her life and continues to enjoy the hidden gems of world travel and the feeling of home she has found in Toronto, Ontario, Canada.

2 Liliane Sibonney

S chool was always a bit of a tricky subject for me, as I never really felt too challenged in the public school system. Finding myself constantly bored and looking to get into trouble, I found numerous ways to skip classes and sneak away to the local coffee shop to smoke cigarettes and play cards. I did everything in my power to rebel when it came to my education. High school was already complicated enough figuring out which crowd to hang out with, where to eat lunch, how to avoid getting sent to the office for constant lates and no-shows, let alone trying to achieve a streak of perfect D grades on all classes I didn't already drop out of. I guess you could say I was a bit of an 'underachiever' in school—making friends with all the A+ students to get me through with missed homework was just one of the loopholes I was accustomed to. My teachers always felt me to be a class clown, someone who didn't take things too seriously, and was "not working up to her full potential". That's all true. I failed Math and Science all the time, and after trying three times I eventually gave up. I was always finding little tricks to just get me by and part of my fun in school was getting pushed through the system; contributing the very minimum in all aspects and still advancing to the next grade. A social life is always compromising for teenagers so trying to get a boy to notice you, not forgetting your combination on your locker, and getting invited to the cool kids' parties, were bigger priorities of mine those days.

I never really had a passion or some idea of what direction I was going to head in after dropping out of school. I always fancied being a lawyer as I thought reasoning was a strong point of mine. I toyed with the idea of massage therapy as I always felt like a bit of a healer, wanting to make people feel good in some way—but my subpar average in Biology proved a Science background was not going to do me right with five years of post secondary school education.

One thing that really excited me was dining in fine dining restaurants. I got inspired by chefs and ingredients. Food, to me, became a form of art I never got to experience in school or at home. Coming from a Moroccan background, my mother was a great cook. But she was the kind of home chef who didn't like to share her space and the kitchen was off grounds when she was doing her magic. As my mother was a working fashion designer, I had a full time live-in nanny. Being of Filipino origin, she introduced me to all things Asian. I spent a lot of time eating things foreign to me, fearlessly. I wasn't like many kids who lived on a grilled cheese and macaroni diet—I had tried some really bizarre stuff, which to this day questions why and how.

Familiarizing myself with the tastes of caviar, truffles and other exotic expensive ingredients I was spoiling my taste buds with each weekend, I decided to take the culinary plunge. At this point of my life I had maybe made myself a few omelets, but I can't say I had ever been cooking from a young age. I was more of a mini *sous* chef all of my life sub-consciously. While job shadowing my dad since birth, some of his real estate property tenants owned restaurants. While he had a slew of errands to run I convinced him to leave me behind with the chefs who all gave me mundane jobs to do like opening cans of tomatoes, and of course a lot of potato and carrot peeling. I guess eventually the smells and sounds of the restaurants got imbedded in my DNA, because I never let that mini chef go too far. One day, I decided to try and recreate a few dishes I had tasted in star rated restaurants. I headed to the markets, picked up what I needed, and just by touch and taste I recreated a few of the best things I had ever tasted. It was at that moment I realized I had been given a gift to cook and that dinner was just the beginning of what was to come.

Each summer I spent working with my father. He raised us to be little entrepreneurs like him and he had always been a role model of mine. Being daddy's little girl, I had always had a soft spot for Daddy and found myself working full days for him in his businesses and never receiving or even asking for a salary. I loved sales, interacting with clients and, of course, watching money come in. I always had a drive to work and felt satisfied when I was.

While sitting at the desk of my father's store I decided that my work efforts could extend to the outside world. I opened a newspaper, skimmed directly to the restaurant/hospitality section and in a neat outline was a little ad for a position available for kitchen help in Bermuda. I 'googled' Bermuda, because it was a country I didn't know much about, and upon discovering it was only two hours by plane from Toronto, and that it was covered in pink sands was enough for me to inquire within. I sent a copy of my resume and got an immediate response booking me in the city for an interview the following week. Upon meeting with my future boss, he told me I was over qualified but I convinced him that I was willing to accept the position, if for even just the life experience of travelling and living abroad. He agreed, and two months later, I was off to paradise. Working in Bermuda was lovely, and while not so career challenging, I was immediately noticed for my work ethic and offered many more lucrative positions. I ended up landing a job as the private chef for a politician and his family of six. I spent days off working on my menus, beachside and after work becoming acquainted with the locals. After two years, I started feeling the effects of island fever and had to get off the rock, so feeling reposed and inspired, I headed back to Toronto to the following career move, which changed my life. I am a believer that 'timing is everything' and upon my return was faced with that chance. My father's tenant of twelve years in historic Kensington market had decided to back out of their venture and before looking for someone to continue the lease my father asked me if I might be interested to venture into something with him. Already having spent years working together with him, I carefully considered the option. The opportunity to open my first restaurant as a chef and owner in the market surrounded by daily fresh ingredients made my decision easier. I quickly got started on my business plan. My father left all creative energy up to me, and with the help of a mason—the three of us and our six bare hands got quickly started on building Kensington's. My tribute to Kensington market established in 1918, the home to immigrants, once known as the Jewish market, Portuguese fish mongers, Kosher butchers, east Indian grocers and surrounded by Toronto's famous China town! The concept was a blend of the new hip and trend-setting locals, with a touch of its ancient roots. The menu was to be adorned with local, seasonal 'market inspired' ingredients. Any chef's dream, really. There were days when I literally waved out the window to my grocer across the street to send over a box of mixed greens. Kensington's gave me the responsibility of raising a child from birth. Open seven days a week, twelve hour days, watching the place grow, and expand, and double and then even triple in size. After the first year of being open, I took over the space next door, tore down the wall and the place just kept on growing. Eventually by year three, we were at a maximum capacity seating of seventy, from its original forty seats. As humble as Kensington's was, there was a lot of hard work, sweat, and difficult days, but still, I had to persevere. And I did. I built a good take-away service and catering platters to the surrounding offices. I built good business relationships with my suppliers, I had very loyal and faithful clients, who have become and remained friends. In my fifth year at Kensington's, while business was nearly working as a well oiled machine, I decided to take a personal challenge. After overseeing many industry magazines hosting culinary competitions, one day, I enrolled myself for a chef of the year competition held by Canadian Pizza Magazine. The attractive cash prize and first place offering a flight and a spot in the international sector in Las Vegas, I said there was little to lose by not trying. Sure, I am not a specialized Italian chef, but I have always viewed ingredients to be as versatile and interchangeable in all cuisines alike. Realizing the deadline was that very day, I threw together a quick outline of myself, boasting of my *jeunesse* as a female chef, and proprietor of a restaurant in the famed historic Kensington market, along with my three course menu respecting the rules of thirty chosen ingredients and five secret ingredients in the allotted ninety minute timeline. I spell checked and e-mailed it off to the editor of the magazine. Only hours later, I received a reply thanking me and with positive feedback saying that my entry really stood out from the others. Two weeks later, I received a phone call from them asking me for my chef coat size, and to congratulate me that I had won first place for Canada, and that the following month we would be off to Las Vegas to compete against seven other countries! I had never felt prouder, but also a bit anguished that if I was going to have to compete against these international chefs, I'd have to actually try and cook my menu! So I started training and testing out my recipes, timing myself and making adjustments to the seasonings and improving my technique with the help of family and friends to test the final products. I brought along my cousin to Vegas to play *sous* chef, because, while we never had cooked together, we both were passionate about food and I thought it would be fun to spend a few days in Sin City together. The competition was a blast. Day one was four face-offs of the chefs and of total scoring the top two highest scorers would compete on the next day. On day one I won first place for top scores, to be competing against Scotland in the cook-off the following morning. After foreseeing a lot of sabotage and chaos one might expect in any sort of competition and being the only female and youngest chef on the panel, I had to really rise above the expectations I had for myself. It was the first time I had ever competed, and my father who made it out to support me in the crowds was astonished by my skillfulness and presentability to the judges and filmed the whole thing on his camcorder, literally shocked that he left the lens cap on the whole time!! Day two, stakes were running high and Scotland chef and owner of 5 top European restaurants was making it his business to kick me out of the race. To his dismay, he came in second that day too. I won first place of the competition, and even being sabotaged to the last moment, we were guided that the announced winners would be held 2 hours later than they actually were! So when I arrived, they had already announced that I won, but I still collected my prize, did a few interviews, and smiled graciously for the cameras. It was a good moment. After returning home, with the title, and a spot to defeat my prize the following year, I went back to the swing of things at Kensington's. The media started to pick up on me and I received a few phone calls for TV and radio interviews and was featured on the six o'clock news by Jojo Chintoh for my title as Chef Of The Year. The media buzz continued and I thought to take advantage of the moment and contacted Food Network's Restaurant Makeover. I sold them on my story and situation as a young female entrepreneur, and they decided to grant my wish and give me a restaurant designed by a top designer and with consultation with a top chef and a new lease on the life of Kensington's. The show was a week of stress for my father as they ripped down everything we built from scratch and presented us with a beautiful, but not super functional TV set restaurant. We spent a following month closed to put things back in working order. The show was aired a month later and in 16 countries. The thing is, the episode has gotten a lot of recognition and they have not stopped airing it to this day. I still get e-mails from 'fans' all the time saying that they had seen the show aired and that I have either inspired them to follow their passion, or that they really enjoyed watching the relationship between my father and I. Of course, we followed the directions of the show to keep to their requirements and played a bit of actors, but the base of the truth was always there. After a few months, I decided seven years at Kensington's was enough for me, and the familial situation was really getting under my skin so I decided to spread my wings a bit further.

I decided to head to the sunshine state to refresh things and take a step back from working so hard and took the next flight out to South Florida. I ended up getting a job as a private chef and stayed for two years working on recipes, menus and catering to private events. It was a really fun time for me in my career and I explored many avenues and opportunities that arose. The biggest life changing moment occurred when I met my husband through mutual friends as he was in Miami on vacation. And back to the 'it's all about the timing' thing. He met me when I was on a bit of a hiatus and the economy in Florida had crashed. Having always been a risk taker, I decided to accept his advances. My husband is from Paris, France, and upon his return to the airport he made me promise I would visit. In a romantic love story kind of way, when he returned to France, he never stopped pursuing me and made me keep to my word. I ended up packing my condo up in boxes, and putting it in storage as a month later I followed him to Paris. I was unsure of what my future held in Florida, and did not know when I would return so I thought rather than signing a new lease for my flat, I'd pack it all up and deal with things when I returned to my life on the beach. When I arrived to Paris, my first overdue trip to Europe, he showed me the ins and outs of the magical city. I fell in love instantly, with the city and with my husband. I woke up every morning and ate fresh hot baguettes, and window shopping here meant something else when you were looking into the window of a patisserie. The mini cakes are art, and the food a religion. I felt like I was home. A city mixed of people, fashionable, and snobby—I fit right in like a hand in a glove. French was an easy barrier to overcome as I had studied it all my life and everything I learned came in handy just in time!

Two weeks later, he whisked me away to Thailand (another bucket list destination, I was able to check off) and we toured the country for three weeks. I ate my way through each city, and embraced all the culture and experiences capturing it all on film. We returned to Europe stopping into the Cote d'Azur to meet his family and I ate French food and drank French wines as if I had been born to do so. I grew such a love for the country and its people, I felt like I was living out the days of a young Julia Childs! She was always someone I had a deep admiration and respect for as a female chef, who discovered her passion late on in life, but I haven't had the slightest inkling I'd be living out this fantasy in Paris France. Needless to say, I never made it back to Miami Beach to collect my boxes; we had them shipped here to my new home in Paris. My French prince charming never let me leave, and funny enough, I'm not sure I ever had intentions to! I have started working on publishing my first cookbook, I give cooking lessons to anyone who's looking for a little inspiration, and I spend my free moments walking through the open markets of Paris smelling and touching the local organic products. I have learned a lot of life lessons coming out of high school and I put a little list of them together to remember.

1. Be fearless.
2. Do things with conviction, believe in yourself.
3. There's always turning back. If something doesn't work out, like flying off to a new country—fly home!
4. Live with no regrets.
5. Follow your passion. If you don't know what your passion is, spend your life searching for it.
6. Always try and inspire yourself and others.
7. Nothing is too big, too far, or too difficult. Dream big.
8. Just because you're a woman, don't ever put a limit on your worth. Being in a male dominated industry, I have to always beat out the odds and competition. I find it exhilarating!

9. Let love in. Keeping your heart and your head open to new situations, relationships and ideas will fulfill you from the inside out.
10. Change is good. Embrace everything that can happen to you in your life: change of job, change of country, change of weight (you'd understand if you saw those little mini pastries here in Paris).
11. Love yourself. If you don't, nobody else will. Fact.

3 Shahnaz Khan

My parents divorced before my first birthday. I was raised by my grandmother and father. I considered my grandmother my mother. My father ran his own business which eventually he lost and began working where ever he could find work. We moved around a lot. Between Kindergarten and grade 10, I lived in 9 different neighbourhoods and went to 9 different schools. In the beginning, these moves would bother me, as there was no conversation or preparation. I would come home from school one day and find the house filled with boxes. As soon as I would adjust to an environment and make a couple of friends, I was saying my goodbyes. I felt like my life had no balance or stability. I felt like I never had the chance to finish the things I started. For instance, I would join the choir and went to every practice but never got to perform at the main assembly. I stopped believing in myself and no longer thought there was a point. I began to use these moves as an excuse, because when we leave and go somewhere else I had a fresh start all over again. While attending most of these schools I remember the parent-teacher meetings; I would always go. I never did well in school. Teachers stressed the potential but I just didn't think there was a point because we weren't staying for long anyway and I told my teachers that. I stopped allowing people to get close to me because none of the friendships that I made would last. At that age, we would make oaths to be "friends forever" with letters and keepsakes but I never saw them again. The relationship I had with my father was a good one most of the time. We never talked about anything in the open, but we did things together. He taught me how to ride my bike, swim and helped me with my homework. He had a little bit of a temper and sometimes I got beat for the things I did so I was a little nervous to be completely honest with him at times. I learned to self-soothe. If something was bothering me or made me upset, I would sit in the park by myself, listen to music or write in my diary. I would never speak how I felt about anything to anybody. I was a loner and I didn't care. I was teased a lot about my second hand clothing, my name, my ethnicity and the aromas of food that reached outside from my grandma's cooking. I do recall a habit that annoyed my father tremendously. I would bring home stray animals. Well, I didn't know who they belonged to and if I saw a cat on the street I would bring it home to my room. I was allowed to keep them a week, tops. Again, I would come home and they just wouldn't be there anymore. I never got closure. I began to feel like my emotions didn't matter. I even remember finding a bird's nest with a couple of eggs inside. I brought that home too, wrapped them up, placed them on the vent, thinking the heat would make them hatch and that I would have my own birds. These experiences helped me learn how to find peace within myself.

We struggled financially. I learned at an early age that when I wanted something I had to get it myself. If I wanted to participate in school activities or pizza days, I would find a hustle to come up with the money. At 11 years old, I would find things around the house that looked shiny and expensive sneak them out and sell them on the side of the road. I had no concept of value and cost; making 5 dollars was a big deal. I felt like a queen. At 13, I put up flyers and had started a little babysitting business taking care of young children in the neighbourhood. I found that I loved playing with kids younger than me. They didn't care about what I wore and where I was from. There were no judgements, no name-calling and they respected me. I realized the natural innocence and purity of children. My first official job was at McDonalds at the age of 15 and I loved it. I had the money to do whatever I wanted and I was just entering high school. Second semester grade 9 on April 3rd my grandmother died. I watched her die at home on her bed at about 2:30 am. She was surrounded by her sons and daughters but she stared right into my eyes until the end. After she passed, I crept into my grandma's room. I lay down next to her and slept holding her the rest of the night. For a long time, I felt that a part of me was missing when she passed, but I dreamt about her all the time. My father and I stayed in that house for a little while longer and by grade 10 we decided to move to the other end of the city. I switched schools again for the last time. I worked while in school to help out my father after he suffered from a major heart attack needing a quadruple by-pass surgery. I was terrified and I didn't know what I would do without him. He has been on disability ever since. At 17 years old in grade 11, I found my first job as a makeup artist. Being creative and being able to bond with other women was why I loved doing makeup. I volunteered in the community center one day per week. I decided that no matter what I chose to do in life that I always wanted to remain connected to children in the community. At 18, my father told me when I came home from school that he had found himself a wife from Pakistan and that she was coming to Canada the following year. I had mixed emotions about my father getting married. To be honest, at first I felt angry, betrayed and didn't understand why all of a sudden he needed anybody after so many years. Then, I thought, it would be best for me because then I didn't have to be obligated to take care of him. She came the following year and at first it was good—it worked. I understood she had nobody as I felt like at times I had nobody either. Then, problems began to arise with our culture differences. She didn't like the clothes I chose to wear or the tattoo I got. She wanted to be my mother and I wouldn't allow it. She was my father's wife and nothing more. The fighting got bad between her and my father because he would stand by me in her face but try to talk to me and tell me to change. I didn't want that stress nor put stress on a marriage that my father wanted. I lived with them until I was 19 and I then moved out.

After high school, I had no plans and no idea what I wanted to do for the rest of my life. I worked in the cosmetics industry for the next 8 years. I moved around a lot, although I remained in the same city. If I wasn't moving from where I lived, I was constantly changing jobs but stayed in the same field of cosmetics. The same thing occurred with my relationships. I would constantly meet the same type of men that were completely wrong for me; love them, hate them and then moved on to the next asshole. In some way, I already knew these relationships would never work out. At a time I chose the ultimate douche bag with whom I decided to live with. From the beginning it was complicated but that's what I loved about it. We had the same temper, passion and intensity. After about 10 months, he became abusive. He would slap me around and I would always fight back. It was like a game. The physical fights were more like wrestling, I suppose, and I didn't take it seriously. Until one day he fractured my nose and I got a black eye. A week later after my eye healed, I moved out. I didn't go to work for about a month or two for the first time since 15 and I put volunteering on hold. I haven't been in a relationship since. The only thing that remained consistently positive and that I looked forward to was volunteering with children and youth. I volunteered and participated in many events and organizations in the community. I began to build relationships with the youth and their families. I learned about their backgrounds, struggles, circumstances, fears and goals. Some of them I watched graduate from high school and move on to post secondary school. To witness those, who society expected to be included in a statistic, graduate from school was an achievement for not only them, but the volunteers and the community that helped raise them. In that very community, others had different fates: pregnancies, some ending up in jail, some caught in the drug game, some let the hunger for money get the best of them, becoming strippers, pimps and the ultimate sacrifice is when the community would lose their children to street violence. I felt that loss a couple of times while volunteering. It's a feeling of helplessness and hopelessness that comes over you. When you hear a mother screaming, crying for her child, one can't help but think what could have been done to save that life? What did we do wrong? Did we spend enough time? Did we listen? Did we work hard enough? It was very difficult watching and hearing about the ones who couldn't be "saved." I had no choice but to walk away or let go. It's when you come to the realization that it is completely out of your hands and you have no control; especially when their own parents sometimes played a role in their hardships. It broke my heart. It was becoming stressful and I began to let guilt get the best of me. I spoke with many people who worked in the community, sought advice and guidance for myself. How could I tell kids to go to continue their education when I had to do the same? I finally made the decision to go back to school.

I enrolled in the Child Youth Worker program. This was a blessing for me in the sense that I was beginning to learn so much about myself. I learned the specifics about communicating with children, how to handle stressful situations and coping with the emotional stress. During this three year program, I took my first trip to volunteer with underprivileged children and youth internationally. I came across the opportunity while on the college website. It was with the organization Students Crossing Borders and that year they were going to Riverton Jamaica. I felt that this would be a great opportunity for me. I had been on vacations to the Caribbean in the past. I always thought that I came to enjoy the natural paradise of these countries only; but this time I wanted to give back. I didn't want to be a tourist who came and released her stress in a country that concealed all their troubles. I didn't want to stay blind. While on this trip, I experienced working in a basic school for children 2 to 6 years old, a shelter for teen moms, an orphanage for children with HIV/AIDS and an orphanage with special needs children who have been found on the road abandoned. During this trip, I experienced something that would forever change my life.

Every place I worked at was special to me. Every child/youth I met on this very first trip will remain a part of me. While I was volunteering at the orphanage for the special needs children, I assisted with bathing and feeding. Every time I looked up he was looking right at me. His eyes were fierce filled with curiosity and wonder. Eight years old, paralyzed from the waist down and strapped to a wheel chair. His wrists were tied to his chair so he couldn't move his hands. I was told this was done to prevent him from hurting himself. He moved his upper body and head from side to side. It was the only movement he could make. One of the caregivers had said he didn't speak and he was hard of hearing. Through his eyes, I felt his soul. The orphanage was run by a group of 3 women taking care of over 20 children, all having special needs. Those who did not need a wheel chair were tied up with pieces of cloth by their wrist to the poles on the perimeter of the common area. I was told this was done because with such little help, the kids could not be supervised regularly and this was their only option. The women were overworked, underpaid and had received no training in taking care of special needs children. I can't express what exactly it was about this particular boy that made me feel like I couldn't breathe. Like when you're having a bad dream and you want to scream but you can't produce a sound. Looking at him and his piercing eyes evoked so many emotions within me. Looking back, I realized that maybe it was the fact that he was living my fear—being totally, completely restrained. Although I was not permitted to do so, as soon as I had the chance, I took this little boy outside of the grounds to a local garden/park. I had this urge in me, like I had to release him somehow, because selfishly, I believed that I felt what he was feeling. I untied his wrists and picked him up out of his wheel chair. With him in my lap I sat on a swing, swaying back and forth. He was numb to it, no matter how high I went, his face remained expressionless. I felt hopeless and disappointed in myself. This child was not like any other child I had met before because there was no "fixing" a circumstance or situation. There was no talking, no listening, no family, no friends, no support, no advice, no resources that I could use to somehow make things a little better or promising. His life will remain what it always had been and there was nothing I could do about it. As I was walking back to his chair carrying him in my arms, the wind began to blow a little stronger. I was with him standing under a tree and he began to laugh hysterically trying to grab on to the branches that danced over our heads. It was at that very moment that I knew that working with children was what I wanted to be involved in for the rest of my life. It is these bitter sweet moments that I live for. It took that specific experience and that little boy to make me realize my passion. It was him who taught me that it is not always about changing a person's life but that it's about changing moments. This boy's face will forever be ingrained in my mind and the sound of his laughter will remain in my heart. He is my inspiration, my motivation for all that I have done and for all that I am striving for. Sometimes, it takes an event or an experience to make us realize what we already knew. Like when you're so lost that you didn't even know it until you were found.

I am working towards obtaining my BSW and MSW and I continue to work and volunteer in the community and internationally. I believe that no matter what your profession, we should all take the time to give back to our community and our youth, because you never know how you can affect a life or another for the better. It could be as simple as one conversation that creates the impact and influence to change a decision or offer a perspective. If deciding to become a social worker or if choosing a career in the humanitarian field, I suggest volunteering, because it prepares you and gives you insight to the type of work you may do. Volunteering is also great for networking, meeting people and it opens doors for opportunities. To become a volunteer in a specific community, the best way is dropping by a community health center or checking out the website. You can find organizations that are best suited for your interests in how you want to be involved. Women are especially important and needed because there is a lack of focus sometimes in how girls are affected by their community.

I asked a group of grade 10 girls what their definition of a woman is and to describe the qualities that make her a woman. A woman, a human being that possesses the strength to fight the inner and outer battles and while feeling the pain of these wars still manages to sustain the power to love, forgive and nurture. They replied by saying that a woman should have confidence, faith within herself, elegance, beauty, ambition and determination. The woman who is a corporate lawyer, the woman who is a wife, the woman who offers her temple, the woman that flies to the moon, the woman who walks miles to provide water for her family, all share an element of depth that only us as women can understand. The young women in this world who are still trying to find their place and purpose should know that they are not alone in their fears and only within themselves they will find the courage to overcome these fears.

4 Polly Shannon

There is something about the title of this book that makes me nervous. It uses the words "Making It." I am really not convinced that anyone ever really feels they have "made it." I certainly don't. There is always more to achieve, more to experience and more to give. There have been moments in my life where I have felt proud and fulfilled and then the next morning I awoke to the panicky state of "What do I do now?" I have lived a very blessed life with opportunities thrown at my feet, some I have been brave enough to take, others left me hiding under the covers. I think I am going to go with "making it" meaning being happy and fulfilled. I feel comfortable offering my experience on that. So to start at the beginning...

When I was little, I thought I might like to be the President of the United States of America. It didn't phase me that there had never been a female President nor did it bother me that I wasn't American. My parents told me that I could be whatever I wanted. Being a gullible child, I believed it. Sadly it wasn't true. I did not make the rugby team, nor was I any good at power mechanics, and I was too tall to be a ballerina or gymnast. It never crossed my mind to become an actress; that just happened.

When I was seven, my father was posted to Ottawa from Victoria. He was a military doctor. My parents found a place in Aylmer, Quebec, just across the river. I remember very little, but that they had taken the ocean and tall trees away and that everyone spoke another language—French! I was luckily allowed to continue my education in English (back then that was rare in Quebec) but had no friends. Also probably important to mention is that soon after we arrived my parents divorced. It was a scary time that left me with an unwell mother who suffers from Lupus, a Down Syndrome brother and a father that no longer lived at home. I used to say "the world went dark." The kids at school and on the bus didn't embrace my brother, Micah, right away. Put it this way, I have been in more school yard brawls than most young boys. I was lonely and a little afraid. Somewhere in that time I had lost happiness and was desperate to find it again. I say this not to invoke pity, but to explain where some of the drive came from.

My brilliant mother had the idea for me to go around the block and ask kids if they wanted to put on a play. Well, we managed to gather a group and put on a play my mother had written. This was the beginning both for me and my mom. She went on to become quite a successful children's writer and I, well, I fell in love—in love with all the attention and with the make believe. The Grimes Road Theater Company began and so did the beginning of lifelong friendships. Someone from the CBC had, just by chance, seen our little around the block play and asked my mother if she would write a special for Christmas. All the kids were given roles. That was my first TV experience. For a minute, as my whole family gathered to watch the show, I felt happy. And then it was over. We continued to perform all over the Ottawa area and the Company quickly grew. At some point in there, I stopped eating. I lost so much weight that the lunch ladies at my elementary school had to watch me eat everyday. I didn't understand why this happened but I was convinced that if I could get skinny enough I would be happy and the world would be right again. It turned out that I would never find "skinny enough" and therefore happiness was never to be found in not eating.

Soon it was discovered that some of the drama group could sing and I was one of them. I was a tiny little thing that could sing un-miked over rock bands. I think I had actual talent here and although I never became a singer, it is part of my work as an actress. I have songs that move me to tears or make me feel strong. I find music for every role. I had sung on Parliament Hill main stage on Canada Day with big bands, on local radio and news programs. All over really. It was so much fun until the concept of being cool hit me at about twelve. I began getting horrible stage fright. I bulldozed my way through that, but singing really gave me anxiety because I thought everyone knew when you are not perfect. At the same time I grew, my bad perm had worn off and somehow my features started to fit together. I finally began to get noticed by boys and modeling agents. This I thought was great! If I could become a model then I would really be something! So ridiculous, but I was twelve. I began a career modeling and by the age of 17 had modeled in New York, Tokyo and Paris. My father made a deal with me: if I maintained high grades and all in Science, I could do whatever I wanted after school. So I worked hard. I had very little free time. I would go to school in the Advanced Science program then go to ballet or opera class then hit a rehearsal for whatever play I was doing at the time and then do as many modeling jobs as there were in Ottawa (not the fashion capital of the world). This taught me about commitment and that I could push myself much further than I ever imagined. I was allowed, on summer holidays or breaks, to travel with my modeling. Unreal to me now, but I went to New York with Elite when I was only 15 years old and at 16, I left for Tokyo and Paris. Well, I was way too young for Paris. Modeling taught me many good and bad things. I learned that I was fearless in front of a camera, I learned not to trust old men who offer you nice things, how to survive on very little food, but most importantly that spirit outshone physical beauty. One night I was in a big night club in Paris where all the top models were hanging out and I started to feel a little insecure. It crossed my mind that the world's most beautiful women were all in the room with me and that I didn't belong. I thought what if they find out that I am just Polly from Aylmer, Quebec? I looked around at all the shiny beauties and recognized Pia from Carlsbad, Sweden, and Meagan from Gainsville, Florida. We were all just girls from different places and we all were there to make a little money, then go home to our families. I let go of any need to stand out and just started to dance with some friends, and somehow in that we became the popular girls that night! Everyone wanted to party with us and hang out. The most beautiful were not always the most fun.

Paris was a strange place for me all alone. I had gone with a different agency this time and when I was there I had worked quite a bit but I could never be skinny enough for them. All my childhood craziness about being fat surfaced again. Just to be clear, I was 5 foot 8 and a half and under 110 pounds. One day I got a call from my agent saying that they had spoken with my mother and she had agreed to me getting an operation where they would remove my bottom rib. This would make my waist smaller they said and then I would book lots of jobs! Right away I knew they were lying and that my mother would never have agreed to that. I was 17! I called home and explained the situation to my mom and was on a plane home the next day. I decided to quit modeling for a while, because I had this bad taste in my mouth from Paris. Once again, what I thought would fix this problem of being unhappy had not worked.

I was a little depressed, underfed and unclear about my future. Finally, out of the blue, we got a call from a talent agency in Ottawa saying that they were looking for a pretty girl who can act in *Are You Afraid of the Dark*. I auditioned and booked the job. I then booked a small role in a Denys Arcand film. I remember saying "Wow! This is so easy!" Little did I know, very little. I packed up and moved to Montreal. I decided to continue modeling in-between acting gigs instead of waitressing and took some acting classes. Things were going well but there was just not enough English work in Montreal so I started auditioning in Toronto. I finally booked a series called *Catwalk* and moved to Toronto. I left behind my little house, a lovely French boyfriend and two cats named Lui and L'autre.

It was hard at first to get accustomed to what felt like a very different culture in Toronto and even though in French I had an English accent it turned out that in English I had a slight French one after spending the prior few years speaking mostly French. The American producers hated it. I worked hard at getting rid of it by watching lots of American TV and mimicking what I heard. People in the States often make fun of Canadian actors for the way they say words like 'out,' 'mother,' 'sorry' and 'house.' These were not a problem for me. I was adding a 'no' at the end of every sentence and pronouncing 'th' as 'd.' Funny how now people think I am from Texas!

Luckily I made good friends right away and looking back I would not have survived otherwise. I moved in with my best friend Lexa Doig, possibly one of Canada's most beautiful and for sure one of my most favorite women, who I am still friends with today.

I really feel like I became an actor when I began studying with David Rotenberg. He was so hard on me and made me so angry that I began to grow in the craft and book bigger roles. I did *The Girl Next Door* and *Sheldon Kennedy Story* within a year of David's help. It is one of the things I suggest to every actor and so few listen. You should always be studying. I am still in class today. If you are not studying even when you are working, someone else is and they are getting better and will soon replace you.

I got to travel a lot with my job, which I loved. I shot a movie in Prague and then went to South Africa, Barbados and most recently Argentina. I have always loved shooting on location and each trip brought a different gift of experience. South Africa really changed my life. I had fallen for an African man and after the filming was over I took off with him and his cousin four-by-fouring all over the country for a couple of months. This was a life different than anything I had ever known. We slept in the back of the pick up trucks and went places no Canadian girl should ever go unescorted. I loved it there. I learned to be more fearless and to feel the Earth in a different way. I would have stayed if it weren't for the fact that I had a dream of being an actress and couldn't see how to do that there. I often wonder what my life would have been like had I just stayed. Jean Roux came to Toronto and we tried that for six months but he couldn't live with all the cement. It was a little like the *Crocodile Dundee* movie. The city just didn't make sense to him. I couldn't survive in SA and he couldn't survive in Canada. So we parted ways.

I think my career really began when I booked *Men With Brooms* and then *Trudeau*. Both were highly publicized and people began knowing my name. There was a lot of pressure with playing Margaret Trudeau. Everyone, it seemed, was waiting to see this miniseries that would portray the nation's most famous couple. I grew to care very much for Margaret. I had done so much research to try and find out who she really was that I felt like she was a friend without having met her. I fought hard to keep her integrity in the show and I did my very best, but I am still not sure it was enough. After shooting *Trudeau*, my Toronto agent kicked me out to LA. I really didn't want to go. I liked being in Toronto with my friends and family and in an industry that had just given me the approval I had been looking for. I had no visa to work but went anyway. I got an agent and a manager right away but really couldn't work. It took three years for my Green Card to come through. I pretty much wasted my time and money in LA for those three years waiting for a little plastic photo ID. Once it finally came through I booked a pilot right away. It was amazing! It was the favorite pilot going into the season. Then it got picked up and I got replaced! That was a tough time. I luckily got some great words of encouragement from friends and managed to pull myself together and move on to other work. I worked a lot but something started happening. I was really unmoved by it all.

I was always happy when I was busy but was unable to sit alone. I couldn't stand it. I have done many stupid things to avoid it. When the universe finally took away any options, I had to look at my life and what was happening. I had done everything you think could make you happy, traveled all over the world, dated movie stars, partied with the coolest people, dined in the fanciest restaurants, had the nicest clothes, and worked with the best artists and still I felt nothing. It all just blurred into one big nothingness. I really stopped caring about any of it. Just as I had suspected all along, something was wrong with me, I just didn't know what. My self-loathing hit an all-time high and down that spiral I went. I thought how dare I be so ungrateful when the gods had given me everything and sitting right next to me is my little brother who has Down Syndrome? Micah goes about his life with the courage of a soldier and the heart of a lion, and I can't get off the couch.

I had been in a long and very hard relationship and wanted to blame that for feeling so rotten, and I did for a while. We were terrible to each other—cruel actually—but I can't hold him responsible for my lackluster feeling for life. I had also put the false notion on that relationship that it would fix me as well. Seven years we tried to make that work and it just got worse and worse. It was my best friend Fawn who called me in midst of all of my relationship drama and said, "This relationship is killing you. You are a shell of who you once were and I will not lose my best friend! Get out and get out now!" I listened. I left with nothing. No home, no money, and most importantly, no self-esteem. It is weird how the person who hurt me the most has probably also helped me the most. Through the healing of that relationship, I found the most important thing; I found me. The thing I had assumed was so awful for so long was not all that bad. I know that sounds cheesy von cheestein, but it's true. I had looked everywhere and done everything to like myself more, but I should have just let myself be instead.

Today I act, because I feel like I have something to share, I can get off the couch, because the world is where all my friends are, and I can look into my brother's eyes and say I get it now. He is just him and he is good with that.

I hope I get to go back and dance with friends in Paris. I hope I get to work on more great projects with great people. I hope I get to go back to Africa and see that crazy moon. I hope I fall in love with the right guy and make him happy, but I know nothing will make me any more fulfilled than I already am.

I guess the point of all of this is to see what the universe offers you. Take what moves you, make sure you have good girlfriends, they are the ones who will see you through, and never think something or someone else will make you more than you already are.

5 Vanora D'Sa

My name is Vanora and I would like to share with you my journey of success and failure and what I have learned in my life. From reading this I hope to inspire you so you can make the necessary changes in your life and lead your life into a positive healthy direction.

I was born in India and was raised by a single mother. From the very beginning I felt different. My name was original and none of my peers were from single family homes. You see, Indians pride themselves on 'nuclear families' and men and women stick together no matter what.

Although my parent's divorce was unfortunate, my mother and her family were very loving and maybe even extra loving and because I was the only baby in the household, I grew up with lots of love and attention. I never felt unloved or unwanted or as if I was missing something in my life. I think that's what spurred my confidence and my 'I-can-do-anything-I-want' attitude.

When I was 9, my mom decided to move to Canada for better educational opportunities. Back in the early 90s, India wasn't the growing superpower it is now. I grew up a happy child with big dreams of becoming a doctor to save my then dying grandfather from his diabetes.

In Canada, it was just my mom and I. No family, not much money, but lots of dreams. I come from a pretty well educated family so getting a University degree was expected, but how to become a success was yet unknown. My mother had no knowledge of the opportunities in Canada and the education system was very different from India. So finding a University and choosing what I wanted to study was all up to me. And so I did. I went to the University of Toronto and graduated with a degree in Psychology and Industrial/Business Relations.

Soon after I started UofT, I saw my dreams of becoming a doctor fade away. Getting straight A's in school was hard and nearly impossible. So I graduated and began working in the corporate world as a Business Analyst.

Fast forward 2 years and the economic crisis of 2008. Everyone including myself was scared for their jobs. Companies were restructuring, laying off many people and others were going bankrupt. I ended up losing my job at Hewlett-Packard but was fortunate to find another right away. Still, I was unhappy. Is this what happens every time there is a shake in the economy? I was young and single with no kids, but I can't go through this stress when I have a family.

I started to look at options to make me look like a successful candidate no matter how the economy was doing. What skill can I offer that is high in demand and I would never be out of a job? I recently bumped into someone who was telling me about medical schools abroad. Then I thought to myself that I have friends going to med school in Eastern Europe, Ireland, India and the Caribbean because of the competiveness of the Canadian system and come back to work in the US and Canada. I looked more into it, and did extensive research.

The next few pages outline how I went back and fulfilled my childhood dream of becoming a doctor.

Med school in the Caribbean:
I'm sure you have heard this a million times, but here it is once more, "With hard work you can achieve anything."

That's how I feel about medical schools in the Caribbean or any offshore med school for that matter. Making the change wasn't easy. I had to head back to school after nearly 3 years of working, learn something I have never done before, dedicate 4 years of my life towards it and put nearly $150K towards doing so. But I did it. I did it, because I knew I could and I wanted a stable and secure financial life, but more importantly I wanted my work to mean something. There is a good feeling that you have when you are following your dream. Something just feels right and everything seems to fall into place.

School was hard. Not only because of the curriculum, but because I was away from home for the first time, away from my friends, and in a stressful environment. You would think that medical students would be the helpful generous type, but I tell you the stress and competitiveness gets to people and I witnessed backstabbing and utter disregard for people. Through all of that I grew. I stayed true to who I am and never lost sight of my goals.

Tips for changing your career:
Think about what you like to do. Think of a few things. You might like fashion for example, but not everyone can be a designer. Think out of the box. Maybe you can be a buyer for a major retailer, or how about a personal shopper at a high-end department store? Explore your options.

Research your options. Speak to people in the field. You don't know anyone? No worries. Get to know people. Part of developing your career is taking charge and learning to approach people in a friendly and professional way. Most people are happy to help. If someone doesn't want to, don't be discouraged and keep your head up. There are others who are more than happy to help. Don't be afraid of rejection.

Ask for opportunities which allow you to sample what you could be doing. I interned with a cardiologist—an opportunity I got through extensive networking. This gives you direct insight into your future career. Maybe it's exactly what you wanted, or maybe its not. Knowing earlier will save you some time and money and give you the confidence that you are making the right decision.

Lastly, be confident. People can sense if you are unsure of yourself. If you try your hardest and give it your best you can never fail.

Tips for finding a school:
Contact the school for information about your program.

Ask the school if they have a counsellor you can speak with to plan your career. All of this should be free and most schools have someone available free of charge to help you plan out your career.

Ask to speak to students currently in the program and to students who have graduated from the program so you know what to expect and can learn from their successes and failures.

Arrange your finances. Are you able to pay for school? If you don't have the savings, talk to the school about potential loans.

Lastly, try your best and think positive.

Not all degrees are made equal:
These days, many people think of success in terms of school. While I agree that education empowers you, it may not necessarily be the key to success.

While on average, people who graduate from Universities earn higher wages than people with a high school diploma, it is important to choose your educational path carefully. Degrees cost tens of thousands of dollars and you may not be able to find a job in your field of study. You want to ensure you are entering a stable work environment, where there will be jobs in the future and the pay is good. Make your education worth the investment. It is also important to look at the careers in which there is a shortage of and what will be required in the future. This information is available at resource centers of many schools free of charge and on the internet.

I chose medicine because there is a shortage of doctors in the US and Canada and I love helping people. Although competitive, I know that there would be a job waiting for me when I graduate. The career is stable, and I can make a difference in the world by healing the sick or at least trying to. Another bonus is that my skills are global and can be applied in nearly any country worldwide. That gives me the flexibility to travel and find work if I desire to do so.

If you like healthcare, but the doctor route is too expensive and long, try becoming a medical assistant, a physician assistant, a nurse, a dental hygienist, or dental assistant. There are some jobs where your education is around a year or 2 and the pay is great and much higher than the average University graduate.

Network, network, network to get you where you wanna work!

Did I mention how important it is to network? This means going out of your comfort zone and meeting new people you normally would not meet.

While I was in business, I was on the board of Wired Women. It is a wonderful organization of women, created and supported by women. There were events that enabled me to meet and network with women in different roles within the community and make some real connections.

I also joined NetIP, an Indian network of professionals, which allowed me to interact with people similar to me, who were very successful and inspirational. It made me think, if they can do it, so can I!

I frequented many Meetup.com meetings with both professional and social gatherings which allowed me to really engage with people in and outside of my field and make connections.

I got my cardiology internship through NetIP. I happened to meet a woman who was listed as one of the 100 most successful women in Canada. I asked her advice based on her experience in health care and inquired about a possible opportunity within her organization and she helped me!

Although I listed some opportunities which worked out very well for me, there were often times that I got rejected or ignored. There were empty promises and people who just don't care to help. I never let that bother me. I always kept pushing for connections and opportunities and developing relationships with people.

Act your wage!

The key to being an independent woman, who can change her career or anything that she wants in her life, is financial investment. Ladies, that means putting down the Gucci (for now), and investing in your future. I see too many ladies who invest in their closets rather than in their bank accounts.

Always put aside money each month in a secure savings account and make a budget for shopping and entertainment. We should all enjoy life but not at the expense of our lives. Emergency money is the key to living a stress-free and liberated life and you should have about 6 months of savings.

My career change was costly. Med school cost around $150K, which I solely funded through my property investment. I have been working since I was 16, and made sure that every month I saved for my future. Right out of school I was able to purchase my first property based on my savings. And since I always paid my credit cards in full and on time, I had good credit which enabled me to be accepted for a mortgage without a co-signer.

In this age of materialism, us women need to act more financially responsible. There is no reason to have a $3k bag on your shoulder if you are taking in $3k a month. There are many stores that have super cute clothes at a bargain price. Look for sales, and spend your money wisely. Like designer goods only? Well look for designer sample sales, or cross the border. I hate to say it but clothing is significantly cheaper in the US, since their stores are able to provide a much bigger discount due to demand and supply. Money is hard to earn and very easy to spend.

Putting items on credit card and paying the minimum payment means that you will likely pay twice what the item cost you with all the high interest rates. So those really cute shoes on sale don't really look like a bargain anymore, or do they?

Being financially independent also means not relying on a man for money. Always have your own bank account along with a joint account when you are married. Make sure you're always making your own money, because that will give you strength and the ability to leave if your man ain't acting right.

Changing your mind and protecting your image:

Life doesn't always go as planned and it's ok to change your mind. Making the shift from corporate to medicine was not easy. I had to tell everyone that what I devoted 4 years of my life studying in school, and subsequently working 3 years in that field, was not something that I was completely satisfied with. I had to face judgement from a lot of people, but was surprised to find so many people supportive of my decision. In fact, a lot of people found it inspirational that I was making this switch.

If you asked me 6 years ago, if I would be going to medical school and moving to the US I would think you were crazy. But here I am some years later doing something I never thought I would be doing. An important point here is that because you don't know where life is going to lead you it is always important to protect your image.

In this era of Facebook, Twitter and loads of other online social websites, when you are young and partying it up you may not think twice about your image. But it is important to protect your privacy and your images. Employers, and clients like to Google your name before hiring you, and inappropriate images will not get you the job. Neither will a criminal record. Every job does a criminal record check before hiring you, so you need to have a clean criminal record. This means walking away from fights and staying away from negative people.

On Facebook, I ensure there are only appropriate and tasteful pictures posted. I also limit the amount of pictures I pose in at parties with drinks in my hand. No one wants to visit a drunk doctor!

I followed my dreams and although I had some detours, my path is clear and my future is bright. I have laid down a solid foundation and look forward to building upon it. I wish you the same! Take a risk and continue to dream, because if you can dream it, you can achieve it.

6

Dr. Dame Daphne Sheldrick
DBE MBE MBS DVMS

I was born in Kenya of British pioneering parents, my father having come to the country from South Africa as a child of seven in 1907, after his father had been killed fighting for the British against the Afrikaner Boers during the Boer War at the turn of the 20th century. At that time Nairobi was just a small railroad staging post which had sprung up beside a large swamp when the railway line linking the Port of Mombasa to the interior inland and on to Uganda, just happened to reach that point.

When my father was grown, he managed to acquire a small farm comprised of 6,000 acres of virgin bush in the rift valley at a place called Gilgil. There he built our childhood home out of stone quarried and cut on the farm, and wood sawed on the farm from dead standing cedar trees in the beautiful cedar forest that clothed the slopes of a nearby hill. In order to reach the forest, he first had to build a stout bridge to ford the river that ran the length of the farm and which was a favorite playground for us children as we grew up.

At that point in time, the country was wild and nature pristine, filled with an abundance of wildlife of every species. Leopards, which took a heavy toll of my father's calves and sheep, were common in the nearby forest. Forest dwelling antelopes were also numerous, as were beautiful black and white colobus monkeys, baboons and other primates as well as buffaloes and herds of elephants who wandered through from time to time on their long range migrations to meet family members and friends in far-off places. The open plains not far from our home were filled with huge herds of different antelope species, enormous herds of zebra and wildebeest, thousands of elands and many prides of lions, as well as rhinoceroses. The human population of the country was small, made up of

47 different tribes, each with its own tribal language– (no more than some 5 million souls compared to today's 45 plus million) and crime did not exist when I was young, since the Africans retained their tribal discipline woven around witchcraft and ruthless punishments meted out by the elders, such as the cutting off of a hand or arm, and sometimes even death.

Missionaries were amongst the early european explorers that opened up Africa to the civilized world, and they created a common language known as "Swahili" to enable people of different tribes to communicate with one another and them. Swahili rapidly spread inland, so by the time I came along, we used Swahili to talk to the local people around us, some of whom were recruited as workers on my father's farm. We children regarded the farm workers as our friends and treated them with respect and affection. I especially liked the man who worked in the garden, who was from the Wakamba tribe, and had filed teeth which he could put in and out of his gums. I would sit with him for hours, begging him to do it for me! Our cook was named Sega, and he was a strict disciplinarian to us children, on whom we enjoyed playing tricks which he endured with good humor. Unlike many other colonial powers of the time, the British were benign rulers and during the colonial era that extended from the turn of the century until Kenya was granted independence from Britain in 1963, Kenya was ruled from Whitehall in London. The white settler community always felt that the London based administration favored the local Africans rather than their own people who had settled in the colony and developed it. As the country developed, it enjoyed an incorruptible judiciary and police force, an efficient civil service, free primary schooling in schools that were counted amongst the finest in Africa, an excellent veterinary service and airline, and a wonderful rail service that delivered excellent standards. Passenger and goods trains ran on tight schedules, the passenger trains fitted with sleeping berths in the carriages, with a plush restaurant car where waiters in starched white uniforms served excellent meals to travelers. By the time I came along the railway ran the length of the country from Mombasa at the coast, through the Rift Valley past my childhood home of Gilgil and on to Uganda.

Relations between the white community and the Kikuyu tribe became tense when this tribe and its allies began the Mau Mau insurrection. Employers were advised by the colonial government to get rid of Kikuyu workers, since many had been coerced into taking a secret oath to kill the white settler community and take over the land they owned. Even then, one of our employees took his own life rather than obey the dictates of the oath he had been forced to take, the measure of the affection in which he held us which spanned the racial barriers of the period. Most other Kenyan tribes were loyal to the colonial government and were not affected, many tribesmen even fighting against the Kikuyu Mau Mau insurgents who claimed that they were fighting for independence. In fact, the colonial power was anxious to rid itself of its colonies after the second World War, and both Tanganyika and Uganda gained their independence from Britain ahead of Kenya.

Besides the domestic animals that my father farmed—pedigree cattle imported from Australia, sheep and pigs, we kept horses that we rode around the farm, and, of course we had dogs, cats, pet rabbits and a host of wild orphan pets, amongst which was a young Impala called "Bob", a waterbuck called "Daisy", a baby kongoni whose name I forget, a zebra foal, a tiny dwarf mongoose called Ricky Ticky Tavey and a very special baby bushbuck whom I named "Bushy", who was given into my care to look after when I was just 3 or 4 years old. I loved him unreservedly and with all my heart and fed him religiously every four hours with milk from a baby's bottle. I sat with him cuddled in my lap for hours and tied a little bell around his neck so that I would always know where he was when I was not with him. My parents told me that mother bushbucks hide their newborn babies when very young, so I made a little thicket for him out of cut bush in the corner of the chicken run until he was big enough to allow to roam the garden as he wished. In between time with Bushy, I enjoyed being with the mother cat and her 6 fluffy kittens born in a little box in a small room attached to the back of our home, which my mother called The School Room, since that is where she tutored my two older siblings each morning, teaching them the alphabet to prepare them well for the boarding school they would attend when 6 years old. I liked it when they were incarcerated in there for their lessons, because it gave me an opportunity to play with my sister's dolls' house (which was normally out of bounds) and my brother's train set (which was definitely out of bounds). When I turned six, I joined them at the nearest boarding school which was in a town called Nakuru some 3 hours journey away by car, on a very rough dirt road. In those days there were no tarred roads in the country—just dirt tracks originally made by wagons which were impassable when they turned to mud during the two rainy seasons a year.

The day came when my little bushbuck was grown, and began to feel the call of the wild. He took to spending time away, when I feared he would be devoured by a leopard, and worried endlessly about him, but my parents insisted that wild animals can never "belong" but are only on "loan" for as long as they are dependent. Thereafter they must return to where they truly belong, there to respond to the dictates of Nature, for they are programmed by evolution to fulfill the role within the environment for which they had evolved over millennia. They taught me about the chain of life where every wild animal has a role and a niche to fill that is beneficial to the whole—the whole being the welfare of the planet, since planet Earth is home to all life that has evolved within it. Every night my mother walked outside to gaze up at the stars and explained to me that Earth was just one of billions upon billions of other tiny cosmic dots suspended on a sunbeam as it circled its own star, our sun. Having to say goodbye to Bushy was the hardest, but most important lesson I had to learn which would equip me for what lay ahead in the future.

During school holidays, my parents took us camping in beautiful pristine wild places, many of which are now National Parks. Then there were no roads there, just miles and miles of wilderness, and all it contained, so I grew up accustomed to wild animals. My sister and I slept under a tarpaulin that had been used to wraps salt, and lions used to come and lick it during the night, their raspy tongues literally inches from our faces as we slept inside. My mother barricaded the entrance and sides with camp chairs, but through the legs of the chairs we could see the lions, hyenas and other nocturnal predators strolling past the camp fire which was kept burning all night as a deterrent. When the lions roared, the ground seemed to shake, and so did we, but we were quite accustomed to such sounds and knew that my father always had his gun beside his bed just next door in my parents' sleeping tent. I loved camping out, and the magic of wild Africa and nature became interwoven deep within my psyche and has remained with me ever since.

When I had completed my Primary Schooling, I joined my sister at the Kenya Girls' High School in Nairobi, again as a boarder, taking the school train at Gilgil station which picked up pupils all along the line each term, and brought them back home again at the end of each term three times a year. I eventually graduated from high school at the age of 15 with Honors in the Cambridge School Leaving Certificate which was the final exam we had to take based on the English curriculum. This made my family very proud and they wanted me to go onto University and become a medical doctor. However, when I was 15 I had fallen in love with my brother's best friend, Bill Woodley, who was 7 years my senior and who had joined the Kenya National Parks Service having left school, as had my brother. Both were Junior Assistant Wardens in the new Nairobi National Park which in those days was wild country far from Nairobi city itself, home to lions, leopards, massive herds of zebra and wildebeest and hosts of other antelope species. The last thing I wanted was to have to be banished to far-off England and University, and eventually I persuaded my parents to instead allow me to take a stenographer's course in Nairobi, which lasted 6 months. This taught me to touch type at 60 words per minute, and to take down dictation in shorthand at 120 words a minute, which qualified me for a good job with a firm called African Explosives and Chemical Industries in Nairobi where I could earn 30 pounds a month—in those days a very good wage.

When I was 18, Bill Woodley and I married. He was the first and only "boyfriend" I had ever had, and although my family thought I was far too young to make such a momentous decision, eventually they capitulated, and we were married in the same Church in Naivasha town where my parents had been married in 1927. My two sisters were bridesmaids and my brother, Bill's best man. The reception was held back at my childhood farm, and people traveled from all over Kenya to attend, for weddings in those days were an opportunity for a get-together for friends and relations from all corners of the country. Travelling was not easy in those days, for there were no tarred roads, and heavy rain often rendered dirt tracks impassable. By then, Bill had been transferred to the Tsavo National Park, midway between Nairobi and Mombasa, Kenya's largest National Park—a huge stretch of very arid country unsuitable for agriculture due to its low rainfall and also unsuitable for domestic livestock due to the presence of tsetse flies which carried the deadly livestock disease Tryanosomiasis which killed domestic animals. It was the only large tract of land that was uninhabited by humans that the colonial government could set aside as a wildlife Sanctuary in 1949. Only bands of traditional elephant hunters from the small Waliangulu tribe frequented the area in search of elephants to kill as part of their tribal tradition. It was an area covered in dense thickets of scrub trees that shed their leaves in the long, hot dry seasons, but which came to life after rainfall, turning them into a lush tropical jungle. It was home to the largest single population of elephants in the country and also the largest number of black rhinos on the African continent and it was equal in size to Michigan State, Israel, or Wales. And it was a hot, inhospitable place, very different to the gentle climate of the Kenya Highlands where I grew up so I did not relish the idea of having to live there, having traveled through it during our annual holiday spent at the Kenya Coast in Malindi, where my grandfather had a small bungalow—the first, in fact, to be built on a beautiful pristine beach where the surf thundered send spray into the house at high tide.

We loved our coastal holidays. It took 5 days to get there, travelling in my father's farm lorry, us children in the back under a shelter rigged above us to shade us from the sun. We camped each night on the road, and again, those nights were filled with excitement with lions, rhinos and elephants often passing by easily visible in the moonlight from our beds in the back of the lorry.

With time, I came to love the arid low country of Tsavo. It held a special magic of its own in the dramatic contrast between the wet and dry seasons of the year. During the dry seasons the trees stood stark and bare, barbed with thorns and spikes, interspersed with low shrubs and wild sisal. Tsavo's unique red soils gave the Tsavo elephants the specific red color for which they are known to this day, since they plaster themselves with red mud at the waterholes to protect their skin. Every day in Tsavo was filled with excitement for we were charged relentlessly by elephants and rhinos during car journeys overseeing the development of the infrastructure of the park. We explored new places and camped under the stars, sleeping on small Hounsfield camp-beds with just a mosquito net hung on a tree as protection. I was told by Bill and his Boss, David Sheldrick, that no one had ever been taken by a lion from under a mosquito net, despite the fact that the Tsavo lions were renowned for their man-eating tendencies. During the construction of the railway at the turn of the century two man-eaters devoured over 70 workers brought from India to lay the track before they were finally shot. Today, these two notorious man-eaters are stuffed and housed in the Chicago Museum in America. Even in our time, Rangers were often dragged from tents, and it was not unusual to happen upon the body parts of poachers killed by Tsavo lions during the foot patrols in the bush. I well remember one night when a lion clawed the wall of our bedroom trying to dislodge horns which Bill had hung on the wall, and another occasion when a lion chased a man onto our verandah at night, as he was walking back to the Labour Lines after dark. We emerged from the bedroom to find him cowering beneath a verandah chair, with a lion standing on the steps about to snatch him!

With Bill, I had one daughter in 1955, and named her Gillian Sala (after a hill in the Park) and Ellen as her third Christian name, which was the name of her paternal grandmother and great grandmother. Bill and I were married for seven years, but eventually he and I decided to separate, since we had fallen out of love, yet remained good friends, more like brother and sister than husband and wife. Bill was promoted to become the warden of the Aberdare and Mountain National Parks based at Nyeri in the Northern Kenyan highlands, and found and married someone else with whom he had three sons. I eventually married David Sheldrick, the founder Warden of Tsavo who was 15 years my senior and with whom I had fallen deeply in love. However, David never wanted to be the catalyst that had influenced Bill and my decision to separate, so he never hinted that he was even fond of me. It was therefore with a sinking heart that I left Tsavo and returned to secretarial work for a firm in Nairobi, moving in with my older sister and her family, and putting my little daughter into a daily Kindergarten school.

Despite the age difference, David and I were soul mates that were meant for each other, so compatible that every moment spent in each other's company was Heaven. I was away from Tsavo for a full year, but whenever my parents went to visit my brother there, who by now was working as an Assistant Warden under David, I joined them if I could, eager to be with David and back in Tsavo again. I was always desperately unhappy to have to leave and return again to Nairobi.

When my divorce came through in 1960, to my astonishment and surprise, David asked me if I would agree to marry him. We married quietly in Mombasa with just my close family present, and joyfully I returned to live in the Tsavo I now loved, this time as his wife. I could not have been happier, as was Jill, my daughter, who told everyone that she now had two daddies and two mommies! Bill and his new wife, Ruth, remained good friends, and Jill divided her holidays between them and us. We had a host of wild orphans—elephants, rhinos, buffaloes and different antelope species that we hand-reared and loved. Like my father, David endorsed the fact that wild animals never "belonged" and that they must be set free to lead a normal wild life in the fullness of time, since a wild life was their birthright and for them, a quality of life. He was a fine naturalist, so knowledgeable and so wise, and he taught me many things about nature and the bush, not just about animals, but also about the birds, the snakes, the insects and their ways and the purpose of each towards the wellbeing of life on Earth. With time our elephant family grew in numbers, as did the rhinos and antelope orphans, either found abandoned during drought periods or orphaned when poachers killed their mothers. The demand in the far east for both ivory and rhino horn fuelled the illicit ivory trade, and constant aerial surveillance and foot patrolling was needed to counteract this menace. I helped my husband in his office, and was in charge of the orphans in our care, and as the years passed, many returned to the wild, there to lead a normal wild life. Yet, because they had been handled only with tenderness and love, many of them still kept in touch, returning periodically to spend time with us.

In 1963 I gave birth to another baby daughter, whom we named Angela Mara, the Masai Mara being David's favorite haunt after Tsavo. Whenever we had leave, we used to return to spend time there, immersed amongst the millions of wildebeest and zebra on their annual migration from the Serengeti in Tanzania.

I was totally bereft when my husband was transferred from Tsavo to head the Wildlife Planning Unit in Nairobi in 1976. Tearfully, I had to say goodbye to all our still dependent orphans, entrusting them to the care of a new Warden, and moving to a house in the Nairobi National Park. Six months later, my husband suffered a heart attack, and died very suddenly at the age of just 56. I was only 41, still with a lot of life ahead of me but I knew that I would never ever find another man that could even begin to compare to David—and I never did. The Government of Independent Kenya was extremely good to me after David's unexpected death. They gave me permission to build a small prefab house in the Nairobi National Park so that I could continue my work with orphaned animals and that is where I still live. David's friends created The David Sheldrick Wildlife Trust to honor his memory and perpetuate his work and the Government gave me the orphaned newborn elephants to rear. Today, some 35 years later, I and my daughter Angela, head the Trust, and we have been able to make a significant contribution towards Kenya's conservation effort, not least hand-rearing over 130 orphaned elephants from early infancy—the first time infant orphaned elephants have ever been successfully hand-reared and also successfully returned to the wild when grown. 69 of our ex-orphans are now living wild in Tsavo, many having their own wild-born young, which they proudly bring back to show the Keepers that raised them, who are still based at the Trust's two Rehabilitation Centers in Tsavo, steering another batch of Ex Nursery Youngsters into adulthood. Angela has given me two beautiful Grandsons and Jill has given me two beautiful Granddaughters, but I have never found another David, and nor would I ever want to! I cherish the years I spent with him, and think about him every day, missing him sorely. But, I am nevertheless, blessed indeed, having enjoyed a rich and meaningful life, surrounded by animals throughout, who have given me immeasurable pleasure and satisfaction, but also a lot of heartache and tears whenever tragedy strikes. Rearing wild animals is a mixture of highs and lows, as is life itself. The lions still roar at night around my small Nairobi Park home, and although I live alone, Angela and my grandsons are just next door in a guest house and I am still surrounded by wildlife of every description—antelopes that visit the small salt lick we put out for them on the rocks abutting my house, the birds whom we feed each day, orphaned elephants and rhinos housed in stables and Stockades in the back yard of my home. When one befriends nature, and breaches the barrier that normally segregates humans from the natural world, one is never lonely or alone, but surrounded by friends of many species, whose lives one can share, living their highs and their lows, and deriving satisfaction from knowing that one has, indeed, made a contribution that is worthwhile. More details of the work of The David Sheldrick Wildlife Trust can be found on our website www.sheldrickwildlifetrust.org and within the Autobiography I have just completed that will be released in spring this year entitled "An African Love Story—Love, Life and Animals".

7 Tina Pereira

For as long as I can remember, there have always been two personal truths of my life that inspire all of the decisions that I make. The first and foremost is my love—whether for my family, friends, ballet, fashion, pink, or sparkly things. My passion and my happiness are born and sustained from how I apply my love consciously, each day. Honouring this truth has allowed me to fall in love with life, and my life, which I surround with the people and things that I adore; love is my ultimate virtue.

My second honoured truth is that I never want to regret not expressing anything I feel inclined to do, or say, big or small, in any given moment of my life. I believe in the beauty of every moment, and since inconsistency is the only one thing consistent in life, I embrace my spontaneity and have faith in the truth behind my impulses. I rely on my instincts, since within them are my greatest desires in life, work, love, and ultimately, the path I feel inclined to follow. As a result of my no-regrets principle, I have risked losing it all, and once, I have! Some of my life lessons were trying and isolating indeed, but on the other side of them came the catalysts to make positive changes in my life and the motivation I needed to achieve my greatest aspirations. What I have learned from life thus far, is that all I can ever do is my very best, to be healthy, to work smart, and to maintain a life in balance to the best of my ability. Most amazingly, I have learned most about myself and my dreams. This being said, I have made the choice to dedicate myself to endless growth, to honour even the tiniest of steps that I take, and to replace my fears with my love, as I continue to journey through life.

I basically grew up in a dance studio; from the time I got my first pair of shoes, until the age of 12. I danced everything the studio had to offer, and was often picked up from school by my teacher and stayed until the studio was closing, cramming dinner and homework in between rehearsals. I competed in endless dance competitions and I even spent the little free time I had with my friends putting on our own dance productions in our family's homes. To this day, I can't help but pirouette in the kitchen while grabbing a spoon, or trying to balance for as long as I can on one leg, while I wait for the water to boil.

While I loved all forms of dance equally, my whole world changed when I saw my first full-length ballet. I suddenly realized what a career in ballet looked like, and the dream of becoming a Prima Ballerina was my new reality. I was so fortunate to have spent six years training at Canada's National Ballet School, where I trained intensely, studied academically, and had the time of my life boarding with young dancers from all over the world.

In my senior year at school, I danced the lead role in a ballet by a Dutch choreographer. He saw a lot of potential in me, and encouraged me to join the Dutch National Ballet when I graduated. As appealing, foreign, and exciting this engagement was, I accepted what was always my dream to be a ballerina with the National Ballet of Canada. Joining the company, I was so fortunate to be given a full time contract just a few months into my two-year apprenticeship, as well as a leading role thereafter amongst soloist dancers in the company. And in my second year, my opportunities became even greater, but unfortunately, so did the increasing pressure I was feeling to keep up mentally and physically with such experienced dancers; and it was beginning to get the best of my confidence. While my struggles and insecurities were only growing worse throughout my third year in the company, I began to reconsider the idea of dancing with the Dutch National Ballet. My thought being that I could expand my training with new coaches, dance new repertoire, gain inspiration and learn from many new dancers, and most importantly, live out on my own for the very first time, and really get to know myself and hopefully come to terms with my fears. The icing on the cake was that my best friend was dancing with the company at the time, so I wouldn't be completely alone! I knew I had to give it a try, and when the offer was on the table, I knew I would regret not taking it. It was undoubtedly the toughest decision I had ever made. As far as everybody was concerned, moving to a different continent seemed over dramatic, and they believed that I was throwing it "all" away. While I wasn't looking for approval for what I know I needed and wanted to do, I struggled with the disapproval of most of the people who cared about me. To a large degree, I think my decision also came out of the fact that my life was already so predictable and nearly prosaic. I could see the rest of my life, career, and my relationship at the time, and it terrified me because I was only 21! However, when I had made my final decision and the time came to embark, there was nothing but love, support, encouragement, and best wishes, as I happily packed my life into two pink suitcases and was off into the thrilling unknown!

My time living in Europe was unforgettable and still, to this day, I am so in love with the European lifestyle and miss it very much. I learned so much from the culture, the company, my new friendships, and from all the travelling I did around the continent every chance I had. Not to mention, living out on my own for the first time! In hindsight, it seems like a lifetime a go. What I never predicted, however, was the severe homesickness I would endure, or the fact that it would eventually overcome me. I had missed my family so much over the 10 months that I was away, and I realized that as amazing as my experience was, my life was meaningless if I couldn't share it with the people I love so much! By the middle of May, I made the decision to return home a changed young lady, so proud of my new self-sufficiency and with new resolve to make my home my home. There was only one small problem. The National Ballet of Canada was in the midst of changing directorship and I would have to wait out the process to speak to the new director, who would have to make the decision to hire me back into the company. For the first time in my life I wasn't a ballerina, I wasn't even dancing, and these few months seemed like an eternity. I literally didn't know how to start my day without ballet class, and I quickly found myself without the only self I knew. Thankfully, everyone kept their "I told you this could happen" to themselves as I seemed to board a whole new life rollercoaster. For a while I hadn't the slightest clue what to do with myself, and I could sense the worry in my family and friends. I had gone to Europe to learn to be independent and self aware, but it seemed to only be the prelude.

Looking back, it was only through this experience of being forced out of the comfort of Tina Ballerina, that I really had the opportunity to get to know and honour the real Tina Pereira behind her. I had no choice but to make the most of my new reality and I did my best to stay positive and enjoy my new life. I needed to find a "normal" job that still allowed me to take ballet class each morning, because eventually getting myself back into dance was undeniable. I experienced a bookstore, a clothing store, and even bartending! I met many interesting people along the way and my eyes were opened to a world I had been sheltered from my whole life. (I graduated from boarding school with only nine classmates). Although the situation was less than ideal, at the time, there was definitely something fulfilling about the experience that allowed me to not regret not having it, if you know what I mean. But as novel as it was, it wasn't long before I knew I needed to dance again! Soon! No matter what! My positive outlook was being put to the test, and I began to really struggle emotionally, as I was getting less optimistic in my efforts to rejoin the ballet. For a while I even stopped taking ballet class, because it made me so sad and perhaps a small part of me thought that it was time to move on. However, I remember attending a performance one night and crying the entire time. Deep down I knew that I wasn't ready to give up, not even close.

After nearly five months that seemed like an entire lifetime, I was invited to perform with ProArteDanza, an independent dance company in Toronto. And after only a few weeks into rehearsals, I was also hired as a guest artist for a season in which there were many injuries at the National Ballet. I can remember exactly where I was the moment I received that phone call, and I can't express how great it felt to be back where I knew I belonged! ·

As luck would have it, I was given a full contract at the end of my temporary one, and just 3 months later came the biggest surprise of my life!

The Erik Bruhn Competition is something similar to the ballet Olympics; it is an event that was established by one of the greatest dancers of all time, Erik Bruhn. Tailored for 2 young dancers from 5 international ballet companies in which he was closely affiliated, and something of a jump-off point to promising careers. It was less than 3 weeks before the competition, when I was asked to represent the company due to the fact that the young dancer originally chosen to compete was suffering from an injury and wouldn't be able to continue to train for the event. As if there was even a cloud 10!

Entering the competition so late, I was pretty realistic about my odds of taking home the best female prize. It was truly "Just an honour to be nominated". However, there was no time to think much beyond that. I had to learn and perfect one Classical piece with a pas de deux, solo, and finale, and learn a brand new 6-minute contemporary pas de deux. There were literally blood, sweat, and tears, and I ate, slept, and dreamt ballet from the time of my first rehearsal to the night of the competition. I was overwhelmed and exhausted day after day, but I lived in each moment, pushing myself further than I ever thought I could go. I was determined to represent myself, my partner, my coach, my boss, my fellow dancers and the company I loved so much to the very best of my ability. And so, I made a point to make my one and only goal to go to bed each night proud that I had done my best in my rehearsals and knowing that I had improved, if even just a little bit each day.

Finally, the day had arrived. When I had finished my very last rehearsal, had my dinner, and was ready to begin to prepare for the show, I returned to my dressing room to find it showered with cards, flowers and gifts from my fellow dancers, friends, family, and my teachers from the National Ballet School. It was such a beautiful sight and so overwhelmingly sweet, that I felt like I had already won.

The competition began smoothly, and my partner and I were doing really well, when disaster struck. Just as I was re-entering the stage to finish the last part of our classical repertoire, I could sense that something was terribly wrong. I glanced at my partner, who had hurt himself badly just seconds before and he was struggling to exit the stage in a bewildered limp. My heart literally sank into my stomach and I knew I couldn't continue.

I ran back into the wings and into Rex Harrington, a dancer I grew up idolizing, and now one of my favorite coaches who was co-hosting the evening. He looked straight into my vacant eyes and demanded "Tina, go do your fouettes" (32 consecutive turns on one leg), but there was no way I was going back on stage! I remember just standing there paralyzed not even able to form thoughts into words when he literally grabbed me by the shoulders, turned me around, and pushed me back onto the stage. I was beside myself, and I had no choice but to get started. As I began to turn, I could hear my friends clapping from the wings to encourage me on. Then later, I heard the audience clapping in rhythm, and then cheering, and like magic, I just kept on going. I exited on the other side of the stage, still in complete shock and wondering the whereabouts of my partner. I turned back to the empty stage with the grand finale music playing and the audience was clapping louder and louder in rhythm to the music when Principal dancer Greta Hodgkinson came from behind me and gave me another little push forward and said "Go finish!" So I went back onto the stage and improvised something similar to the ending I should have danced with Keiichi, and I finished the piece on the music. And the crowd went wild.

It turned out that my partner tore his Achilles tendon mid air and needed to be rushed to the hospital. I sat backstage still in shock and worried sick about him while the other competitors prepared for their contemporary pieces. Once I knew he was well taken care of, I became calm and at peace with the situation. I was so proud of what we had achieved together, and for me, that was truly priceless. Moments into the intermission however, I was collected and carried away by a very ambitious ballet entourage. Apparently, there had been a plan in action, and like sheer fate, I was able to change my contemporary repertoire to Romeo and Juliet. It turned out that Principal dancer Guillaime Cote was watching the competition from the audience and was willing to step in as my new partner, the Juliet costume I would wear just happened to be displayed in the lobby of the theatre as a part of a Shakespeare exhibit, and the orchestra was already prepared, because the English competing couple was to perform another version of Romeo and Juliet to the same score! What were the odds?

I was hurried to my change room where one of my friends did my hair, (which included securing a friend's pearl necklace she was wearing that evening to my forehead with eyelash glue) while two other friends gave me a mini performance of the pas de deux to help remember the choreography, since I had only performed it once before; and another friend altering the oversized costume. I remember saying a somewhat vacant "ok" to whatever I was told as I was led by the hand around the theatre to prepare.

The situation was so beyond overwhelming that I had no choice but to trust whatever was happening to me.

Just before entering the stage as Juliet, I will always remember how my coach looked me in the eye and said "bless you" in a way so sincere that it was so touching and sweet, but also in a way that made me think that the moment was terribly more serious than I was prepared for. It's not that I didn't want to do amazingly well, but it was just that I actually felt so calm and free knowing that I was no longer competing, but instead allowing myself to enjoy every second of performing for an audience that was so supportive of me, and wanting to give them all I could.

When I entered the stage, I had never felt so calm and relaxed ever before in my dancing. Part of the reason was that it was actually a relief to become Juliet and for those moments to escape into a world much more quiet than my own.

When the time came for the awards ceremony, I remember standing calmly on stage without a single thought, but instead, just the feeling of being overwhelmed. I don't even remember hearing my name being called as the recipient of the female prize. I just remember feeling a little push from behind to go forward to accept my award. When I did eventually realize that I had won the prize (as the presenter began filling my arms with flowers), I literally felt like I was going to explode! My emotional state was already at such full capacity; I could barely take it in. The remainder of the night is more of a blur. That is until the night was finally over and I was back in my apartment with my best friend Brett, who helped bring all of my belongings, including all of the thoughtful gifts I had been showered with back home with me. We sat in my apartment until the early hours of the morning reading the cards, arranging flowers in vases, and opening presents. I was even more overjoyed! Not only did I take home the award that night, but I also took home the greatest friend I could ever ask for to celebrate it with me. And I felt like the luckiest girl in the world.

That one single event has changed my life forever, and has set a foundation to the life that I live. I continue to set goals for myself, big and small, and realize the importance of my daily work and how the little improvements I make, and the smallest opportunities can lead to success greater than I can imagine.

Finally, as much as great goals require a lot of dedication and serious time commitment, I also strive for a well-rounded balanced life. My beautiful art form of ballet dancing, for example, requires a lot out of me, including a lot of working time in the studio, rest, good nutrition and sleep. But equally, I value the time I get to spend with my family and I am lucky to get to see them often and I have a loving boyfriend I am fortunate to share my life with. I am passionate about my blog about fashion and ballet, and designing and sewing leotards which have easily become my favourite pastimes. All of these things combined, are what keep me inspired, energetic, busy, and happy. When I am engaged in one, I know that it strengthens all the others, and this is how I know that I am on the right path, following my instincts, living in spirit, and moving in the direction of my dreams.

www.blog.tinapereira.com

8 Denise Wade

The Denise Wade Show

W hen I think back on my life it seems to be so episodic. Maybe that explains my love of television sit-coms; *Three's Company*, *Andy Griffith*, *Bewitched*, *Will and Grace*, and my favorite, *Friends*. It's everything I've looked for my whole life. In between the laughs and the good natured wise cracking, there is a lot of love and belonging; there is home. These ultra human characters, flawed and sometimes foolish, are still always there for each other. Like the theme song says "I'll be there for you." Isn't that what we all want? I love the way they name different episodes of *Friends*. There is one called "The one that might have been" where they explore various "what ifs" concerning each character. There is also one called "the one where everybody finds out" when it is discovered that two of the characters have fallen in love. Looking back over my life, I see how easily it breaks down into episodes.

The One With The Red Satin Dress
It took my breath away.

Nanny Ellis watched me untie the ribbon, slowly open the box and push aside the cotton candy colored tissue; there was the most beautiful dress I had ever seen. A red satin dress. I was sure I had seen Audrey Hepburn wearing a dress just like it. I couldn't believe it was for me. I would parade around in front of my mirror for hours at a time singing into a hairbrush or giving my Oscar speech. I was five years old when she gave me that dress, and I was sure that if I wore it, I would someday be on stage or on the screen. Dorothy had her ruby slippers and I had my red satin dress. When I was very little, I was a total show-off. I loved to sing and I lived to entertain. On weekends, I would put on backyard shows for the neighborhood, charging fifty cents at the door (the backyard gate), and perform skits from the Carole Burnett show that were half remembered, half improvised. Then, for the final act I would come out in my red satin dress and sing "I'm All Outta Love" by Air Supply. When we added up the baked goods and lemonade I would sell, I made a killing; I was a real entrepreneur. Those days were full of music. I remember days when I stayed home from school "sick" with my mom and an old tape recorder she borrowed from my uncle. I would sing and sing and we would have the best time together.

Then, something changed.

When I was six years old my parents split up. I don't recall much about it except the four of us, my brother David, and my mother in the front seat, my sister Dawn and I in the back driving down Kennedy road away from what had been my home, and our suitcases falling out of the hatch back, spilling all over the road. None of us spoke at all. We just helped our mother gather up the clothes and drove on, but looking back, I see my innocence still laying there all over that road. After we got settled on our own we were okay for a while and Mom made us feel like we were a family on our own.

Then she met a man and got married.

It seemed to happen as suddenly as that. Everything changed; we all moved in together. There were two more brothers and another sister. Do you hear the song in your head "Here's a story...of a lovely lady?" We were the Brady Bunch in numbers, but this was no feel-good family sitcom. I think we all tried to make the best of it at first. I wanted my mom to be happy so I tried to keep smiling, but that smile faded over the weeks and months that followed. The nice man with the three children we had visited changed. He was now my stepfather. I was afraid of him and my step brothers seemed to be so mean. My brothers and sisters changed; we seemed to lose each other, and in that big house full of people I felt all alone. We moved to a new neighbourhood and I changed schools. I changed. My red satin dress didn't fit anymore and I didn't like the person I saw in the mirror. At school I was terribly shy with the other kids and I found the teachers to be so impatient and intimidating. It was so hard to make new friends. The closest I came to a new companion was a girl who would send me little paper cards she made up with little messages that said how ugly or stupid I was. Life just felt hard and people felt hard. I spent most of my time at home in my room and in many ways, I locked myself away behind a door deep inside that I didn't open for many years with my red satin dress pushed way back in my closet, nowhere in sight.

Don't you hate it when you start liking a show, and all of a sudden they replace an actor you really like with one you really don't? It always feels like the beginning of the end. The little entertainer was replaced with a lonely little girl.

The One With The Doctor's Wife

There I was all alone in my room and I know that doesn't sound like a good thing. I started having some issues with my body image too. I realize that doesn't sound like a good thing either and I guess it could have taken a very unhealthy turn, but another character emerged in that room. I started doing sit-ups, push-ups, and any number of other exercises I picked up in magazines or on TV. Maybe I was still depressed, but the endorphins from working out made me feel good and I have to think it gave me the sense that I was in control of something in my life. It started a life-long love of fitness and it balanced perfectly with my love of KitKat bars. School, as I said before, was an awful experience for me. I was so sensitive, and felt so defenseless, disconnected and intimidated that I really didn't get much out of it; I just wanted to get it over with. So when I signed up to sing in the school concert, I was as surprised as everyone else. Some fearless alter ego took over and just went for it. Nobody knew I could sing; I wasn't even sure I could anymore, but I did. A whole cast of characters were emerging in me, begging for their turn in front of the camera: a fearless showgirl and a dreamer, a shy little orphan curled up in bed crying, a runaway with her suitcase packed by the door, and a hard working no-nonsense female version of my father. That would prove to be the good news and the bad news in this story.

By the time I was about to turn 18, things were were starting to look up. I had a best friend named Jennifer, and a little bit of popularity from my involvement in music. On my 18th birthday, Jenn took me to the Keg. We had a waiter, who I thought was kind and very handsome. We kinda flirted all night but nothing really happened. The next day my out-going twin self took the reigns. I found myself calling the Keg to ask to speak to our waiter the night before. We went out on one date and hit if off right away.

I realize now that meeting Doug was not just about finding a boyfriend, but about finding a family. It was like throwing out a canvas covered with paint that I didn't know how to finish and starting a new one. Doug and his family were unlike anyone I had ever met. They were spiritual, musical, and close to each other. I tucked into the middle of that group and became a part of it very quickly. Doug was the most intelligent person I had ever known at that time and it seemed to balance out my life so well. I was not much of a talker; I might be able to start a sentence, but I would always lose confidence that anyone would be interested in anything I had to say, lose focus and leaving it hanging three quarters of the way through. Doug finished my sentences for me; eventually it was like he could have whole conversations for me. Doug's mom, Tammy, was an accomplished pianist, and both Doug and his sister Amber sang, so we would often all sit around the piano singing together. It was idyllic. It was as if I'd leaped into a television screen and was living in the spin-off of some warm cuddly family show—*Little house in Scarborough*.

At 22 I said "I do." Doug and I got married, and he entered The Naturopathic College Of Medicine. I held down the fort financially with as many as three jobs at one time, paying for a condo and a couple of cars while Doug was getting his degree. Still, I had the sense that there was something more I wanted to do. I had been taking lessons on piano from my mother-in-law, and followed up that education at the Royal Ontario Conservatory. One day sitting at the piano with Tammy she told me about a music program for young kids called Keynote Kids for children ages 3–5 years. I thought the program was brilliant and with my love of music and for children, it was perfect for me. I was able to start classes at the library, and within a year or so my programs had grown into a full blown successful business, so it was time to find my own place to rent. After months of looking, I found a place and hired a team to renovate and build music rooms until it was perfect. My school thrived over the next several years. Eventually, in what I thought was a very good deal, I accepted an offer by a much larger company to join forces, but six months after, I had become part of a big franchise and I came to realize that we had very different ways of doing business and I packed up my sheet music, said goodbye to a couple hundred students and parents, who had become like family and had trusted and relied on me.

To say that I was devastated would be a great understatement. I was angry and depressed and desperate for something or someone to hold on to. I had felt Doug drifting away for quite some time with his school friends, while I took care of things at home, and I was resentful of him for being self involved and not being there for me the way I was for him. By this time, Doug's parents had moved in with us and when I needed so much to have a place to lick my wounds and retreat, I found I was not the center of anyone's attention. Again, I felt like I was surrounded by strangers. It wasn't a pretty time to say the least. There were break ups and make ups and the whole thing felt like barreling down the highway in a messy car trying to look for a map. After Doug's graduation, he was invited to join an established practice in Saskatchewan and since I didn't know what else to do, we sold the condo and our furniture and moved to Moose-Jaw where I became the doctor's wife.

There seems to be something difficult about telling my own story that I didn't expect. First of all, its not like walking through rooms, looking at pictures and trophies and ribbons and simply giving a guided tour. It's more like wading into a flooded basement and trying to figure out what's still worth keeping. Secondly, if I were making up a story, I would have a clear beginning, middle and ending. Each part of the story would unfold with my eyes fixed on the eventual glorious conclusion. In my story, the mountain top is realizing there is a mountain at all; that there is a brass ring, or a ship to come in. To tell the truth, I had forgotten about my red satin dress until I started out trying to put my own story on paper. It's hard to look back and see that so much of your life is like watching a child trying to build a sand castle as the tide is rising and the waves keep crashing in, wiping it all away.

The One With All The Singing

By the year 2000, I think I thought I had what I wanted; a nice house, 6 cats, and I was the doctor's wife in a very friendly, quiet prairie town. I had someone looking after me for a change. I had all the time, and money I wanted. I had a marriage that "worked." I obviously didn't see the parentheses back then, and the doctor didn't notice that our relationship had suffered so many contusions at that point that by then, we had settled in to what we were really best suited to be—just friends.

One of our favorite things to do was to join Karaoke contests, and after winning a few, someone suggested the idea of a one woman show starring ... me! Using Karaoke gear, a sound man, a couple of light stands, and a lot of Shania Twain, Faith Hill and Martina Mcbride tracks, I did regional festivals, corporate shows and cafes around Moosejaw to rave reviews. Enter the fearless me. I was still the girl who couldn't finish a sentence, but I could stand up in front of any number of people, sing my heart out and flirt and kibitz with the crowd by myself from one hour shows to sometimes entire evenings.

It is impossible to look at it now and not see the cracks that were forming around our life together that were directly related to me stepping out on a stage by myself, totally in control, under my own power. Back then, it felt like the world was crumbling, but now, it seems more like the shell around a baby bird.

I started to be aware of the controlling from Doug and from Doug's family (who had moved out there as well). At first maybe there was a safety in not having to be the one who knows, but as I began to grow and gain my confidence, I resented it more and more. I felt myself growing out of my life. In 2001, I auditioned for a spot on the *Telemiracle;* a nationally televised telethon hosted by the Kinsmen Club of Saskatchewan to raise money for children with special needs, which is shot in Saskatoon. It was a pretty big deal for me; there were some big names on the show and I and my karaoke tracks would be right in the middle of it all. Amazingly, I was chosen out of quite a lot of talented singers from Western Canada. Doug and I made the two hour trip to Saskatoon for the weekend. Then, when the moment came for me to get up on the big stage, with a theatre full of cheering people, bright lights and live cameras, it was fearless Denise who went out there and gave it her all. It didn't even occur to me that this was the biggest thing I had ever done and the closest to my dreams that I had ever been. I sang two songs, got off stage and signed autographs as if it were the most natural thing in the world... as natural as doodling on a piece of paper.

"The Bob Newhart show" aired in the mid-seventies and was based around the life of a New York city psychiatrist, his sweet and understanding wife Emily, his wacky neighbours and his neurotic clientele.

"Newhart" aired in 1982 to rave reviews. Some good old Bob. But that's where the similarities end; different wife, different wacky neighbours, now he's an inn keeper in Vermont. Wow, doesn't that sound a bit far-fetched?

The One With The Big Move, And The Little Apartment
Fade from prairie grass to a bumper to bumper busy city street and pan across the tops of the cracked and littered rooftops, sweeping in a panorama that continues around revealing the CN Tower, partially concealed by the midday smog of Toronto, then finally resting on me standing on a roof top overlooking Danforth Avenue with the new love of my life—Thomas.

Doesn't it almost make you feel like you're in a Quentin Tarantino movie? I know, I didn't say it in so many words, but tucked away in the story you must have seen the truth of it; that Doug and I were not meant to be forever. I didn't really see it either, until it was well past time to leave. It was a mutual agreement, but as the song says, "breaking up is hard to do" even when it is as easy as it was for us. I wasn't just leaving him; I felt like I was leaving a community, friends and family I had grown to love, but it felt like the right move. The September before, my sister had given birth to my nephew Alexander, and I wanted to be more than the occasional greeting card in his life. I drove across Canada from Saskatchewan back to Ontario with a few bits of furniture and two of my cats with the bitter sweet feeling of both leaving and coming home. I met Thomas at a studio in Oshawa, where I was recording some demos. I had no idea I was going to fall in love with him. There are pictures from the two day session I still have today, and you would swear that we were already together. At the start, I did everything I could to resist it, feeling like it was too soon; I would say "I'm not going to call you", then... I called him. I said, "this isn't going to happen"... but it did. Before I knew it, we were living in the heart of Toronto, something I had never wanted to do, in his little apartment where I never would have seen myself living. No matter what you think you will or won't do, when you fall in love—I mean really fall in love—all bets are off. I remember standing on the roof of Thomas' building when we first dated and saying "I don't believe there's a 'right one' for anyone." He remembers it too. He tells me when I said that, a little voice in his head said "she's the one".

So there I was in this little apartment with Thomas, with my two cats and every other week I was stepmom to a five year old red headed boy named Faron. Reading it now as I write it I have to ask the question: Was I crazy?

Hitting the bottom—people who have never really been there use that expression in a different way than people who've spent some quality time there. It's like saying the word "love" to describe how you feel about a pair of shoes. The bottom is not pretty, but for some it is essential. For those who have been lost, or never really even had a sense of purpose or direction, it does provide a clear place to start from. It tends to be very murky down there and there were lots of times I would have said I had "hit bottom" only to find that it had only been a rocky point jutting up from it. When you really hit it, you really know it.

I don't really want to go into a lot of detail. There were cries for help, expressions of anger turned inward and outward. You don't have to be a CSI to figure it out.

The One With The Bottom
Picture a toy boat in a full bath tub when the plug is pulled out. See how the little boat seems to run a circuit around the outside? That's the way it was for me. It was a gradual emptying of all that had buoyed me up 'til then. I no longer had the lifestyle I was used to. Divorces aren't usually as amicable as break-ups are, and the result of my divorce was the financial opposite of what most women experience. I simply didn't have the money to fight it and though Thomas would have given me both kidneys if I needed them, he is a successful Canadian singer/song-writer and that rarely translates into wealth. To top it off, he was going through his own hell with what we thought at the time were voice problems.

I no longer had my little show; "Just Denise" wasn't going to cut it in the Southern Ontario market where there are full bands, who don't make what I was making alone. I was part of a blended family again. I didn't see that one coming. I felt like I was a little girl competing for the love of a parent again. Nobody who goes through that likes to admit it, but that's how it feels. I didn't know what to do. My instincts said "get a job...any job." My family said "get a job, any job." That's just the way we think. I was losing myself a little at a time, at least who I thought was myself. I tried to tuck into Thomas's arms and just let everything be okay, but it was more and more not okay with everyday that passed. I see the tub almost empty, spiraling quickly in smaller and smaller circles and then comes the bottom.

The One With The Question

The Chinese philosopher Confucius says "things must get worse before they get better". I wouldn't ever have wanted to believe that before, but it's true.

Thomas' voice problem turned out to be a neurological disorder called Oromandibular Dystonia. He could no longer sing, and eventually would hardly be able to speak at times. The prognosis was "nobody knows, we'll see". He began working in construction with my mom's boyfriend Bob and was going through his own identity crisis. At first, I thought I would start up my music program again. Thomas and I plastered Toronto neighbourhoods with flyers to little or no reaction. I then thought I would go into the handbag design business. That ended up being a bust; I still have a hundred of them (want to buy one?). I began to work at Shoppers Drug Mart in the cosmetics department, which felt like giving up at the time, but ended up being very educational. I became very passionate about cosmetics and skin care. The most important thing I had to do was put myself back together. Seeing a psychiatrist was the first step. Learning how to listen to my own thought process and hear the tapes I was playing from my childhood and realizing that I was depressed; not the "good grief Charlie Brown!" kind of depression, but a chemical imbalance. It took a while for me to come to grips with it, but as my treatment progressed, through therapy, medication, love and support, I started to get to know myself really for the first time. In the meantime, Thomas and I put together a show called "The Covergirlz". In the beginning, it was just a way to get me out there singing. Just to let you know where I was at in those days, it took me over a year to even get comfortable enough to sing in front of Thomas, but after a while, I learned that I was good at singing harmony, and had a love of jazz standards as well as the country and rock I had grown up with. The Covergirlz ultimately became a show that took me across Canada and through parts of the States and has given me some of my favourite memories. It was while I was singing with The Covergirlz that I was spotted by Beverley Mahood, a popular country singer and former lead singer for the group "Lace". They loved my energy, and wanted Thomas and I to help resurrect her girl group career. So much has changed since then. When you are depressed, you see life through a tunnel; coming out of it, I began to see so many people who were there for me. My family, my dad and stepmom, my stepson, and a whole cast of new friends who help me keep growing.

So, how do you know which moment was the one that changed your life? I quit my job at the drug store, joined a new version of the group "Lace" and toured Canada with it, even doing a month of shows in Afghanistan. I have been a print model and commercial actress since 2005. That was the year I auditioned for the Shopping Channel. Good old fearless dreamer me walked right into the lions den, in front of the brass; with no net and no script, I talked about the special selling points of a pencil for ten minutes (try it sometime). Even though I had zero experience, the girl who used to need someone to finish her sentences was talking on air for a living and meeting so many of my heroes; Joan Rivers, Suzanne Somers, Marie Osmond and connecting with living rooms all across Canada every week. Thomas and I had a beautiful wedding in 2007 with our friends Marc Jordan and Amy Sky singing for us, Faron giving a beautiful reading for us, new and old friends, family, my nephew Alex looking so dapper and so happy for us. Surely, that would be a contender for the day that changed my life. But I don't believe any of those days could have come without one little piece of the puzzle. It all came down to one simple question.

The moment that changed my life seemed so small. It's like what they say about the flutter of a butterfly's wings being felt on the other side of the world. One day, Thomas and I were driving to a rehearsal and talking about what I wanted to do with my life. I was still working at Shoppers, and my blue collar ethics wouldn't even consider quitting. I was considering going back to school and taking a computer course. We drove along, trying to sort it out and as usual, my head began to spin just looking for a solution that felt right. Then, Thomas asked me the one thing no one had asked me for years; not since I was the little show-off in the red satin dress. "What is the first thing you ever wanted to be?" he asked. And in a second, in that moment I knew. The earliest memory I have of wanting to be or do anything is this one thing.

I wanted to be on television all of my life. It had never occurred to me that I could just decide. I always felt like I was stuck in someone else's script. It just hit me like lightening to realize that it was really all up to me. It changed the way I looked at the future and the past. I stopped feeling sorry for myself and saw that everything that had ever "happened" to me gave me everything I needed to be successful in my life. There didn't have to be any excuses or reasons or doubts or fears. I stopped looking for other people to define me and I knew that it was me writing the story all along.

So, what's the first thing you ever wanted to be?

9 Reyhan Sofraci

Y ears ago I wanted to start a venture and pursue a dream I was not even aware that I could bring to fruition. I had to break mental, traditional and emotional barriers as I pursued what I believed I was destined for. Financial woes, fears, loss, joy, panic, you name it. Every single emotion would coexist in my days to come.

I moved to Canada when I was ten years old. I still remember how different things were here. I used to live in Turkey and London where a ten year old was still a kid. I found things here were so different and children were expected to grow up so quickly. I went to great schools and remember seeing many councilors as I was trying to explore the right career path for me. University—what was the point? I come from a family lineage where the men have always been the breadwinners and the women the housewives. The only reputable lines of work that were worth pursuing and deserved any respect and recognition were lawyers, doctors or engineers. Saying you wanted to pursue anything other than those were just pointless.

I was still supported by my family with the understanding of the importance of education and started University at the age of 17. I really had no idea what I wanted to do with my life; even though suggestions like the above were made, I recall wanting to be a professor, a teacher, or even maybe a writer and photographer for National Geographic. Fashion just never seemed like a possibility to me; it was never something I ever pondered as a business as needlework and design were always seen as only hobbies in my family. I graduated from the University of Toronto at the age of 20; having studied Sciences and completed a specialty in Psychology.

Following my graduation, we moved to Montreal. Depressed, lacking the ability to speak French, I felt lost and hopeless. I did not know what to do with myself. But I had to jump back. I got jobs in condo projects, hotels, and started saving my money in hopes to pursue and start something of my own. I knew I could not be a homebody and there was something missing; there was this ambitious fire burning inside of me.

So one day I woke up and decided to do it. My friends had been encouraging me for a long time. I would take my purchased bikinis and change them up and people would want to buy them off of me. Friends encouraged me by stating that there was something there and I should pursue it. Years later, I even remember discovering sketches on the sides of my notes in high school and University. I was always into taking swathes of fabric and making it my own. I just never thought I could pursue it beyond a hobby.

I knew nothing of the industry but decided to take a huge leap and jump in to see if I would sink or swim. I still remember my first investment—a 3 in one serger that cost me $2000 to purchase in Toronto. The sad part was it was no good for the job and we never even used it! I had to buy more machines in the months to come and eventually raised enough money in my savings to hire someone with experience to bring my sketches to reality.

I still remember the first time I sewed a slip with a simple domestic machine. It was absolutely terrible in construction but the style came across nicely. I went to see my dad with excitement. He was being funny: "Wow beautiful, but isn't it a little small?" he stated with a perplexed expression. He always felt that I was just playing around and investing in a hobby. I remember when my dad finally realized that I was not pursuing a hobby but was actually pursuing something more. He started seeing me and reading about the brand in various media. I remember the excitement in his eyes when he would google the brand and see his daughter and the company. He became so proud of me and that alone is something so priceless to me. Now, he laughs as every time he sees a swimsuit on TV, he no longer admires the women and the beautiful form but actually analyses the swimwear. It is funny to see such a huge shift in his perception of bikini bodies and of my 'hobby'.

I remember our first fashion show, it was way too late in the swim season but I really wanted to see if anyone would even respond well to what I designed besides my loving and supportive friends and family. Days later, articles came out on our launch and I was so excited and thrilled by what these people had to say. It felt so incredible to be recognized even though I lacked a foundation in fashion design. People took me very seriously and I was so amazed by their kind words and support. To be acknowledged by industry professionals was the ultimate form of flattery.

I remember the first time a stylist called me up from Elle magazine and wanted to come by to borrow samples for a photoshoot—I was in complete shock. I spent all night trying to bring the office to a state that was presentable and impressive. I was so excited and nervous, yet when she came by I was truly surprised by how wonderful she was and then reality struck me. There was no reason to be nervous, she too was a person and she was sweet and interested enough to want to come to see me. She borrowed a whole selection of suits and took a few pieces that I had actually removed from the collection with her for the shoot.

Then, we actually made it in the magazine, the cover of Elle Canada! I could not believe it. It was one of the suits we had removed from the collection. A look that portrayed a high wasted panty that only started becoming a trend in the years to follow. The phone was ringing like crazy and I had no idea what to do. It was just me answering the phones and trying to help people who wanted to order it. Just to order fabric, grade the pattern, get it all rolling would have taken up too much time and as we all know, people have short attention spans! It was such a great opportunity and I will forever be grateful for that recognition.

Sports Illustrated—the bible of swimwear. They receive thousands of suits for the issue and when yours is selected, it truly is an incredible form of flattery. I will never forget the excitement when we had received the call. WE had made it in.

So how did my degree end up relating to anything I ended up doing? Well, the key thing is that I love people and I love to create. I love the power of perception and can see how even the smallest tangent can redirect one's attention and make them forget what they were thinking about or seeing a minute before. The power of perception! Swimwear became my calling and the human body my canvas. I wanted to play with fabrics, with lines and draw attention to the beautiful female body and accentuate all the positives that it possesses. Such small fabric with the power to do so much.

Pursuing a dream is something that everyone is encouraged to do, but the hardships involved in making it a reality is something that requires understanding and preparation. Always ensure that you are prepared as much as you can be. Gaining experience in your field is something that I did not do which I highly recommend. It is important to get to know your industry and see if it really is the path for you. Sometimes you do not realize all that a certain business entails and once deep inside you may realize that you took a wrong turn.

You will meet many people along the way—Some good and some not so good. You will have to make ethical decisions and these will determine where you will go. I remember I was approached by an ex-partner of one of my competitors who wanted to partner with me. I knew at that moment that if I took that path, my business would be on overdrive. But I had an ethical issue with this and chose to take my time and do this the right way.

I wanted to ensure that I never stepped on people's toes to get on top. I have never believed in this. It is sad, but I have witnessed most of the time how people step on others to rise. I never wanted to do it this way and this is why it has taken me longer to get where I am today. But I am happy and have no regrets in my decisions. I have always believed in the importance of appreciating other people's work and even though I have definitely witnessed such things, I would never bash anyone's hard work to put myself on top. One must appreciate others' talents and learn and develop to improve their own.

Nothing in life comes easy and everything has a price whether that is personal sacrifice, monetary investment or loss of time with friends and loved ones. One has to be prepared for all the joys and challenges that will come one's way. I remember when I first started. My entire life was dedicated to the business. I worked every day for at least 12-14 hours and weekends had no meaning to me. I still remember driving in old Montreal with my brother one summer weekend with my face glued to the window crying. I was watching people hand in hand walking down the streets—families, couples, friends. I felt as though I would never experience that sort of weekend again. It was overwhelming.

Never attempt to do everything by yourself. It is impossible. You need to have a support crew, be it emotional, physical or mental. I was blessed, I always had a family that loved and deeply supported me. My mother would run around and do anything for me. My father was always there for me. My brothers always went out of their way for me and my then boyfriend and now my husband always did everything to take away stress from me. Even my grandmother would stay up late into the hours of the night and do all the swimsuit packaging for me. Nothing would be where it is without the support of my loving family.

I had times where I was about to burn out from stress, where I wanted to just stop, but their words of encouragement, their hugs and their love always gave me the courage to move forward and not to give up. I am lucky; extremely lucky. People are important and love was the fuel that gave me the power to push hard and keep going.

In business, as in life, you need to partner with people who balance your weaknesses and compliment your strengths. I could not be anywhere without my partner in crime, my brother or the support of my entire family. Over the years I built a strong team of talented people around me. This company's success is a result of all the hard work and talent that was put into the company by everybody. It is always important to give credit where it is due. It is not me, but we, all the people who have been involved and who have brought the company to where it is today.

When you wake up in the morning, you should have a smile on your face. We spend most of our lives at work so I have always been a strong believer that it is important to love what you do and do what you love. Chase your dreams but don't dream blindly. Life is not easy and many hardships may come your way. Just be as prepared as possible for the challenges that may come—be it financial, emotional, physical, or mental. It's not easy and hopefully one day, when you look back at everything that you have surpassed, you will feel a sense of pride and joy like me.

We did it.

Melanie Groom

I was born in Orillia, Ontario in 1979 to my amazing parents Rob and Sue and an older sister Christie. We grew up in a small town of about 28 thousand people and for as long as I can remember, I always desired to move to a big city where I could be "something" or "someone".

I was very fortunate as a child; my parents put me in dance lessons, piano lessons, golf lessons, skiing, and my true love, horseback riding. Prior to my tenth birthday I was experiencing an abnormal amount of back pain that my mother insisted was just growing pains. My complaining got to the point where she finally decided to take me for an x-ray. I actually love my parents for being so calm about sickness and pain as they have made me a stronger person for it. I actually rarely get sick, because I tell myself I'm fine. However, the x-ray that I had actually showed something much worse than anyone had expected. I had a spinal condition called Spina Bifida Occulta.

Just a couple of months after my 10th birthday, in November of 1989, I had a spinal surgery at Sick Kids hospital in Toronto. The doctors told my parents after my 7 hour surgery that they were so lucky they operated as my lower spine was nothing but mushy cartilage and could have resulted in paralysis. I remember my hospital stay very clearly and most of what came after it.

I was put in a pink, fluorescent fiberglass body cast for four months. I was homeschooled for the second semester of grade 6. It was so cool how all of my classmates wrote letters and sent get-well cards. It wasn't much more than a year after my surgery that I was riding horses and entering competitions every weekend. My life from 10 to 19 was pretty awesome. I had dedicated my weekends to my horse shows and my weeknights to training myself and my horse. Having this focus definitely kept me out of trouble and fed my ambitious and competitive nature.

I didn't have a ton of friends in high school—I knew a lot of people, but I only had one really close friend. She was the 'bestest'!

When we graduated high school, we knew that her parents were going to move out of Orillia and that we would be separated.

We worked our butts off the entire summer after high school and bought our tickets for a trip around the world; literally. We were able to choose 8 countries; they just had to be headed in a westerly direction. First stop: Vancouver, Hawaii, Fiji, New Zealand, Australia, Singapore, Amsterdam, and New York City! Best time of my life!! Well at 18.

As I developed as a teenager, I had a strong desire to be a model and an actress. I had a hard time admitting it as I never liked the reactions I got from people. This is probably the reason I started pursuing it so late in life, something I would do differently now. If I desire to do something now, I go for it.

My first apartment in Toronto was on Roncesvalles with one of my 'besties' that I met working on promotional tours. We would travel Ontario promoting products for companies such as Labatt, Proctor and Gamble, Unilever and so many more. It was a really cool gig. We met tons of people and developed communication skills that were priceless.

I was 21 when I started college and my mindset was in the perfect place to get decent grades at school. I had moved to Etobicoke and lived with a roommate I met off craigslist. Lucky me, she was really cool. For anyone that is contemplating college for 2 years, honestly, just do it! It was probably two of the fastest years of my life. For me, it was really important to get a post secondary education. I never had a desire to go to University or be a doctor or someone people would think is really smart. Funny enough, I actually believed for a very long time that I wasn't very smart. I surprise myself everyday now; most often with my spelling. In middle school I was a terrible speller. Now, I rarely have red lines on my e-mails! It's funny the things we tell ourselves. I think that small incidents happen in our lives and we let those incidents shape our lives. That is, until we realize it was only a small thing and we have the power and ability to create whatever we want. I really do believe anything is possible for myself and others.

During my college years, I worked as a model and bartender. It was around my second year that I started to take part time acting classes. I was sick of telling myself I wanted to do it and not doing anything about it. Bartending was an awesome gig. I made great money and met some really amazing people; many of whom paved the way to where I am today. My advice, always be a networker and always stay in connection with people that could possibly influence your life. Fortunately for me, I was able to stay away from the partying that is aligned with bartending. It was all around me all the time, but thankfully, I chose to work at night and still get up in the a.m. to train clients and fill my days. Some paths you just choose not to go down, and sometimes you do and you are able to escape. I was always afraid of the unknown.

Around 24, I was a couple years into auditioning and working in Toronto on commercials and small parts in film and television, however, for me it just wasn't cutting it. So many people would say "if you want to be an actress why don't you just move to Hollywood?" so sure enough I did. Obstacles and all, I packed up my little black sun fire and drove to California. I had no job, no working visa, and no agent. But I did have a friend, who introduced me to another friend who happened to have a whole lot of connections. This friend that I met in LA is still one of my closest friends to this day and the person responsible for introducing me to my current business associates.

LA was tough. But I learned how to do it on my own. I really had zero clue what I was going to do once I got there, but I somehow figured it out. I stayed 6 months in LA and it is an experience I am extremely grateful for.

I obviously needed to start making money again and get an apartment back in Toronto, so I went back to bartending and started auditioning in Toronto. I had a different outlook, which was great, more confidence and a sense that I could definitely make something happen with my acting career.

I worked as a bartender and struggling actress for another year and a half, until my urge to travel elsewhere kicked in. I had heard a lot of actors talk about Vancouver and how many TV shows and movies were filmed there. So I thought what the heck, I'll give it a try! Moving to Van was much easier, because I knew I could work there, and I had some friends that could show me around. I had planned to go to Vancouver for 3 months and ended up staying 8.

I absolutely loved it there. While I was there, I had plenty of time to soul search and be in my head. I read a lot of books and really questioned if I wanted to struggle for the rest of my career. I had promised myself that Vancouver was the last kick at the can when it came to acting as a career. I had met so many people in the industry, had studied at numerous acting studios, had moved to LA, and now Vancouver. I made a deal with myself that if something significant didn't happen for me, I was going to explore other career options. I just had zero clue what they may be.

While I was there, I had set up a lunch with a friend of mine to just casually catch up on life. Little did I know that my present career would come out of that meeting.

My friend happened to be an extremely successful business man, who was introduced to me by my friend I met in LA.

I asked him what he was doing in Vancouver and he said he had just purchased a company that he was going to franchise. This company happens to be *blo* Blow Dry Bar. He casually asked me "would this be something you would be interested in bringing to Toronto?"

I was automatically intrigued. I went home and called my best friend Tara in Toronto and asked her what she thought and would she do it with me. Tara and I had always wanted to open a business together, again, we just had no idea what that may be.

She was instantly on board. I had had that lunch meeting in January of 2009, Tara and I really didn't have much experience with lawyers or contracts or anything business at all. We asked our family and successful mentors around us for tons of advice. We had our first store open in Toronto by July of the same year. From the moment we opened our doors, it became really clear that our lives really would never be the same. We now worked 7 days a week and had responsibilities bigger than we could have ever imagined. The best part was that we had each other to lean on.

We quickly opened a second store within 6 months and a third within a year. Tara and I had partners in our three Toronto stores that owned the first US *blo* location located in San Francisco. These partners felt that Tara and I were doing such a great job at operating our stores that they gave us the opportunity to take on the operations of *blo* San Fran! So cool for Tara and I as we got to fly out to California quite often to get this store up to its potential.

I remember saying to myself "all I want to do is be busy, and have something to do everyday I wake up." That is one wish that came true in a big way.

The crazy part was Tara and I actually had no idea what we were doing. I truly believed that this has helped us get to where we are. We had to work extra hard to be successful. Getting the money to open the stores was not exactly a piece of cake. It definitely took a lot of effort and connections and relationships we had built over time.

All of a sudden, I had gone from an actor/trainer/bartender to running 3 businesses not to mention just under 30 staff, all of whom are in their early to mid twenties and some even older than I.

Everything was a learning curve, well, still is.

I never knew how difficult it was to run a business and actually keep your doors open. Bills, bills, bills.

My father always told me "make sure you pay yourself first." Why don't we listen to our parents?

It took us until year 2 to finally understand why you should in fact follow that simple rule. However, when you are so committed to making it work you will do just about anything to keep afloat.

When year one came to a close we were in the position of finding more money to keep the stores going—not a fun place to be in. However, it is necessary in most new businesses. My life began to resemble a rollercoaster. There were weeks where everything was going smoothly and then all of a sudden a massive dip downward. But sure enough, we would come climbing back up and stay steady for a while until another dip would come. It took me a while to accept that this was life and likely how it's going to be forever. It's what makes it interesting and, most importantly, has trained me to understand that no matter how low, I will always come back up.

Needless to say there is most often a desire to make more money, and Tara and I had it. We wanted to make another stream of income so that we could make more money without taking it from the business, as it couldn't afford it. Seeing as Tara and I spend everyday together, we had plenty of brainstorming time to think about something creative.

What better than starting our own product line that we could sell throughout the chain of *blo* stores? So that's what we did! We created a company called MANE TEEZE by T&M. The T&M stands for Tara and Mel. Our first product is a line of premium hair perfume. It took us a year to get prototypes out. However, once we did, we sold out of all 500 in less than 6 months. By this time, *blo's* head office had grown to over 15 stores across North America. Tara and I had used our own money to create the 500 prototypes and we wanted to expand and make our product better. The search for more money began. With success, we were able to secure a supplier that funded our project to develop 10 thousand bottles of MANE TEEZE. We designed new packaging and a third fragrance. We are currently selling our product in 10 *blo* locations as well as other salons across North America. We have a plan in place to expand our MANE TEEZE Brand by adding new products and potentially an entire clothing line. Everything about this new company is exciting to us right now. We have the potential to create something very unique and, most importantly, our own.

I am currently living in Toronto with the love of my life and enjoying every minute of it.

I feel my future is wide and open and sure to be full of ups and downs. I decided a while back to hop on my rollercoaster and enjoy the ride!

11 Tara Dawn McIntyre

I was born and raised in London, Ontario. I have an older brother and younger sister making me the middle child. My mother and stepfather (didn't know he wasn't my biological father until later in life) were your typical blue collar family.

My mother was a dental assistant, my stepfather a maintenance/landscaper at the local hospital. My mom had me involved in Highland Dancing at a very young age, which I came to be quite good at through the years. I was training hard all week and competing and winning all around the country.

I was also very involved in sports in elementary school. Cross country running, gymnastics and diving. Doing sports was great until I found a new love for the arts. The arts kept my mind busy on fun, creative activities, which I believe is an essential part of the development of children.

During elementary school I had lots of friends, was outgoing, an athlete, public speaker, in the school choir and winning awards for art and highland dancing. However, there were distressing events that were taking place at home and it didn't come to the forefront until around grade 5.

No one, including my mom, would ever know of what secret I was keeping until now. I remember having sex education class in grade 5 and learning about child molestation. As soon as the class started and the teacher started to talk about what it was, everything she was saying was happening to me and had been for as long as I could remember.

How could this be true? I thought my father (stepfather) loved me. Why would he want to hurt me? Such were my thoughts. I believe that this was an every-day event for all little girls. I even believed that this is what father's do to their daughters.

All these emotions ran through me for several days before I knew that this was something that needed to be addressed. The secret that was supposed to be "our little game" was going to be told.

My mother worked days and my dad nights so he was always around when my mom was at work. It was the perfect setting for him to do what he did to me and to also belittle and beat my brother without my mom knowing. My father and my brother were never on good terms it seemed. I guess it was easy for him to do what he did to us, because we weren't his biological kids; there was no real connection for him. My sister was his one and only biological child and he never did anything to her, thank god.

I finally found the courage to tell my brother about the abuse. I thought he was going to be so mad at me and blame me for what was going on. He believed me from the second I told him. He wrapped his arms around me as we were walking home. He told me "You HAVE to tell mom." So I did.

My mother was driving me to dance class that evening and it was a moment I will never forget. My stepfather was originally going to drive me that night, but I insisted my mother take me. I could tell by her face during the ride to class that she was wondering why I was so persistent on her driving that night.

We arrived at my dance class and the whole car ride I was trying to recite how the hell I was going to bring it up. What was the right way to tell her so she wouldn't be mad at me? Was she going to believe me? Was she going to make me go back and face him?

He had a crazy temper. What if he beat my mom because of me? All these scary but real thoughts raced through my mind. I finally got out of the car and said "Mom, I have to tell you something". She replied "What honey?" I got scared again and said casually "I will tell you later". She looked me right in the eye like she already knew what I had to say was serious and said, "No, tell me now". I held the door open with my gillies (dance shoes) in my hand gripping so tight and said "Dad's been touching me". She said "Get in the car" and put her foot so hard and fast on the gas pedal I flew back in my seat. She started to cry and began asking me 1000 questions. She had her arm across me like moms do when they are trying to protect you. She said "Honey, I'm so sorry, why didn't you tell me sooner? "When did he do this?" So many questions! She drove us right to the police station where I would stay for the next several hours giving my long, detailed statement.

It was over. She believed me, which was crucial for me and my state of mind. I believe that this is what started the healing.

He was arrested, charged and plead guilty for what he did.

The biggest thing I learned over time was to forgive him to set myself free of guilt and I did just that. I will never forget, but the moment I forgave him, I was set free from anything he had over me. They say everything happens for a reason; I wonder all the time what lesson God was trying to teach me and my family. I still ask myself "Why would he let this happen to us?" I guess I will never know, but I know it shaped me into the strong and determined fighter I am today. If I can get through 12 years of sexual abuse, seeing my mother and brother mentally and physically abused, I can guarantee you I can get through almost anything life can throw at me.

Grade 6 was a fresh new start for me, a time for positive change and a new direction in my life. My father was gone so we all felt safe and were one strong family again.

I applied and was accepted into Lester B. Pearson School for the Arts. I thrived for the rest of elementary school in music, dance, drama and art.

Banting Secondary School was my next stop, which was already home to my older brother and all of his friends. After 2 years at Banting I was accepted again into a prestige art program at Beal Secondary School. Once again, I flourished in this art school, several years later I graduated high school.

The arts always seemed to be where I belonged. That said, I enrolled in Hotel & Restaurant Management at my local community college; this was of course at my mother's request. My mother wanted to see me get a stable, respectable job and always reminded me of how important a good education was. I did see later in life how important it is to have some education in your back pocket. Community college did not last long for me as my heart and mind were never in it. I was bored and needed/wanted more.

I had always wanted to be a makeup artist and I knew London, Ontario was not the place to get an education/training for what I wanted to do. I had visions of being the lead makeup artist for a Steven Spielberg movie or being a personal make-up artist to a huge "A-lister" in Hollywood.

I didn't even know where to start looking or how I would even pay for my schooling, but I knew I would figure it out and I did!

I always knew that London was too small of a city for my big dreams. After all, I am a Pisces and a HUGE dreamer of things way beyond my reach—or so I thought. I couldn't wait to move to the big city of Toronto where I knew all my dreams would come true.

Now, how the heck was I going to get there? What would I do when I got there?

I was never very strong in Math, Science or History, so relying on my GPA to get me anywhere wasn't really going to be effective. Like I said, I spent a majority of my school life in Art schools and I was going to have to use that time to jump start a career in Toronto.

My big move to Toronto was here! I finally arrived and settled into my apartment, that I shared with 5 other people. Not really the glamorous living situation I dreamed of, but I made the best of it. The School of Make Up Art was a block away from where I lived, which was a bonus as I was not familiar with this new city. I went to school almost every day and loved every minute of it. I felt like I had really found my calling. I didn't really like the beauty side of makeup classes; it was the special effects and camouflage classes that I absolutely loved. Camouflage or corrective makeup was for burn victims, people with defects and birth marks. I graduated a year later with honors and started to look for jobs in my new field.

It didn't take long to get hired at a makeup counter downtown in a huge mall. I always wanted to work for MAC cosmetics, because it was the monarch of makeup and a great paying job to boot. I had a friend who worked at MAC and eventually got me in. I worked there for a few years and did some freelance work on my days off to gain more credibility in this very competitive field. I ended up partnering with a friend of mine who was amazing at hair and owned her own salon. She would book the hair and automatically recommend me as the makeup artist. We were a fierce match and made a lot of money together. I eventually got bored of makeup and wanted to do something else but what? Fashion was next in my list to tackle.

After many months of cold calling fashion houses and wholesalers in the city, dropping off resumes in person, checking craigslist and other job sites, I finally landed a killer job as a couture wedding gown designer. This was my dream job for about 2 years. I got to spend and work alongside a very powerful and successful fashion designer, who was cool and scary at the same time—can you say "The Devil Wears Prada"? I learned a ton about different fabrics, colors, textiles, pattern making, dealt with real models and fit them for runway shows in New York City. I also got to travel all around the United States and Canada doing trunk shows for her, which was what I really liked. Dealing with brides was a job all on its own. After a few years with her I felt like I had learned a lot, but needed to move on.

I really felt like I needed an office job to be credible or to feel respected in the working world. So I found a job in a bank as a teller and bartended at night in this hole-in-the-wall bar. I made more money working one night in the bar. I felt respected and good about myself waking up at 7am to be at work at 8am in business attire at the bank. I stayed at the bank as long as I could.

I was approached by a friend to come and help him open a cool new gym in the city and I immediately accepted. That's where I met my future business partner and best friend Mel. I was the front-end manager of this new concept gym and she was a spinning teacher and personal trainer. We hit it off right away. I got her a job working with me at the hole-in-the-wall bar as we both needed to make more money than the gym was providing.

We travelled together, went through many boyfriends and friends together. She was there for me when I got really sick with my thyroid and that's when I knew she would be a friend for life. They say you don't need a whole lot of friends just a few good ones. Mel and I spent many nights just the two of us over a glass of wine either in her apartment or mine thinking of what business we could open together—a consignment store? Shoe store maybe?

Well, many years passed and many jobs in between and no business. We really didn't take it that seriously, but it was something we always seemed to come back to and always revisited over wine.

Mel moved away a few times, but we always kept in touch. This time she had been back for a few years and was on the move again following her dream of being a successful actress. I was always her biggest fan and knew she would someday be famous. Mel had made a lot of very important and influential friends while bartending all over the city, which would eventually pay off for us both.

Mel decided she was going to give it one more shot and moved to Vancouver. Before leaving, she got me a job as a personal assistant with her friend who was a very successful entrepreneur. While working for him, I was able to learn an abundance of new skills, which would help me in operating a small business.

That summer was life changing for me. I ended up finding the love of my life, moving from a basement apartment and buying my first home in Oakville with my husband to be. The trek from Oakville to Concord was so far and I felt like I needed a job closer to home.

I was lucky enough to be hired by another top Canadian entrepreneur in Oakville and sometimes, things just happen for a reason. My new boss was very inspiring and I absolutely loved working for him. Once again, I absorbed as much information from him as I possibly could. It was life changing, because he would eventually end up helping me achieve my very own dreams of being an entrepreneur.

While in Vancouver, Mel ran into an old friend from Toronto, who would change our lives forever and this was when our "*blo* baby" was conceived.

Mel called me right way and asked if I would be interested in bringing a new "salon like" concept to Toronto. It was apparently the new hot thing in Vancouver. I believed this was the break we had been waiting for. *blo* Blow Dry Bar was the name and it was North America's Original Blow Dry Bar. Scissors and dye are forbidden. No cuts, no color: Just WASH BLOW GO. Hair Cadets (aka Clients) choose from 7 styles featured in the *blo* Hair Menu. These styles include the sexy razor-straight "Executive Sweet" to the rocker-chic inspired "Sex, Hugs and Rock & Roll". How cool was this?

And it was PINK to boot. We were chosen out of hundreds of applicants to be the *blo* ambassadors. In less than a year we opened up 3 locations in Toronto and one of which is in the Four Seasons Hotel in the Yorkville area of Toronto. We eventually took over our first US store in San Francisco, California.

We are going into our third successful year and with that being said, it has not been an easy ride whatsoever. We have definitely learned the hard way on many different important business issues like staffing, labor laws, HST, payroll and the list goes on and on. We have come a long way not having any real schooling or business training under our belts. I think we have done a hell of a good job. We still have a lot to learn in the world of small business ownership, but we welcome every challenge and any learning curve this world has in store for us.

Not that we don't have enough already on our plates with almost 5 stores, over 40 staff, keeping up with friends and family, married life and did I mention I'm 8 months pregnant? Mel and I needed more. One thing we knew for sure, we couldn't take too much money from our business until we were almost debt free or close to it which is typically 5+ years. Also, having two of us made it that much harder to take a reasonable salary you could live on. But we just take what we both need in order to survive in life and it's a sacrifice you have to be willing to take as a small business owner. Having three stores made it a little easier, but we knew we had to come up with a way to supplement our income. Do I go back to makeup on the side? Should Mel go back to bartending and personal training? When the hell would we have time? We already put in over 70 hours a week.

We had to think really hard and be very creative and realistic to our situation. So Mel and I had an idea to create our own product line. Over the past year, we have created a line of premium hair perfume called "Mane Teeze" by T&M. Our line was successfully sold out in the first 6 months of launch and has now been implemented as a retail product for *blo* franchise stores in Canada and the US. There are about 18 *blo* locations and growing by the day.

I can tell you that being a creator of something, being able to say this is your baby and your idea is so much more rewarding and fulfilling. Don't get me wrong, I am very proud of owning a franchise, but at the end of the day, it wasn't my idea. Mane Teeze is all ours and the sky is the limit with our product. We also have such a perfect set up with having 5 of our own retail stores to showcase Mane Teeze in. It has done incredibly well after our huge launch of the line in November 2011.

This will not only be a hair perfume line but a hair accessory line. We will be growing the Mane Teeze line with exciting new products like dry shampoo, travel size hair perfume, shower caps, umbrellas and more. Some top retailers in Toronto have already picked up the line soon after our launch, and places like Alberta and even Russia are also on board. Mane Teeze is sold in other *blo* locations across North America including Oakville, Vancouver, San Francisco, Texas, Miami, L.A. and growing day by day.

I guess you could say the girl next door from London with not a perfect upbringing or silver spoon has made quite a name for herself. I married my soul mate and had a beautiful baby girl named Noel. I'm not rich, I'm not stress free, but I am a strong, determined woman and I will do whatever it takes to make not only my business successful but my life. It's about taking chances, trusting your womanly instinct and following your dreams no matter how big or small. If it's your dream, then no one can take it from you. As American business woman Mary Kay Ash once said "Most people live and die with their music still un-played. They never dare to try."

12 Aimee Agresti

s my heels clacked against the shiny lobby floors of bustling 30 Rockefeller Center in New York City—esteemed home of *NBC*—I felt myself walking just a little taller. I couldn't keep from smiling. I wanted to feel proud of myself, for this milestone I was about to hit, but I was completely and utterly nauseous. My hand trembled as I reached for the elevator's up arrow. I took a deep breath, and gave myself a pep talk. Somehow, I lectured myself as the doors opened, whisking me up, you have become a staff writer for one of the hottest magazines around: Us Weekly. Somehow, you write stories that millions of people read and now, incredibly, you have even been drafted into service as a TV talking head. Somehow, you're now getting out of the elevator and walking into the offices of Access Hollywood, a show you've watched religiously forever and you're about to make your first major TV appearance. This is national television, Aimee. Smile. And just don't blow it.

The rest was a blur. The producer ushered me into the studio, sat me in front of the camera and pinned a tiny microphone to my dress—I hoped it wouldn't pick up the rapid-fire beat of my racing, nervous heart. I also hoped I wouldn't draw a blank, that I would say all the right things, that I would say anything at all. But then the camera went on; and so did I. I could feel myself flipping into some other mode, like I was having an out of body experience. The producer asked her pressing questions—mostly about Britney Spears' latest ups and downs—and I gave quick, sassy sound bites, smooth as can be. I even made some jokes. In no time, she was thanking me, reminding me to watch the clip on that night's show and sending me on my way with a promise to have me on again.

I was back in the lobby again before I granted myself a moment to fully take it all in:

A national TV spot? And it actually went well? Not bad for a girl who was once voted "Quietest" of her high school class.

Yep, Quietest. And it was a title, I'm sorry to admit, I had rightfully earned. It was something I thought about after every subsequent TV appearance—and there were a lot of 'em, spots on everything from E! to

VH-1, each one slightly better than the one before it. I had come a long way, baby.

But in school, and for a long time afterward, I owned that dubious Quietest distinction. It wasn't so much that I was scared to talk to people, that wasn't really it. It was more that I just didn't have any confidence in general, at all. And people could see that from a mile away.

Sure, I suppose some girls are born with confidence—how nice for them—but for the rest of us, confidence is something you have to remember to put on in the morning before you leave the house. It isn't natural at all at first. It's something clumsy that takes practice and skill to wear properly, like liquid eyeliner.

Growing up I had a close-knit group of pals who knew the real me—my penchant for corny jokes and my sarcasm and my uncanny ability to remember lyrics to every pop song ever written. But to the general population, I was a straight A, type-A, super-introvert. I studied like a madwoman to get perfect grades, ran myself ragged doing the full menu of extracurriculars (newspaper! chamber singers! French honour society!), but it didn't matter how hard I worked or how well I did, I only saw how much further I had to go to reach my scarily big goals. I put my head down and my guard up and I hid behind my work. Luckily, there would be people scattered along my path to spur me on and pull me out of my shell. And with their help, and plenty of trial and error, I managed to find my way.

In the process, I started making mental note of what propelled me and what held me back. In the magazine world, we're always making lists and ranking things: "Sexiest Celeb Couples!" "This Season's Top Trends!" "Five Steps To a Hot New Bod!", so I've boiled my story down to a handy guide I like to call "Ten Tips For Chasing Your Dreams." Here it goes:

#1 Turn your negative into a positive.
So, all that studying in high school paid off and I shipped out to my dream college, Northwestern University in Chicago, to major in journalism. Writing had always been something I loved, because I could do it on my own. I could write, rewrite and edit my thoughts, then send only what I thought was perfect out into the world, into the school newspaper, or even just into my journals at home. It felt like the only thing I had power over; it seemed that if I kept at it, I would always be able to get better.

Freshman year I heard about a national college magazine run out of a nearby Chicago suburb and I latched onto the place: it focused on entertainment, which I dreamed of covering, having grown up reading every celebrity magazine I could get my hands on. They put me to work writing tiny blurbs on city hotspots for the magazine's dining section with the idea that I would eventually graduate up to writing actual stories. But one day, a few weeks in, the editor-in-chief went scouring the office for anyone who had seen this one hot new TV show. One of its stars was coming to town and the magazine could get 15 minutes with him for a cover story. But no one in the office watched his sitcom.

"I love that show, can I do it?" I asked finally, after the editor had exhausted the senior staff members. Reluctantly, he said yes.

I hadn't actually seen a single minute of that show. I had been studying too much for TV, but I got a crash course from friends who were fans, read everything I could that had already been written about it and by the time I sat down with the star, I was an expert. I was terrified, naturally, but I was incredibly prepared. I asked good questions that got him talking and for the first time it dawned on me that there was a great flipside to being quiet: it makes you a good listener. People appreciate when you're paying attention, when you're engaged and you care about what they're saying.

Over the course of the next three years I spent all my spare time writing and editing for the magazine. It felt unreal: the staff was so small that anything I wanted to write about, I could go for it. I hung out backstage at concerts talking to every band I could; I had film and TV stars calling my dorm room for interviews. ("I need the phone, Drew Barrymore is calling in five minutes!" I would have to warn my roommates.) My writing improved, but, even better, I was learning how to interview, how to get people to open up. I still always half-expected them to realize that I wasn't cool enough to be talking to them. But, then again, to them I was a reporter, time had been booked, and a story would be written and there was value in that; there was value in me. Over time, the interviews became less formal, more of a conversation. I stopped looking at my notes and found I could just chat without any prompting. By senior year, I had become editor-in-chief of that magazine.

#2 Shine at even the smallest of jobs.
I planned to move to Manhattan after school. I hadn't ever been there, but that's where all the magazines were, so that's where I would be. And the summer before my senior year, I scored an internship at one of my favorite entertainment magazines there. The city itself swept me off my feet from the start. I loved the energy of this place that so many of my favorite authors had once called home: F. Scott Fitzgerald, Dorothy Parker, Truman Capote. My eyes were so wide and my heart so full, just to be there. Not everyone thought I was cut out for it though. A few people took one look at sweet, polite, little me and shook their heads, telling me with a smile,

"This city is going to eat you alive, darling." I'll never understand why people feel the need to say things like that. But I wasn't going anywhere.

At the magazine, there were a handful of us interns stuffed into this one little office down the hall from all these writers whose names I read every week. I was starstruck by them. They were god-like to me, every day felt like being in the presence of the Dalai Lama or something, and, of course, I took a respectful "don't speak unless spoken to" tack with them.

The work itself was much easier to adjust to. No writing to speak of. We sorted mail, read mail, and typed reports about which stories generated the most mail. We answered phones and took messages. We Xeroxed layouts and distributed them from desk to desk. And we did odd jobs for the various editors. One day, for instance, I was dispatched to the artsy shops of the Village to try to hunt down heart-shaped sunglasses for the style editor. It took me all day but I finally found them at a street vendor's display. I bought five pairs, one of every color. They soon put me in charge of typing the data for the weekly box office chart: numbers, titles, figures. I got to write a headline, and it was particularly thrilling, because I got to stay late on closing night. I felt a part of things on those nights, even though the majority of the time I was just running around with Xeroxes or sitting there waiting to be told the page was ready to go.

The summer flew by and before I knew it, it was my last day. The intern coordinator, a sharp, kind and well-established woman, whom we all desperately wanted to impress, would be giving us individual evaluations. I racked my brain for anything I might've done that would have gotten me noticed and, save for a few clever headlines, came up with nothing. The whole idea was to make them want to hire you when you got out of school. I didn't think there was any way I had left this kind of impression.

I took a seat in her office and, nervous, launched right in, telling her what a wonderful time I had had, how much I had learned, how exciting it had been to be there. She smiled and nodded, then looked me straight in the eye.

"Let me tell you what went on here this summer," she started, her tone mischievous. "You probably think we didn't give you much to do. We know all of you interns can write. We know you're all talented. So we use our program to see how you fit in, how you respond to the tasks we give you."

Whoa. The revelation hit me like a 2x4. So they were paying attention to all those mundane day-to-day activities?

She continued: "The key to success here is showing what kind of person you are, that you'll do the grunt work with a smile."

"So, um, how'd I do?" I asked, tentative.

She smiled. "You did great. Everyone loves working with you. You're a great fit." I was stunned. I guess you never know what will get you noticed. On my way out I spun around and remembered to tell her that I had trained another intern on how to do the box office chart. She smiled and studied me, surprised.

"You did, did you? You are a quiet force, aren't you? People don't realize how much you're always thinking a step ahead," she said pleased. She shook my hand before sending me off: "Be sure to keep in touch."

She got me my first real job, but it wasn't at her magazine. Timing is everything and there weren't any openings when I got out of school. But after four long, painful months of temping and job hunting in the city, while living in a lonely little room in a grungy, dorm-like all-women's residence with no air conditioning and shared bathrooms, I got a call. She had a friend who was an editor at a movie magazine (one I happened to love) and needed a new assistant. I applied and got the job.

#3 Don't wait for opportunities to come your way, make them by thinking outside the box.

At the new job, they told me I wouldn't be allowed to write for at least the first six months but then, if I had mastered all the daily clerical duties, I might get some small assignments. So, I became the best administrative assistant I could: booking meetings, typing memos, transcribing interviews, answering calls, filing expense reports. Unlike the kind of magazine bosses you see in movies, mine was an incredibly nice, smart man who told me when I was doing a good job and wanted to see me succeed. And when the time came, true to his word, he started sending some stories my way: little blurbs on that month's movie releases.

One day, he called another assistant and me in: he had tickets to a movie premiere that night and he couldn't go, we were welcome to go in his place. I couldn't believe our luck. Neither of us had ever been to a premiere. We were mesmerized by everything from the klieg lights that you could spot blocks away from the historic theatre to the fact that even nobodies like us could walk the red carpet (it was the only way in the door). Later at the after party, we sipped cocktails, nibbled on canapés and gawked at the celebs. I got mistaken for the director of a hot Indie movie that had just been released, which, of course, made my night. I later spotted that very director chatting by the bar, and, gathering up my courage, I went over, waited for a break in her conversation and introduced myself. I had interviewed her on the phone a month earlier and she remembered me and was so warm. I felt like a different person being at this party, mingling with people I never dreamed I'd be mingling with.

By the time the other assistant and I left, thoroughly dazzled by the 'fabulousity' of it all, we had cooked up an idea to pitch ourselves to my editor as party reporters. We laid it all out in a memo we had waiting on his desk the next morning. He went for it. Soon we were covering a few events a month. I would proudly stake out my spot beside the other reporters on the red carpet to interview the stars, then, after the movie screening, I'd hit the after-party searching out any celebs I may have missed. Of course, typical me, I wasn't content just being there, my stomach was perpetually tied in knots: what if I don't get all the stars? What if I don't get good enough quotes? I had to do a good job to prove to my editor that I deserved this assignment and to encourage him to give me more. It was survival of the fittest too: You had to be aggressive nabbing the celebs and keeping them engaged enough that the other hovering reporters wouldn't trounce on your time. I studied these stars, their sparkle, and tried to reflect it back to them, radiate the same vivacity so they would want to talk to me. Some nights went better than others, but every night ended the same way: I would tuck my tape recorder away and make a lap around the party, revelling in the unmistakable irony that the girl who had never gone to high school parties and barely gone to college ones, was now hanging out in places like this.

#4 Don't blame other people if you're not as happy as you could be. Instead, find a way to make a change <u>yourself.</u>

It was a fantastic job. But, whenever things get too comfortable, you find yourself moving back the goal posts again, and I soon got restless. I had gotten to do some editing here and there, but writing was still my dream and I couldn't quite convince them that I could pen the longer stories. It frustrated me and I started to take it personally, even though I knew I shouldn't. The truth was I still wasn't speaking up as much as I should have in the office. My work was good, but I didn't lobby hard enough for new opportunities. I didn't present myself like a person who deserved them.

I began toying with the idea of freelance writing fulltime so that I could spread my wings and try contributing to a bunch of different magazines. Also on my mind: my boyfriend (later to become my husband, who I met when he was working at the magazine next door) had moved to Washington, DC, to work in politics. We had been long distance nearly a year. I thought, if I really do go freelance, why not do it in Washington, which also happened to be my hometown? It was a gutsy move: I worried both about giving up the stability of a fulltime job and taking myself off the magazine track. I feared that I would lose a certain lustre leaving New

York, that it would be harder to get assignments and that it might be nearly impossible to get back onto a magazine staff if I wanted to return. But, ultimately, I decided it was an exciting risk: it could be good for me to be my own boss. I was right: during that time, I wrote the kind of meaty stories I never could've if I'd stayed at the magazine. It wasn't easy. Some months I had too much work, others not enough, but it all taught me how to hustle and forge new connections. I even started writing a novel, something I had always dreamed of doing but never had the time.

#5 Don't be afraid to take that detour, you can always find your way back.

I had finished a very rough first draft of the novel when I started longing for a steady gig again. (Luckily, my boyfriend was open to a change too.) So I checked in with my New York magazine pals and heard through the grapevine that *Us Weekly*—which I adored—was looking for writers. I applied and they hired me on a trial basis as a staff writer, with the possibility of staying on full-time if things went well. I got the call on a Thursday and they wanted me to start that Tuesday. We were still living in DC, but I hightailed it to New York and slept on a friend's couch for a few weeks until we could find a place and get settled. Thanks to good timing and good contacts, I was back in Manhattan faster than I ever could've guessed.

Us was like all my past journalism experiences amped up on steroids. Everything was more exciting and intense: the deadlines, the amount I was writing, the run-ins with stars who would just drop by the office to have lunch with the staff. The pace was frenetic; the people were superhuman in their ability to juggle so much. I'd never had to churn out stories so quickly in my life. I'd never considered myself much of a daily deadline writer: I generally needed the time to let a story knock around inside my head, decide how to structure it, perfect the writing. But here, if it was closing day, you would get assigned a story in the morning, turn in a draft that afternoon then keep rewriting, stitching in new facts as updated info poured in, until after nightfall. And, of course, every stage of the process happened lightning-fast even though you might be there until after 2am. I remember a friend describing the workflow as feeling like your head had exploded and you had to put the pieces back together again. That was about right. But, slowly, I got the hang of it: I learned by watching smart writers I admired and by getting edited by some of the sharpest editors I'd ever worked with.

#6 If you're determined to enjoy the whole experience, you'll end up doing better work.

Rather than just trying to be the best writer I could, I went into this job with grander aspirations: to make the office a real home. I wanted to be that person everyone enjoyed working with. The funny thing about that kind of goal is it actually makes you do your job better. I made wonderful friends. We lunched together, hung out on weekends, went to each other's weddings. They were people I adored, respected and learned so much from, and by getting to know them, it made me more confident in my work. If I turned in a story that, unfortunately, needed some rewriting, I didn't beat myself up or take it personally. Instead, it felt more like my editor was a pal wanting to help me improve. By opening myself up, letting people get to know me, it brought on new opportunities too: the woman, who booked staffers for TV interviews, thought I had the right personality for it. I jumped at the offer and she put me in the rotation for media promotion.

I spent four years there and could have stayed forever. But when my husband came home one night and said he'd been offered a job in Washington again and one that we both decided sounded too good to pass up, I took it as a sign, yet again. I had struggled to find time to work on the novel during those years at *Us*; what writing I had managed on weekends and evenings had been slow and difficult. I needed to devote more time if it was ever going to be finished. I knew what I had to do.

My *Us* friends gave me a lovely, heartfelt send-off, promising to keep in touch, and many even telling me that I had had the best attitude on staff and they would miss that; that meant so much.

We moved back to Washington and I started freelancing for some of the local city magazines and got back to the book.

#7 Dream big. And don't let anyone tell you not to.

I finished the novel. I revised it. I polished it. I made it as perfect as I thought humanly possible. It was my baby. And with the help of my wonderful, supportive agent, it went out to publishers. I crossed my fingers and checked my e-mail obsessively for word that one of these fine editors wanted this book. And I waited and waited, like a girl sitting at home by the phone waiting to get asked to the prom. And one by one, they all said no and broke my heart. But

#8 If at first you don't succeed, try again. (Even if you feel like you must be delusional to think you could actually pull off whatever it is you're trying to do.)

That hit me hard. Few of my rejections even contained any actual constructive criticism. They all liked my writing, a few didn't know how to market the book, some thought it was predictable while others found it surprising, a couple didn't love my main character but others did. One person, most perplexingly, admitted they'd started reading on a bad day and that that might've colored their opinion. The bottom line: there wasn't any one thing everyone universally disliked, which made it harder to know what to change or whether I should be changing much of anything at all. What the heck was I supposed to do with that kind of feedback?

Where I had had good timing in the past, it seemed now I was just completely off. For whatever reason, this wasn't a book these folks felt like publishing right now. And I felt pretty low and burned out too. It seemed like a sure sign from the universe to just stop writing fiction. Worse still, it seemed there weren't any magazine jobs to speak of anywhere I looked. No easy refuge, no backup plan. I would just need to keep freelancing. But I had been bitten by the fiction bug and once that sting of rejection started to fade, I realized I was still infected: I couldn't give up on it yet and I didn't want to.

Through the years I'd kept in touch with a writing professor I had back in college. We kick it old-school and write actual letters from time to time, something about that always makes the words feel weightier. So I wrote to him and asked, how do I know if I'm really supposed to be writing fiction? He wrote back that it's pretty simple, if I'm meant to be writing fiction then I'll just keep writing it. He meant that the more I write, the more doors I knock on to try to get published, the greater my chances of finding success. If you keep at it, it will eventually happen. And I think that's true with any goal, whatever the field. If you don't give up, at some point you'll find a way into wherever you want to be.

So I did the only thing I could think of: I started writing another book. I'd had an idea bouncing around anyway, for a book much different than the first, I just needed to take a chance and give it one more shot. And this time I gave my attitude a makeover too.

#9 Believe in yourself. If you don't, then who will?

For a long time I hadn't told anyone I was writing fiction at all. I figured it would be safer not to tell, then if my books never got published, no one would know I had failed. But then I realized that that was just the old Quietest side of me rearing its ugly head again. I couldn't let that happen. If you don't believe in yourself, no one else is going to believe in you. I've been lucky enough to have found people at every stage in my life to give me encouragement, but it occurred to me that I had to find confidence within myself too. So I started telling everyone I met that I was working on this new novel, hoping it would be a self-fulfilling prophecy and that if I acted like it's just a matter of time before this book found a home, then it really would.

I finished the book, it went out to publishers, I crossed my fingers and this time my story had a happy ending. ILLUMINATE, the first book of my Gilded Wings trilogy, was published in March 2012.

#10 Cut yourself a little slack and realize that you'll never have all the answers—I know I sure don't—and that that's OK.

No path is ever totally smooth and I certainly still have hiccups in my confidence. I'm about to begin writing the third book in this trilogy and I will inevitably sit down in front of my blank computer screen (scary! so scary!) and worry about how well the words will flow to fill it up. And whenever I do eventually finish, then I'll sit down again at some point and begin writing something entirely new and have to hope all over again that it'll be something a publisher wants to publish and readers want to read.

But then I'll remind myself to take a deep breath and just give it my best. If I've learned anything so far, it's that if you keep working, keep improving, keep knocking on doors, then eventually one will open. So this quiet girl will just keep making noise until she has everyone listening.

13 Emily Field

My story is not one of great tragedy nor is it one of extreme ease; I would say I was middle of the road when it came to life. Looking back however, it was the struggles and challenges I faced that made me the person I am today and I would not change any of it. Growing up, I would have benefited from a book like this, just to know that there were other people who had endured challenges but had figured out a way to succeed. There were many people along the way, who helped me to become aware of who I was and who I wanted to be. I am by no means finished my journey, but I do feel like I have come a long way with the help and guidance of those closest to me.

My mum is my closest friend and role model. She is the one person who I can count on and that I know will always be there for me. To many, our relationship is strange, as we are more like friends than anything, but it is hard to share experiences with someone and not be close with them. After my dad passed away when I was two, it was just my mum and I. Although there were stepfathers and step-siblings along the way, it was always the two of us trying to find a place to fit in. It felt like we were always on the move, changing locations as our lives changed directions. This was hard for me, and was at the source of my shyness and anxiety growing up. It was never easy to make friends, because I didn't know how long we would be in one place and I became good at only getting close enough to people to have acquaintances and not really getting too attached, always anticipating a move. This was also when I became jaded and angry at the world. I never felt good enough or that the life we had was enough because we were always on the move searching for something more. I see now, that my mum was only trying to give me the life she thought I should have and deserved to have.

When I was thirteen, my mum met her current husband and my new stepfather. Needless to say, I was not very embracing of this new relationship. We moved in with him about a year after they met and never looked back. I was just starting grade 9 when all this was happening: new house, new dad, and a new school all over the summer. It was a lot to take in. I was never great in school, and I certainly was not about to apply myself when I hated life. I managed to make friends as I did in every new school, and I managed to squeak by in my classes. I also began to realize that this guy was not too bad. In fact, Craig turned out to be the best thing that had happened to us in a long time, and I was shocked that he not only put up with, but embraced my attitude, and still does.

I remember being in grade 8 sitting in my friend's kitchen telling her that one day I would live on a farm with horses and dogs and other animals. She looked at me like I was crazy and told me that it was unlikely that a city girl with little money would have that life. But that never entered my mind, because as long as I could remember, my grandfather, who had a love and passion for animals, influenced me. The summer of my grade 12 year of high school was the year I realized the dream of getting my first horse. We were out for dinner to celebrate my birthday and Mum and Craig gave me a card. When I opened it I started to cry; they were going to help me buy and care for a horse. I still had to work to contribute to her, but they were willing to help me. I still get emotional when I think of that day, because that was a turning point in my life. Not only did I realize a dream of mine, but I also realized that I had a strong support in my 'parents'. My last year of high school was devoted to my new horse; I spent as many hours as I could at the barn, even when I should have been in class. This amazing animal had quickly become my best friend, someone I could trust and would never have to move away from.

After high school, I decided to go to Trent University, because I had an aunt who lived nearby on a farm so I could bring my horse and dog with me. I had the opportunity to reconnect with my dad's sister; Claire was not only a friend to me during that time, but a teacher. Claire taught me about my family, as well as independence and self-love. She was always honest with me about her past and always encouraged me to live my dreams no matter how hard they may be to achieve. It was during my time on the farm that I realized who I was as a person, and who I wanted to be.

Many experiences shaped who I am today, one of which was my first major car accident in my first year of University. I know, everyone has accidents, but I was not one for admitting I was not perfect. Not long after my accident, I faced yet another set back. My dog was killed when a cement truck hit her one morning on our road. This was one of the most difficult things I have ever gone through. This experience brought on the worst bout of panic and anxiety I had ever faced. I became unable to perform daily tasks. Everyday was a struggle, it was then that I realized I had to seek professional help to deal with this anxiety if I ever wanted to be successful and lead a full life. I have since learned how to manage my anxiety and am a happier and healthier person, because I was able to get help when I hit rock bottom.

While I was doing some soul searching on the farm and figuring out who I was, I was also doing the same thing in a professional capacity as well. I knew I wanted to be a teacher, but I had little guidance and understanding of what it would take to get there. I started volunteering at a local high school and met my most significant professional role model. The principal of this school took me under his wing and guided me along the path to success. He not only gave me many opportunities and experiences within his school, he connected me with other community members and schools giving me a rich volunteer experience. I never had great marks in University. I was always so busy doing volunteer work or riding horses that I rarely went to class and was happy to pass with minimal effort. When I applied to teacher's college, though I hoped, I never thought I would get in. My marks were not where they should have been, and I felt that there were more suitable people out there than me. But I did get in! I was accepted to two schools and decided to go to York University. I learned a valuable lesson in all of this. There is more to life than how well you do on a test or an assignment. It was because of my hard work and determination that I was accepted to teacher's college, and I am a better person for having those experiences rather than top-notch marks.

Teacher's college was one of the most challenging years of my life. I was overwhelmed with lesson planning and placements but I had a blast. I learned so much about my teaching style and myself while there and I really realized that teaching is a passion of mine and something that I was born to do. When I graduated from teacher's college, I was hired at a school board for supply work. I have been in this board now for three years and continue to find Long Term Occasional jobs every year. This year, I have one of the most challenging and rewarding jobs I have ever had: teaching young mums. These young women come to school with their babies and work to get their high school diplomas while learning to care for their children. Although I am the teacher and I am there to teach them academics, they are the ones who teach me on a daily basis. There is not a day that goes by that I am not blown away by their strength and determination to hold their heads up high in the face of hardship. These young women fight everyday against the cycle of poverty and abuse and stand up to stereotypes in order to provide a better future for them and their children. This has been one of the most rewarding experiences of my professional career. I have learned about myself as a teacher and a human being as I am reminded everyday to be mindful of others' struggles and to always treat people with compassion and understanding as you never know what battles they were facing that day. I am also reminded everyday of how strong women can be.

Not only am I living my dream professionally, but personally too. I did realize my dream of living on a farm with dogs and horses. I have two horses that bring me so much joy and love. I also have two wonderful dogs that make me laugh on a daily basis. My animals are the ones who remind me to slow down and appreciate the small stuff and that to laugh is the greatest medicine. Although I always knew this is where I would be one day, I am not sure that this is where I always will be. I now realize that life is constantly changing and that is a good thing. Without change, we would never grow and learn about who we are and who we want to be. I feel like I am starting a new chapter of my life and that I am in a place of love for others and myself and I am excited to see what great things are coming in the future. I know there will continue to be challenges in my life, but I am confident that I will be able to face and overcome them; with my support system and the faith I now have in myself.

14 Krista Napier, BBA, MBA

Imagine walking into a room and being engulfed by a sea of dark suits. That's a typical day for me as a female technology analyst. The technology industry in Canada is one that is dominated by middle-aged, Caucasian men. So, as a 24 year old fresh out of University, this was, needless to say, extremely intimidating.

I'll be honest. I did not dream of becoming a technology analyst while growing up. I had no idea the job even existed, and I certainly was not a tech geek. I'd consider myself more of a business geek, so I guess "geek" was the common factor here. I was on track to getting into the financial services industry and was attending business school at Wilfrid Laurier University (Ontario, Canada). I went there specifically for the co-op program so I could try my hand at financial services. But during the first round of co-op placements, I came up against a problem: there were no co-op postings in the financial services sector that term. I was stumped. So instead, I applied for jobs in different industries. One of the jobs I applied for was as an Associate Analyst at a technology company. Why did I apply for this job? Not because I liked technology. Not because of the pay. Not because of the company's brand name. I applied, because it had the word 'analyst' in the job title. I figured, if I learned what it meant to be an analyst in the technology industry, I might be able to apply this insight to the financial services industry later on. My roommate had also told me her boyfriend had worked there and that the people were really nice, and that they had a foosball table. I was sold. I love foosball, and people make all the difference no matter where you work. So I gave it a shot.

I found myself in an interview with my soon to be boss. In retrospect, he took a chance on me (I had a straight A+ average, but no tech experience), and I took a chance on him (I had no idea if I was going to like being a tech analyst for the summer). But it turned out to be a match made in heaven, and I ended up falling in love with technology. It was a summer romance that started with that co-op job, and it's lasted 8 years now and it's still going strong.

What I didn't realize at that time was that I was entering an industry where I would be the minority. You know that game, "which one of these things doesn't belong"? That's how I felt when I started my career. Everywhere I went—the office, an event, a client meeting—it was all men, in dark suits, all older than me with tons of experience in this sector. I, on the other hand, had almost no tech background at all; I was petite, with blonde hair. I hardly fit in. Upon meeting people, the first thing they would ask me was, "how long have you worked here", singling me out as the newbie.

So I needed a strategy to survive, and this was what I came up with: I'll dress like them. I bought a bunch of dark suits, and wore my hair up in a tight bun, wore nude nail polish, and dressed very conservatively for about 2 years while I focused on learning as much as I could about the industry. It seems a little silly now. However, at the time, I thought I had to conform to fit in and gain credibility.

The other part of my strategy was to work really hard. My first day, one of the very few women in my office came up to me and said, "it's great to see another woman in the industry—but I have to tell you , it's sink or swim here. I hope you can swim." Luckily, not only could I swim, I had my lifeguarding certificate. Seriously though, I knew from the start I was going to have to work my butt off. That was a given. But I had to figure out where I could add value.

At first, I thought working hard and adding value meant I had to know everything about the very technical aspects of the industry (computer programming & building technology). I remember going to my boss and asking to take some night courses on programming so that I would be able to keep up with conversation with my peers and customers. My boss very kindly said that was not necessary. "You have a business background Krista— leverage that! There are lots of technical customers of ours who need help positioning and marketing and selling their solutions. You can help them understand how to best position themselves in the market and the trends they need to watch out for." He was right. That's essentially what my business background had taught me. I didn't have to know C++ or Java programming to make my mark in the tech industry. I had to know about the technology at a high level and I had to be good at math to track data and identify trends, but telling a programmer how to program was meaningless. Once I realized that, things got a lot easier. Figuring out where I could make an impact was an important first step in my career, and in my job as a technology analyst.

So what exactly does a technology analyst do, anyway? Simply put, it's my job to be an expert in one specific area of technology. My areas of expertise are mobile devices, which includes devices like smartphones, media tablets (iPad, etc.) and eReaders. I advise manufacturers, resellers, government, and end user organizations on how they can develop/sell/use these products better in their organizations, how many of these devices are sold in Canada, device trends, etc. I also do commentary for the press, and I'm a frequent speaker at events. It's at those events that I've had some interesting encounters.

For example, a few years ago, I was presenting as a keynote speaker. The event had attracted about 500 people, however, this was at the beginning of my professional speaking career, and so many people in the press and the industry did not publicly know me yet. Before the event started, I was in the lobby mingling with guests and networking. I decided to walk up to one gentleman I did not know to say hello. Keep in mind, I was wearing a black sleeveless A-line dress (which just happened to be similar attire to the wait staff). The man turned around and said, "oh, could you grab me another glass of red wine, please dear". When he realized I was not a waitress, he apologized profusely, and asked if I was looking forward to hearing the keynote speaker. "I think she will have some interesting things to say," I said with a wink and walked toward the stage to take my place as the event got under way. Encounters like that didn't make me upset or angry, but they did remind me that I still had a lot of work ahead of me to prove my place in this industry. Luckily, I had a lot of inspirational women to keep me going.

While women are scarce in technology, those that I've had the pleasure of meeting are very impressive. There seems to be a close connection with women in technology and a respect for one another as we each take on the industry from our own angle with gusto. Some of the women I've met have risked it all to start their own businesses, have raised families as single mothers, and have gone to school full time while running a business full time to pay the bills—and they have succeeded despite those intimidating situations. Seeing and hearing about that kind of inner strength has inspired me to continue my trek in tech.

The two women who have inspired me the most though are my sister and my mom, because they helped me realize I didn't have to conform at work to be credible and respected. I was at my mom 's place one afternoon with my sister, and I was showing them a new pair of shoes I had bought that I was planning to wear on the weekend. They were a fun pair of black high heels with black sparkles covering the toe. "Those are gorgeous," said my mom and sister. "They would look amazing with one of your black work dresses—it would add some glitz—in an appropriate way for the office". I was unsure. Wearing sparkly shoes to work? No way could I abandon my plain black (and boring) high heels for something a little more fun and daring, or could I? I hesitantly took their advice and I wore them. First time

I did I got so many comments on my outfit, that I quickly realized I didn't have to conform after all to receive the respect I desired in my industry, and the credibility I had worked for. And it went beyond clothes. I realized I could add my feminine touch to many different aspects of my work to add value. For example, keeping a dish of candy on my desk attracted visitors and led to valuable business conversations with colleagues. I've been asked for my opinion many times by developers creating products/apps/solutions targeted at women, and I've also been asked by many companies to speak at their events largely because they wanted "a female's perspective."

Today, I don't wear dark, conservative suits. And I don't own any either. I wear what I feel comfortable in. As my dad always used to say, "Krista, think outside of the box!" That's exactly what I do now. For example, yesterday I had on a floral skirt with an off the shoulder white blouse, with red nail polish (my favorite color). I wear my long hair down, and of course, I always have on my high heels (and sometimes they are sparkly!). I still have to walk into a sea of dark suits most days, but I do so with confidence now. Being different attracts attention, makes it easier to network and meet people, and makes me memorable in a large crowd. Simply put, it's OK to be different.

So don't be afraid to try the unknown, even if it takes you into a sea of intimidating dark suites. And when you get there, don't conform—figure out where you can add value, and then let your hair down, and dare to think outside the box!

15

Lauren Anderson

If you would have asked me ten years ago, at age twenty, where I'd be in ten years, my answer with absolute certainty would not have been where I am today. At the time I was attending college, hoping to become a veterinarian. I am the youngest child of divorced parents; I have an older sister, Kelley. I lived with my mom and step-father growing up, but maintained a close relationship with my dad. In high school, I was a loner who played sports. I was never popular, nor "pretty" by society's standards. I wore baggy T-shirts, no make-up; that sort of thing. I have always had a tight-knit family, though not without issues at times. Both my parents come from large families where hard work was instilled at birth. My mom and my dad's parents both started their own businesses and had reasonable success with them. Both my dad and step-dad are very hard workers, in businesses not related to any family business. I can credit both of them, along with my mom, for raising me to be independent, hard working, and to never feel entitled. They also taught me the value of self-awareness, which has played a huge role in my life.

As I mentioned before, being "pretty" and fitting in, was never something I was overly concerned with. And that didn't change when I went to college. I chose to leave home for my first year, but that didn't work out so well. After my first semester, I went home to attend the University of Florida. I also had a boyfriend at the time so, naturally, I wanted to be closer to him as well. What a big mistake that was. He cheated on me numerous times, broke up with me, got back together, broke up, got back together—you know the stupid drill. So during my senior year at UF, when Playboy came to town looking for girls to represent the University in their "Girls of the SEC" special pictorial, I decided to go to the audition. It was a joke actually. I had never even seen a Playboy before, much less thought about posing nude in one. But I went anyway, and told them I was uncomfortable with full nudity. To my surprise, they said yes and put me in the magazine. It was the first of many pictures of me that would appear for Playboy. The magazine came out in October of 2001. The beginning of the following year, Playboy called and told me they were holding open auditions for a new reality show they were doing, and wanted me to audition. It was going to be on Fox before the first American Idol. I was still in school, but I decided to go ahead and go to the audition just to see what it was all about. A few weeks later, I got the call that I was a cast in the show, "Girls Next Door: A Search for a Playboy Centerfold", set to air in May 2002. Almost immediately I had to pack and head to Los Angeles to compete with 11 other girls all vying to become the July 2002 Playboy Centerfold and cover model. As improbable as it may have seemed to me, and some of my family members, I won. Even after fainting during my first photo shoot, I still became the July 2002 centerfold for Playboy magazine.

As you can probably imagine, my life was turned completely upside down after I won the show. Though school was incredibly important to me, my dream of working with animals had to take a backseat to my new career: glamorous model. Funny as that was, and still is to me and people who know me, it was now my reality. So what did the boyfriend think? Who cares! I came home from Los Angeles after winning the show, and immediately broke up with him. We both knew it was coming, and it was a huge weight lifted off my shoulders. So now came the fun part: Hollywood parties, beauty, money, success! I moved to LA a few months later. The "old" Lauren, as I like to refer to myself before playboy, who was frumpy, who didn't work out, wore no make-up: she had to hit the road. I became very aware of the world I had entered into. Beauty was required, self confidence was an absolute necessity, and the competition was going to be fierce. I was ready. I would go home to Florida pretty often. It was my way of trying to stay grounded in a world where everyone floated high above the clouds. On one trip home, I met Mark (that's not really his name, but we'll go with it for the sake of his ego). Mark was playing sports at the University of Florida, and instantly caught my attention. Love at first sight? I'd say so. We were attached at the hip. I was still living in Los Angeles, but started coming home more and more, of course to see my family, but also Mark. I was in love at 23 years old. I started thinking about moving back to Florida, but I didn't want to just give up my life and career in Los Angeles. I began thinking about starting a business. What could I bring to my old town Gainesville that is part of my world in Los Angeles? I had always been taught that inner beauty was more important than outer beauty, but in the world of modeling, outer beauty was a paycheck. So naturally, I wanted to look good. Tanning was part of Hollywood by this time. If you were tanned, you looked thinner and it hid any blemishes. Perfect thing for me to bring to my small, southern town! As I mentioned before, my family has always worked very hard. And because of that, we had the resources to start a business. So with the help of my mom, step-father and sister, I opened my first business, a tanning salon LAE Tanning, in Gainesville. The "LAE" stood for "Lauren Anderson Entertainment". The theme of LAE was Hollywood. I wanted it to be a place that you would normally find in Los Angeles, not Gainesville. We decorated it with Marilyn Monroe, Playboy and naturally, pictures of me everywhere and a few special salutes to the man himself, Hugh Hefner. The man changed my life for the better, it was the least I could do!

Being a Playboy Playmate has its perks. It has allowed me to do things most people only dream about. I've met celebrities, and yes, even dated one or two. I've made good money, and had fun doing it. I love modeling, and of course enjoy the attention that comes along with it. But not all the attention is good. You've heard all the stereotypes: dumb blonde, bimbo, gold digger, whore, etc. I know I've heard them all. So I knew my venture into the world of business would be full of excitement and hardship. My claws would need to be out and ready. But it was, after all, my choice. Sure, I could've stayed in LA and laid on the "casting couch" a few times to land a role here and there or even worse, became some old, rich man's arm candy. No thank you. So I went back to Gainesville.

LAE Tanning opened in August 2004. By this time, Mark and I were in full swing. I adored him. He adored me. I maintained my career in modeling as much as I could while spending most of my time in Gainesville. As any small business owner knows, it's virtually impossible to make any money during the first few years of business. It was harder than I could've ever imagined. But we kept at it and every year, we saw an increase in sales. And it seemed like every day we learned something more about what worked and what didn't. About a year and a half into having LAE, Mark decided out of the blue he wanted to break up. I was devastated and Gainesville being the small town it is, made our break up even worse than it needed to be. He being a well known athlete, and me, the Playmate, it was a recipe for disaster as far as I was concerned. So I started spending more time in LA again, with my mom running LAE on a daily basis. I was still very much involved, though many days over the phone. In 2006, I landed a job hosting a live production in Las Vegas, for six months. During this time, I decided it was time to open the second LAE. I was juggling the show in Vegas as well as both stores at home. It was a difficult time, to say the least. It also left little time for my personal life. No boyfriend and few friends. It was all work. Truthfully, it was the loneliest time in my life. I turned 26 that year. For my birthday, I stayed in my apartment in Vegas, alone with my five rescue cats. It was then that I knew this Vegas life wasn't for me. When the show ended, I went back to Florida to concentrate on the businesses.

I manned the front desks, I worked and worked more. Again, I ventured back to LA where I got an apartment with two of my best friends, who also happened to be Playmates as well. My life consisted of auditions, shoots, flights to Florida, working the front desk at LAE, doing marketing plans, cleaning tanning beds, and occasionally sleeping.

The following year, I ended up back together with Mark. I was thrilled. Yes, this was going to be difficult. He was playing sports in Europe and I was juggling my two businesses with my ever difficult career in the entertainment industry. The most important things to me at that time were my businesses and Mark. My career in entertainment would go on the back burner for a while. That was okay with me as I was already struggling with morality and that self-awareness I mentioned before. I was losing myself in Hollywood. I was caught up in that world. I will never forget my mom coming to visit me in Los Angeles, having a huge fight with her over nothing, and her last words to me before she got on the plane back to Florida. She said "you've turned into a Hollywood bitch" and left. Had I become everything I hated about that world?

Having two businesses with other family members was both a blessing and a curse. The tension between me, my sister and mom was growing every day. At the same time though, who better to trust than the people closest to you? That year, 2007, was set to be the first year we would show a decent profit. Then, the economy crisis hit. We instantly saw a drop in numbers. Tanning and beauty was the last thing most people would spend their last dollar on. But one thing we all agreed on was that we would stick with it and make it through this tough time. And we did—but not without problems. The fighting between me, Kelley, and mom was bad; at times, severe. The stress of a "sticks and bricks" business wore on us. We all walked out at one time or another. I was lucky enough to have the occasional trip to Europe to see Mark that kept me sane. I was still pursuing my career in modeling with the occasional hosting and acting gig. The entertainment industry was fun, but far from the stimulation I craved mentally. I wanted to be different. I wanted to make something for myself, not ride on the heels of posing nude once. And I knew I would always have a stigma to fight where that was concerned. Time went on and we kept going, kept working, kept marketing. But something about just tanning people was again lacking in what I really wanted to do for people. I wanted to give others the confidence I had learned to have. Trust me, as I talked about before, confidence was definitely not something I ever had. What made me feel confident? That's what I want others to feel. How do I, Lauren, go in front of a camera, naked or not, and become someone opposite of who I really am? Am I makeup, hair, tight clothes, sexy eyes?

Heck no! But I become that when I need to be. It took work: physical and emotional.

Kelley is a single mother. Confidence was something she always had. Kelley was the homecoming queen, beautiful, popular girl in high school and college. She and I were and still are, by most accounts, opposites. The one thing we have the most in common is that we both want greatness. We are passionate about what we do. I always joke that she's the brains and I'm the beauty. But the truth is we are both both! She brings a creative side that I don't have, and I bring the strict, business side. She's the one who has a thousand ideas all at one time and on different sheets of paper scattered around our desk, and I'm the one with the typed out list of things to do in order of importance. She's the yin, I'm the yang. We fight like you can't even imagine, but neither of us can imagine a life without the other.

By the end of 2008, we were in full agreement that we wanted to open a one-stop-shop beauty center. A place where a person can come and have all her beauty needs met and walk out feeling fabulous. A Hollywood vibe, with small town prices. But it would take money and planning. Did we want to keep the tanning salons? Did we want to do tanning at all? What did my mom want to do? She was tired and ready to be done. We needed some more time to figure it all out. I was concerned about opening this new place with how much time commitment it would take again. I spent a lot of time visiting Mark, and I didn't want that to change. How would I do this? Well, God and the Universe have a way of figuring things out for you, whether you want them to or not. Out of the blue, Mark broke up with me, again. I thought I would marry him; he had other plans. I was devastated, again. To add insult to injury, my father was diagnosed with stage 4 metastatic cancer just weeks before. This was by far, the lowest time in my life. I had a huge lesson to learn here. You can think your life is going to go in one direction, but it turns out going in the opposite. But that's not always a bad thing. The lesson I learned was that everything happens for a reason. Planning too far in the future was pointless, because things can change every day, every second actually. I was finally figuring myself out after the break-up with Mark and the news about my dad. Before that, I was still searching, trying to figure out who I was and what I wanted out of life. Was I the small town girl or was I more the Hollywood model turned entrepreneur? Answer was, I'm both. Before the break-up, I spent so much time being his girlfriend, rather than being myself in a relationship with him. Unfortunately, that was a big part in our demise. I vowed to never again become my significant other's girlfriend or wife. I would always be me, and only me. And I had finally realized who I was. Kelley and I decided, together, to open the place we wanted and dreamed about.

We closed the two tanning salons with my mom's blessing, as she wanted to be finished with her part in the businesses anyway. We opened LAE Beauty, Inc.—a full service tanning and MediSpa. LAE Beauty is a place for people to come and rejuvenate mind, body, skin and spirit. A key factor often overlooked in the aging process is the balanced life: physical, mental, and emotional harmony. Although our beauty center is a place for rejuvenating, we are not a day spa. Rejuvenation does not always mean relaxation! LAE Beauty brings together medical science and beauty to offer our clients the most current "non-knife" medical treatments available to look younger and feel better. LAE Beauty offers a Medical Weight Loss Program that teaches people to regain control of their body and life. Our skin rejuvenation program includes the following medical aesthetics: Botox (for wrinkles), Juvemedicalillers), and Sclerotherapy (saline spider vein removal). Other beauty services include: Endermologie, chemical peels, a variety of facials, sunless spray tanning, teeth whitening, waxing and more. Our goal at LAE is to teach our customers what LAE BEAUTY is all about: a fresh, healthy, smart approach to taking care of their body and skin. One of our philosophies is to focus on the things you can control: your choices and your attitude. Decide today how you will look and feel tomorrow.

Kelley and I have faced and continue to deal with the obstacles of being a woman in a man's world. Being a small business owner is challenging regardless of gender, but there are some issues women face more often than men. Generally, women face stereotyping/ gender discrimination and I've had to face that times ten also being a Playboy Playmate. People often look surprised when I introduce myself as the owner of LAE Beauty. I think this is due to people's automatic assumptions about women, particularly young women and our ability to own and run a business. I am automatically not taken as seriously, and many times I feel like people are impressed by my business smarts versus expecting it. And I know Kelley feels the same way. Many times I feel like I have to know more, and be more vocal about what I know to gain respect from colleagues.

This was particularly true during the build out of our spa. The contractors automatically assumed we knew nothing about the process. It was not until we were working with them side by side, using the lingo and getting things done that they respected us. It was an obvious gender bias that we had to overcome. Kelley and I found that respect once they realized we were in charge and we knew exactly what we were doing! LAE Beauty came together just as we envisioned. We had found our version of the perfect Hollywood decor, full of velvet couches, Marilyn Monroe pictures, playboy memorabilia, martini glass lights, black concrete floors. We were just off the

Sunset strip, only in Gainesville, Fl. I have learned through the years the importance of having the right people around you, in business as well as personal life. Kelley and I found those people. During the start-up of LAE Beauty, I met a guy who was amazing. Though I was fresh off my break-up with Mark, the idea of someone new was refreshing. I was determined to have this new relationship be different. I wouldn't make the same mistakes twice. I would maintain my life and my independence no matter what, and I have. Sometimes, it's hard when you get very comfortable with another person, not to fall into the trap of making his life yours, or vice versa. But it's imperative. Finding the balance of being happy together but also being happy apart, is one of the most important factors I've found in relationships. But the most important thing I've learned in business and in my personal relationships is how we fare during and after the bumps. One of my favorite quotes is the English Proverb "A smooth sea never made a skillful sailor". I have been dragged through the dirt, on more than one occasion. I've been called every name you can imagine after I posed for Playboy. I've been told I wasn't good enough, pretty enough, or smart enough. I was even laughed at when I went into the bank to apply for a loan for LAE Beauty. I will never forget what Kelley said when we walked out together, after our meeting. She turned and looked at me with a half smile and said "did you feel like we had on bathing suits for that meeting?" The answer was yes. I wasn't surprised we were treated that way. After Playboy, I knew most people would never look at me the same. It worked out for the better though. The funny part is that loan officer calls all of the time now asking if we need money. I have weathered many storms in my life and have always come out the other side. LAE Beauty is living proof of that. When the economy fell, I could've given up and shut down - but I didn't. I knew I'd land on my feet. Of course, there will always be stress and pressure owning a business, but it's worth it. My sister and I have opened this business, literally with our own hands. We spent countless days and nights, painting, measuring, cleaning, hanging and everything else that goes along with opening a new business. It is our blood, our sweat, and yes, our tears.

Everything has its ups and downs.

Life has taken me to the highest highs and the lowest lows. But the empowerment I have knowing I've not only been a successful model, but also a thriving business owner, is like nothing I've ever felt before. I've come to accept and acknowledge everything in my life—the good and the bad. I've been knocked down, but I always got up. I've been dumped, but I've been in love, twice. I've almost had to close the doors of my business; now I'm looking to expand and franchise.

Sure, sometimes I think about how easy it would've been had I decided to be the rich man's "arm candy" for a living, but what else would I have been? With absolute certainty I wouldn't be as whole a person as I am today. I've worked very hard to become the person I am and to have the life that I've been blessed to have. Being handed anything on a silver platter is not my style. I'd much rather have someone hand me a million little pieces and tell me to put them together. Or better yet, find the pieces myself, and arrange them how I see fit. Oh and about that guy I met after Mark, we just welcomed our first child, a baby boy! Life really does go on...

Website: www.laebeauty.com

16 Tracey Baker

I could not have made it in high heels, because there was nowhere to buy them! Growing up in a small town in Ontario, the options were—shall we say—limited. It had its drawbacks but I learned to have an appreciation for my childhood and make it the support I would need later on in life. I would learn that no matter what comes my way, I could embrace it and use it as a stepping stone to deepen myself and nurture myself in this vast and amazing world.

It could not have been easy for my parents. They made the decision to move to the town for good jobs, a clean environment and a great place to raise children. I could have never fully understood at such a young age the sacrifices they made for my sister and I.

At such a tiny school, my circle of friends was small and loneliness was not uncommon. I always bordered on the anxious side, knowing I needed to travel and tread new territory. My parents had exposed my sister and I to it at a young age but I still felt the urge to get out of my comfort zone. I was a very questioning teenager, sometimes frustrated by the geographical limitation. The small surroundings often suffocated me and I turned to the beautiful wilderness around me and found peace in the solitude of the trees and bay. The kids in my town could be harsh. The gossiping and cliques were typical of high school girls, as in most schools. I guess being so sensitive, I took it more to heart and needed to find a way to be more at ease with myself. This is where it gets interesting you see; my father was my teacher in high school so I felt under the radar by those around me. Small town life can be, well, small. It's the way my life was and at the time I did not appreciate fully what this small town would give me later in life.

I loved fashion and culture but am not aware how I really knew what was out there as I did not watch much television or read magazines. That deep longing for more went even deeper. I wanted to wear high heels. I wanted to roam a concrete jungle in them, I wanted them to ride the subway, find hidden streets and shop in China Town or Little Italy, and run through airports to board planes to SOMEWHERE.

I chose to go to Wilfrid Laurier University and I felt it was a good transition from my small town. I wasn't, however, confident in my choice of programs mainly because I still didn't know what I wanted to do with my life. I chose to study psychology as it held the most interest for me but I soon started to feel out of place again as many of my friends knew exactly what career they wanted, and I did not. I worried about passing exams, writing papers, getting my degree, feeding myself, and fitting in. Here I was, presented with some old feelings, yet again, of not knowing my exact path. Everyone around me seemed to be so defined. I was working part time jobs and having fun at school, not taking it too seriously but just focusing on obtaining the degree. I ate a lot of Kraft Dinner and graduated, and ate more Kraft Dinner as I now stressed about what to do in this 'real world' everyone was talking about with consternation. I still felt a little lost but had formed new friendships and connections since my high school days, putting one foot in front of the other so a part of me felt like I was still growing.

I focused on this part of me that was evolving in the midst of a lot of anxiety. This is where acceptance became my new best friend. I accepted with grace, my second new best friend, all that was bestowed upon me in my formative years. A strange feeling of calmness came over me in forgiving the things I could not change, but taking a valuable lesson from each of them. I was not denied opportunities at all, but had been blessed with a safe, healthy, simple upbringing that left me with a childlike wonder and curiosity to new things and adventure. I was in touch with nature and quiet surroundings, I was not dependant on material things, I had an imagination, and my hometown was now a beautiful getaway with a gorgeous long beach, fresh clean water, and an unpretentiousness to it that allowed my mind, body and soul to feel free without the noise and smog of the city.

With this knowledge as a stepping stone, I did marvel at the city in a big way. As soon as I got my degree, I moved straight to downtown Toronto. University had been a great jumping off point and it was time for the next step. I loved driving around the city getting lost, riding the streetcar or subway just to get my bearings and to people-watch. I loved everything about it but I never lost my pride and reverence for that small town that raised me.

But I STILL didn't know what I wanted to do with my life. I had a hard time finding a job and after applying for and taking countless positions that were, what I thought, undeserving of a University educated woman, I felt like I was settling. My post-education debt was growing and I started to feel lost again. I was craving more, and now that I was in the city seeing more, it made it that much harder to handle. In my hometown, you could only desire a certain amount of abundance as you were only aware of a certain amount of abundance. If there were no real malls or television to watch, how could I know what I was missing?

The inner battle of wanting so much but obtaining so little was ever present. It was time to get a hold of myself. I could not compromise my happiness to make others around me accept me or be proud of me. There had to be a way to be happy in life while using my talents. It was far too easy to see all the people that were (what I thought) successful, and wanting what they had.

After working some exciting but meagre paying jobs I began to have more and more opportunities come to me. I started travelling more for work, working as a Budweiser Girl and brand ambassador for some pretty hefty brands like L'Oreal and Virgin. I was paid to go to important events and nightclubs sampling yummy alcoholic beverages and doing make-up artistry with the newest cosmetics. I threw Jagermeister parties and went on some pretty amazing trips. Life became a lot more interesting from here on out. I gradually started to feel like it wasn't in fact that I had been lacking anything; I had a wealth of knowledge and experiences to my life. The more appreciation I held for everything in my life, the more interesting my life became. I encompassed in gratitude all the bumps in the road, hiccups, good friends and bad, ecstatic moments and lonely moments; for each brought a lesson to my life and another ounce of wisdom that allowed me to walk more courageously.

My next stepping stone to not catch my heel in was walking confidently with the decisions I had made in life thus far. I was still feeling that I wasn't defined the way others were. I still saw my friends working corporate jobs, getting married and having children, living a very stable and predictable life. I often questioned myself and wondered if my curiosity and craving for adventure was bringing me down. I knew within myself I did not want the things they had or were doing. It's just that the lack of adherence and conformity to these types of lives was making me feel like an alien in my own world. Some would sit at their desks in their offices speaking to me about the stresses of office life and the lack of vacation time they had. Although I valued their lives and what they were doing, I felt as though because I didn't want those same things, we were having a hard time relating.

A new chord was struck when my very good friend from University told me about the loss of her father and brother when she was younger. To me, this girl exuded confidence. She was outwardly and inwardly beautiful. She was smart and witty and energetic. She had many friends and a wonderful mother who nurtured her as mine did. How could something so dispiriting have happened to her? I felt guilty feeling the way I did without being able to speak of a major traumatic event in my life, or knowing the world wide suffering taking place.

My friend and I bonded over years of friendship. We could talk for hours about the meaning of life and spirituality. I felt so safe talking to her about these things as she truly understood and had lifetimes of wisdom. I felt like I had known her forever. With her help, I was coached in my authentic self and what gifts I had to share with the world. My anxieties about life faded into assurance that life can be beautiful and safe, without always second guessing ourselves.

It was the greatest lesson I learned, that you need to overcome life's toughest moments and accept why they happened and see the gift it gave you. She went through a process of learning how to make her mind happy, not by relying on her outer world and circumstances. Closing the gap of what we want to be and what we are expected to be can be done! If I stayed in fear of life and in disappointment of self, I would be believing I was separate from my true self and source. We could unlearn our minds of old thoughts and patterns to allow for the new plenitude of happiness. All of us together were learning to live without conditions on ourselves.

I had to unlearn my mind from the insecurities, non conformity, and unfulfilled realizations that had been plaguing me most of my life. If I was going to allow in new inner power, or better yet, renew the inner power that was always in fact there—I needed to get to work! Fulfillment was my new goal. Every week I would remind myself that the world is neutral; it's what I am projecting on it that creates my feelings and intentions. My mind had completely shifted since being a teenager and I was now allowing things to happen organically.

I started working for WestJet Airlines in 2006 and quickly became surrounded by a strong group of individuals who all worked in the industry in one capacity or another, but also had intriguing lives outside of the airline. One of my co-workers was a Dee-jay on the side, one leased and sold construction cranes in Dubai, and another was a wealthy woman who simply worked part time for the social factor and to keep busy, not to mention the incredible benefits of travel. I loved this group of people and the camaraderie. We weren't ashamed of ourselves; we didn't need to hide anything, explain anything, or put on heirs. We were simply individuals who loved to travel and make our living whichever way we could. Some of us had degrees and some didn't. This job was a means to an end; the end being job satisfaction, a career in the airline industry, the opportunity to see the world, and lining up with what is important to us.

Everywhere I traveled to I started to blog about it. I marvelled at the world and there was nothing better to me than trying new foods, swimming in different waters, and seeing how others live. I loved staying in hotels and trying out new spas, living like a local in another country, and challenging myself to drop old routines. I kept writing and documenting and soon friends and family were asking me for advice on where to go on their next trip.

With each of these documented experiences I saw more development in my soul. I loved reading over my journal entries and looking at the pictures. I felt so fortunate to be able to go to these places, and I was proud allowing these experiences to represent me and my true self. I spent every last dime on travel and when I now sat down with friends who bought a nice new house or were deciding to have a baby, I respected their life decision and was happy that they were doing what they wished, and we could relate.

I noticed my comfort level with myself started to change. I was having so many fulfilling life experiences, yet still lacking in what society would deem appropriate for someone my age. I started to care less and less about stigmas and saw that many of the people I knew who had for so long defined themselves by their job, were not happy or realized people at all! Many of them maintained a boyfriend or girlfriend at all times, because they were afraid to be alone. All they talked about was their job because they had nothing else of substance they could be comfortable contributing. When the conversations ran dry of office politics, there was nothing to be said. They often dismissed fun events or experiences, because they were too afraid to break routine and go for it. Always worrying about what others would think of them if they did what made them happy, started to eat them alive. They found the monotony of their life easier to handle, and this to me was definitely not true living.

My insecurities with my life lessened, my head and chin raised up when people were speaking to me about what I had been up to the past year, my voice was stronger, the guilt was melting away, my inner child wasn't shaking with fear, my ego wasn't hurt and was no longer controlling me. I was ME and I was proud of the way I was living. My friendships deepened with my friends and when things got tough, we reminded each other that it was a lesson to grasp and to look forward to the opportunity to conquer the moment, with grace and acceptance of course.

I learned not to regret anything. I had heard this repeated to me countless times in the past but it had true meaning to me now. I was ok. I thought of high school and if I had known at the time it would only be but a brief moment in my history, I wouldn't have been so fraught with fear. I thought of University and had I known I would be surviving an exciting life in the city post-grad, I wouldn't have been so anxious about all the 'what- ifs'. I started to watch my pattern of thoughts more and I accepted bad days knowing that life is full of opposites and is in constant change. If I could keep my attitude positive during tough times, I could feel better about things overall. I was surrounded by the best friends, family, and supports. People who encouraged me to be me were accepting. This group wasn't the easiest to assemble but the more I changed my outlook, the more positive people gravitated towards me.

People I know want to control their lives for fear of unpredictability, holding onto control hoping it minimizes risk. Through all my ups and downs of living in a small town where in bad weather the roads close, the local stores only carry limited items, and getting to the city can take you hours, I could not have too much control over my life. Furthermore, going through University as a wandering student where sometimes I had money for bills and fun and sometimes I didn't, I learned to embrace the unknown and let it come to me on its own time and without judgement.

I cannot emphasize enough how important it is to maintain your positivity and put your life first. I learned that if I could do this, I could get rid of guilt and negativity and handle my life minus the rollercoaster ride. I truly believe these life lessons and experiences are what grew my warm and loving heart which exudes compassion for others. I look at a person not knowing if they are covering their true selves up, because they feel like less of a person. I look at someone who seems to have it all and know that on the inside they may feel like they have nothing, yet they shield themselves with outer beauty to distract the feelings away. I look at a friend and see that he has the perfect career yet he cannot stand it and only pursued it, because he feels he has no choice. My friend also gave me the daily reminder that life is a road with bumps in it. Keep moving straight ahead enjoying the journey, but don't stop to look back on those bumps that made things rocky momentarily.

I have become such a good traveler, because, as we know, travel involves a lot of surprises and flexibility in one's personality. Flights can be cancelled at any given moment, Mother Nature can wreak havoc, different cultures can command different adherences, and you encounter many different personalities abroad. I have become a lot more laid back and welcoming to change and surprise. I can be a respectful guest in a foreign country and maintain my personal safety.

I feel so well rounded and complete at my age! I believe that if I hadn't gone through all the bad days, I would not be the same woman I am now. If you tried telling this to the fourteen year old, who just wanted a cool pair of jeans like other fourteen year olds somewhere in the world were wearing, or the eighteen year old who had her father for a teacher, thus never ever being so cool as to skip class, I would have not believed I would be standing here today in my high Louboutin red-soled heels. No way. These very heels as a matter of fact are going to walk through airport security soon to board my plane. I travel a lot now, my true dream. I started my own web publication and business called *'Posh Girl Peasant Girl Travelling'* and I do things I love. I am still wandering of course, only this time knowing that I am ok, I will be ok, and I am living my life the way I want to.

When I was watching giant sea turtles swimming in Bora Bora and everyone was leaning over the boat taking pictures, I stopped and said 'Thank You' to the universe for hearing me and granting me this opportunity. When I was gazing over the edge of the amazing Grand Canyon watching everyone hike busily around the rim, I stopped and mouthed 'Thank You' over the cannon wall. When I sit with my family on our rented villa's patio on the Amalfi Coast in Italy with a giant bowl of pasta, I quietly hum 'Thank You' to the sound of the music echoing off the rocks below. And when I walk along the beautiful beach back home I say a million 'Thank You's' to the place that raised me, and set me free to have a world full of opportunities and acceptance.

It was so important for me to value my roots and learn from them, hold them dear to my heart and let them be the soles of my shoes. I look back all the time on my upbringing and that small little town that nurtured me and cared for me but set me free when it was time to go. The people I grew up with also had a journey to embark on. I paved my own way and that is my history I am creating. My friends now love that I am from beautiful cottage country—I can toast a marshmallow better than anyone, I am in tune with nature and appreciate it deeply, and my dad kept me safe at school in a way him and I never ever planned!

No matter where you come from, do not ever feel that your path is already laid out for you. At the end of the day, sit back, close your eyes, and dream about where you want to go and what you will do along the way. Allow for spontaneity. I much prefer road trips in my travels that are unstructured and allow me to stop when I see something interesting, or rest when I'm tired. Treat your dream much like a road trip: pack your best shoes, hop in, and let the adventure take you.

17 Euraysia Lee

This isn't a story of success. It's a story about succeeding. It doesn't have the story book ending, because it hasn't ended yet. It's a story about perseverance, strength, belief in oneself, and accepting that life is difficult and unrelenting; but if you're resilient enough, you'll make it.

I've contemplated days about how to start my tale of trying to keep on keepin' on. It's never easy to put your life's hardships down on paper. Where do you start? How do you start? Well, how about first I describe the kind of life I've lived. It's not a life of living in the slums, trying to save scraps from every meal. I'm not going to over embellish my childhood hardships. I lived well. Upper middle class family; always had food on the table and clothes on my back. But one should never judge a book by its cover. Yes, on paper my family looked great. But emotionally, we were always strained.

When I was 13, I was diagnosed with clinical depression and extreme anxiety. An unfortunate mental illness I inherited from my mother; it runs in her family. Of course, being young, all I knew about mental illness was the stigma surrounding it. The negativity, the shame; hiding it and not wanting to admit to it. It was embarrassing and my father wasn't supportive either. He thought more sunlight and extra vitamins would make me all better. "There was nothing to be depressed about. We had enough money and a good lifestyle. You're too young to have that kind of stuff" was his train of thought. And that's the problem with the stigma surrounding mental illnesses. My high school and my doctor advised my parents to put me through counselling. However, when it came down to talking to a counsellor, I was too shy and embarrassed to tell her anything and so the therapy was useless. Over the years, I've learned to accept it; it's not something you can avoid or control. It's a disease, like diabetes; out of your control and nothing to be ashamed of. Unfortunately, that was a lesson I had to learn with time.

Well, as mentioned before, it ran in the family. My mother was manic, and I, refusing to be on medication, because I was too embarrassed to tell my mom I needed a prescription for depression, went untreated for years. Unfortunately, I was only hurting myself. My up and down moods, my irritability, and snappy behaviour only worsened through high school and by the time I graduated, my mother and I could barely live in the same house together. I was in and out of my parent's house, because we would fight too much. Finally, one day the strain was too much and the day before a very beloved uncle's funeral, my mother and I got into it regarding plans for me attending the viewing the day before the funeral. That was the end of it; she kicked me out the day before the funeral. To add insult to injury, my University had been on strike and ran into mid-June, leaving me without my regular internship position (which was given away in early May), and unable to find a summer job and without my car, which was left under my parents' name for insurance purposes. I had no money, no job, and nowhere to live. I moved in with a "friend", and while looking and doing whatever I could to find a job, her husband had other ideas about my staying there and did all he could to make me leave. Needless to say, I did. I sold whatever I owned that I thought had any value at all, paid him the rent, and my best friend Missy offered me a place to stay with her. I left to move in with Missy an hour away in Toronto next to my University in the middle of the night after a fight with my "friend" and her husband.

It was Missy that gave me the strength to keep going. She helped me by allowing me to help her with her small baking business, which she ran from home by paying me small sums to help decorate her cakes. She helped me get a job at the restaurant/bar that she worked at, and let me live on her couch for as long as I needed to get myself organized. I was going to enter my second year University, but I was debating dropping out to find a full-time job and was ready to sell my laptop to give her something, anything for letting me live with her rent-free for so long when she sat me down and said to me: "Listen Rae, my mom always told me, if you sell your things, you'll always end up with less in the end, never more. I'll help you out because that's what friends do and I'll let you stay here for as long as you need until you can get your feet on the ground. But don't sell your laptop, and don't you dare drop out of school."

I went into my second year of University when Missy found out one of her friends was moving into a town house, and introduced him to me. He was getting a three bedroom townhouse and agreed to let me live there and when I got my student loan I could then pay him back the rent I owed. I found a part-time job on campus working three hours a night three days a week which wasn't much but it was something. I still didn't have much money left over and I lived off instant noodles, water and mushrooms that my cousin had bought me and brought over for me one night. To this day, I swear I'll be sick if I see another package of chicken flavoured MAMA Noodles.

I didn't have any extra money ever, and so I walked an hour to and from the University morning and late night after work or class. I didn't live in a good neighbourhood—Jane and Finch in Toronto, anyone who knows the area knows it's no picnic—but I did what I had to do to attend class. Some days, if it was raining, I'd scrounge up $2.75 from my low end piggy bank that I kept for emergencies to take the bus to school, because I didn't have any shoes that could keep the water out. On days where I had no change, I'd just have to do my best to avoid puddles and bring extra socks.

Holidays were the worst, because the school would shut down and I'd have nowhere to go. I'd manage to find some extra money to take a bus back to visit friends, however, when they went away to visit other family during the holidays so over Christmas I'd be alone.

My friends from back home never visited me, never called, never facebooked me; I checked every day. I would message them and normally get nothing back. I would later find out they were upset that I had moved to Toronto in the middle of the night without telling them; however, none of them ever offered me a place to stay knowing that I had nowhere to go and I didn't want to ask if it wasn't offered.

By the end of my 2nd year, I had moved four times and lived in four different houses with four different roommates. I was working three jobs and took the occasional week off school here and there to do trade show promotions which ran during the day in order to make ends meet. My grades suffered tremendously, and I was de-enrolled from my four year Honours program to a regular three-year Bachelor of Arts; which was crushing my dreams of going to grad school.

Finally, I got into the student houses owned by the University in which rent was charged to your student account and you didn't have to worry about having it ready for the first of the month. I kept only my part-time job on campus, and my manager would try to get me into as many shifts a week as he could find; however, there wasn't much work during the daytime. I didn't have much money, and lived off crackers, butter and tap water. My friend Missy kept encouraging me and came to see me whenever she could, and on weekends if they needed extra help at the bar, I would work for tips. But even still, I would go days without sleeping. I'd lay awake until 7 am, then get ready and go to class, then work, then home, and again lie awake until the next morning. My depression and anxiety was eating at me and I had a lot of anger/trauma built up that I had never dealt with that was causing an overload of stress. I decided I had to come to terms with the fact that I could not overcome this illness on my own, and I needed help. Even with all the support and encouragement I received, I didn't feel right. I knew that was wrong, and I sought out help.

The University offers free counselling and treatment and I saw a doctor at the on campus clinic for medication. It took me a lot to be able to come to terms—with the fact that mental illness doesn't just go away, and getting help was nothing to be ashamed of.

Since then, my grades went from a C average, to a B+ average, to getting straight A's, and I have been accepted back into the Honours Political Science program at my University. My plans are to get into graduate school and complete a Masters degree in Sociocultural Anthropology in hopes of later working to develop therapeutic rehabilitation programs for children with mental and physical disabilities in a social and physically interactive setting. After living with my own stigma regarding my own mental illness, I have come to realize just how debilitating it is to be afraid of coming to terms with it, because of the fear or alienation. I want others to be comfortable in social settings and to be able to overcome not only mental illness, but physical disabilities as well and hopefully raise awareness to the issue of stigmas related to disabilities.

Before the therapy, even thinking of talking to my parents would send me into an uncontrollable anxiety attack and I would shake and cry for hours, but after therapy, I was able to call my father and actually speak to him on the phone and ask him to bring up some of my belongings that I left at my parents' house for my on-campus apartment.

When my father brought up my belongings, he apologized to me, and we began to rebuild a relationship. I still do not live with my parents, and don't believe I'll ever be able to again; however, our relationship is very good. My friends back home and I have since talked about why things happened the way they did, and have patched things up. Missy and I are still the best of friends even though we don't see each other as often. But when we do see each other, it's as if we haven't skipped a beat.

Through all the pain, I was constantly reminded that there was light. So many days and nights I would lay in bed and cry until my eyes couldn't open because I was so confused and didn't know what to do; tempted to give up, trying to convince myself that things will look up, but not being able to find that silver lining. The dark times were very dark and very common, but after seeking the help I needed, and with the endless encouragement of Missy and everyone that helped me out along the way, I learned to let the dark times be dark, but know that every day is a new chance. It's a new opportunity to do something good, make something good, show and prove to the world that there is more out there and find the strength within.

By strength within, I don't mean find the strength to do it all on your own, I mean being confident enough to know that there is more. There will be better times, and to be able to accept that you can't always do it all on your own and there is absolutely nothing wrong with needing, wanting, and asking for help.

There is no such thing as "raising yourself". Even the most solitary tree needs sunlight to grow. Life is a journey and upon that journey you're going to hit rough patches, get stuck in the mud, forget your route, and get frustrated. But the key is to never give up, find your strength, believe in yourself, and never be scared to ask for help. Take the good with the bad and know that it's never really over; there's always tomorrow and the ability to use that tomorrow as a new opportunity to be the best person you can possibly be.

Life is beautiful; life is what you make of it.

18 Dalia Asterbadi

Y ou determine your own success and how you choose to measure it. My journey seems of the ordinary kind with the exception of one thing: I never take anything for granted nor do I accept mediocrity. I would rather fail trying than take the safe road. In fact, failure is not a word in my vocabulary; there is only learning, detours and milestones. I have taken what some would say is a hard path in an industry that is male dominated. I would like to say it's my destiny and my passion and I am privileged to have family and friends who are my cheerleaders. They taught me to dream, and to dream big.

I love technology, and I enjoy business. After University, I took on a few technical roles to try to implement my newfound knowledge. I also developed a passion for marketing and sales. In my first job, I tried to get as much done so I can experiment with some marketing tactics and support the sales team. This volunteering effort got me noticed, which led to progression towards more marketing-focused positions. Within 6 months of my first marketing job, I was promoted. I became the senior manager responsible for public relations, lead generation, and product marketing. It was a big challenge, but I accepted the responsibility with excitement. I had a team that was smart and whom I admired. The golden rule of hiring is to never be afraid to hire someone smarter than you. If you are surrounded by brilliance, it can only lead to daily inspiration. I was fortunate to have a mentor in the organization, who recognized my talent early on and gave me the support and guidance to advance in the company. I strongly recommend that young entrants seek out a mentor in their company to help them.

My dynamic with the companies I worked for and their managers was interesting. I was always one of a few women in my company and I quickly learned to get used to it. I learned to be aggressive when I needed to, but never overtly masculine. I learned how to be a woman in a man's cabinet, as I always like to say. Most women make a mistake by thinking they need to behave like men, but that is not necessary as men are capable of relating to women. I was simply myself, and by assuming that my gender was not an issue, it naturally became a non-issue for the rest of the team.

My roots were not from humble beginnings. Like many children raised in the Middle East in the 80's, everything material and luxurious was common to us. I attended a very prestige American school with my Kuwaiti peers where the value of a strong education was important. I had a great group of friends; my memory of them is wonderful, and we even used to compete for who can throw the most lavish birthday parties. In fact, I remember for my 7th birthday, I demanded we rent a big truck, so my gifts could be transported back.

Today, a resident of Toronto, Ontario, Canada, I recall these memories as nostalgic, especially in light of the huge change of culture that I've gone through. However, it has also brought me to appreciate the true luxury of life, health, family and joy. On August 1990, we were rudely awakened at 6 am with the sounds of helicopters and emergency sirens. That was the day that Iraq invaded Kuwait. Scrambling for our safety and entering the cellar, one can only think of why? I don't plan to get into this, as my own opinion of it changes over time. I do, however, believe that morning became an integral part of who I am today. We lost everything material, but considered ourselves lucky. We were the last people to leave the country and legally come to Canada. My father had a business and was doing a lot of work in Montreal at the time. Every time he would come home, he would bring us souvenirs of Canada that we cherished. We were planning to move to Canada, we just didn't realize it would come unexpectedly. It was an arduous transition, but it also led me to appreciate the true luxury of life, health, family, and joy.

My family means a lot to me; we share a lot with each other and our journey together is not common. I have two older sisters. They inspire me every day, especially as a young girl. They were unlike anyone I knew—smart, caring, creative and they dedicated most of their time to teach me things. The events we shared growing up in one of the richest countries in the world, living in Spain and travelling together mixes many emotions for me. As we rebuilt our lives here in Canada, we had a lot of growing pains and cultural adjustment, but the most difficult experience so far was getting accustomed to the educational system. School was not the fun, competitive environment I once remembered. This had an impact on me, and it began to change my point of view on education. As a sidebar, at 5 years old, I knew the 12 by 12 multiplication table. In fact, my mother made Math a very important subject for us. We occasionally had bedtime stories, but we rarely missed a drill of Math before going to bed. My mother, who used to be a Math teacher, once shared her thoughts when I asked why Math was important and said; "If you can add everything in your head, you won't rely on others to do it for you. This means you can always count on yourself." I always interpreted it as I will never have to cheat in school, because I would be smart enough to do my own homework, however, a few decades later, it makes sense. I didn't count on others. If there is one thing I can share with anyone who is finding their way, it would be do what you have to and before asking for help, first attempt to do it yourself.

Growing up in Canada was amazing, I had the chance to be Valedictorian and discover many things, and I enjoyed everything. I had amazing friends, but one thing I always remember was it was not challenging enough. In high school, I was so bored that I decided to get myself in trouble; I was a teenager! I truly feel bad for putting my family through so much anxiety.

In reflection, I was not a bad kid at all; I just liked hanging out, going out with friends, and may have gotten myself in trouble one or two times. I mention this, because I think it's important. If you are always sure of yourself, no matter the influence or time of your life, you can always come back to something. I know I pushed myself and others, because I was bored and wanted to see how far I can go. I always knew that I wanted to go to school, in fact, my family was worried I would be influenced by people to not go into University. I was determined to, and I was always in control. I knew no matter what I did, or what kind of influences I had, I have to stick to my instinct, and as much as how cool it was to be free spirited, and take life and school less seriously, I actually found that to be stupid and non-rewarding. I had a goal: to be the best person I can be. In fact, I took it as a challenge when people thought I took the easy way out. This allowed me to bounce right back. It made me work on having top marks so I could get accepted to the best schools. In my graduating yearbook, my note was: "Most people look up at the stars and admire it; a champion climbs a mountain and grabs one. Don't push me for anything, 'cause I will always beat it. Thank you for strengthening me."

I graduated with a Bsc. Eng. in Systems Engineering—it seemed interesting, but someone told me that was one of the hardest degrees you can do. I was one of three girls. This was the beginning of what may seem as me entering a male-dominated industry. I always stood out like a sore thumb. I was intimidated at first, but then realized I had an advantage. Nobody saw me coming.

Why I Chose Technology
Most people would assume that the huge tech bubble of the 1990s was my main motivation to enter technology. Yes, that might have been a factor, but it was not my primary reason. My father was a techie and former employee of IBM, who exposed us to technology at a very early age. Our first home computer was bought in 1984. Our father would sometimes take

us to work, where I recall being fascinated with the impressive buzz and hum of the mainframes. We would trolley around the offices and pretend to be making magic behind those machines. I consider myself lucky that my father introduced us to technology very early. He encouraged us to understand what computers can do, how they can be programmed, and even painted a picture of what the future could look like with technology. Most importantly, he taught me that I shouldn't be afraid of it. That nebulous thought back then of what it could be is where we are now, and there is a long way for us to go. Being exposed to technology at a young age meant that it was no longer intimidating, as children are blessed with the inability to be intimidated by new things.

My father had a huge influence on me. He is my number one mentor and my biggest inspiration. My mother is the rock of the family. She is an art enthusiast and a skilled artist. She took the time to teach us art. My sisters seemed to have the knack for it as they are very talented, and the only canvasses we hang on our walls are originals by them. I seemed to be the between child: I loved soccer, pottery and cars. Both my father and mother were entrepreneurs. My father, however, has started several successful businesses and it was very common to discuss this at the dinner table.

Risk was not an issue in our household. The only risk my father would ever mention is the risk of not getting what you want in life if you don't work at it now. He always had a motto with us: "Work hard now, play later." I have used this in many of my speaking topics. He often spoke to us of what he called the "learning curve", a curve that he would use to illustrate what it's like to accelerate your ability to achieve goals. It also described that hard work was about a balance of knowledge, perseverance and patience. Three words loosely used today to paint a success story, but in his words, these were not the ingredients to success, but the prerequisites to carving your path, not just from a career point of view, but in light of the expectations you set on yourself. It was not easy as a teenager to grasp this, but listening to it often allowed me to appreciate it eventually. Today, as I reflect on my career and my company they resonate like nothing else can.

Knowledge

Knowledge is the art of understanding your discipline, your passion and your skills while striving to be the best you can be. It also represents your astuteness to how you measure yourself with others. Most people fail, because they do not expand their horizons to understand how they fit. The best soccer player always looks at how he compares to his competition, not the rest of his teammates. An architect evaluates what he can do to improve his skills from a global perspective, not how his current project is performing. An entrepreneur never basks in the small successes of his business, but reflects on how these milestones are improving the company's ability to lead in its industry. You can claim knowledge is also about innovation and re-inventing yourself every time you think you reached a dip in your life. Today, you hear a lot about execution. The key to success is focus and execution and you should always set a specific set of tasks that you can rely on yourself to accomplish. This was one of the hardest things for me to do, because as a generalist you sometimes skip over the details and that could hurt you. Know the details, understand how to collaborate and take responsibility for the assignment. If you set a bar of success you can accomplish it by applying knowledge and focus.

Perseverance

Perseverance is about continuing to strive for your goals. I used to ride a motorcycle and loved it. Speed was great, but a life lesson I curiously learned from riding a motorcycle is that your eyes navigate for you. Where you look is where you will go. If you looked down, or away from the direction you are heading, you would likely lose momentum and fall. This is a great concept to keep in mind when you consider the perseverance to achieving your goals. It doesn't matter how long the journey is, as long as you keep your eye on the goal, the target and the direction you want to follow. You don't always hit a homerun on the first bat. In fact, you may strike out! Don't get distracted by the illusion of what you are working towards. Keep your eye on the path and know when to let go. Perseverance is difficult to explain, because there are times you need to steer in another direction. It doesn't mean you quit or stop the focus. Just assess the direction you are heading and if it is worth continuing on that path.

Patience

As a teenager, you want things to happen instantly, and they sometimes do. As you begin to build on your new goals, you discover things do not happen overnight. Patience is a conscious effort to not give up too early, or become frustrated when they don't happen quickly. Enjoy the journey and be aware of how you are spending your time to reach new goals.

I was lucky to have this training at a young age. My father invested so much time talking to us about business, money management and risk. But what is important is that even though I had all this knowledge, it was when you physically put yourself in this position you begin to learn and realize.

This is a great similarity to my first year at University. It was tough, it was emotionally destructive, and there were a lot of bets on you failing. But one needs to remain on the end goal and so I persevered, because I believed my education and training were going to be the first milestone in entering this space and being taken seriously. I did not want to take an alternative path. I stuck it out and it got easier with time. In fact, I told myself, if I can do something well that I like, imagine what I can do with something I love. This, in reflection, was a very important point in my life.

Today, I base most of my decisions on their significance to me in two years. This also applies to how you assess mistakes. Mistakes may seem like a very big deal, but if you do not think they will be significant two years from now, do not sweat it. Keep your eye on the big picture. I developed this way of thinking as I was planning to start my business, realSociable. I had the idea as early as 2006 and had invested some time evaluating its feasibility and waited for our technology to evolve. I waited for the right time, and the right time pertains to the technology available as well as the risk I was able to handle.

I was always told by my father that if you can survive your current lifestyle without earning any income you can persevere and make anything happen. This speaks so loudly to restaurants. Most restaurants don't keep enough capital to run at the quality and standards that they aspire to have, should there be a slow period after opening. Unfortunately, their patience and their lack in ability to maintain its service usually disables them. I knew I had to be in this stage. So I began investing my money—a big risk—but I knew the rewards would be bigger. I waited approximately 5 years to build a portfolio that would yield a good return to do two things: raise my own seed capital for realSociable and keep some money for my own expenses.

Building a team is not easy. In fact, it is often said that not building the right team is the number one early reason start-ups fail. I had a partner; we were diving into this together, and we assured one another we would be there no matter what, but that quickly changed. Six months into our venture and many disappointments later, that journey came to an end. It was amicable, but one of my first lessons. Make decisions fast and do not let them cost your company. I am sharing this, because growing into the person you want to be has to come with bruises and road bumps, otherwise you don't know what to fight for. It was simply a non-issue for him to walk away, although he had created a liability for the company and lost us business. I was depressed and couldn't muster the energy to leave the house. It nearly destroyed me, but then I woke up one day and told myself: if I was able to assemble a team once before, I can do it again.

I quickly moved ahead and never looked back. Some people just don't know how to push themselves and hold themselves responsible. I am not one of those people.

Bouncing back solo

I needed to understand the runway; I had to rebuild the vision I had. I planned to do it on my own until we were in a position to attract talent to join the company's management team. I regained my spirit and energy to do this again. For those supporters I had, I kindly apologized and advised them we are continuing and that their support was important to us. It was a regained spirit, one that gave me the strength to do it on my own.

It is not easy; every day is a new day, you have to be able to think big and climb your way out of hairy situations. I once read a great blog post about the entrepreneurs' journey, which is positioned as a ride on a long wooden roller coaster, bumpy all the way, but filled with ups and downs. It resonates strongly with me as there are some days that are great, where my grin can be seen from miles away. There are also days I was so overwhelmed and frustrated that I wanted to crawl under a rock and stay there. The passion inside me and the sheer determination of achieving the milestones I laid out for myself is what kept me going.

As you begin telling your story and building a team, you have to be prepared that there will be some obstacles in the way. In the beginning, hearing direct criticism may anger or hurt you. It took me a while to understand that it is good to listen to comments and truly understand the feedback that I was receiving. I began to learn more about myself and what people wanted to hear, which gave me an overall better position. I also grew a thicker skin. In business, you cannot mix emotion with conduct. I had a wonderful conversation not too long ago with a woman I admire in Silicon Valley. She told me: "Tell me how your business will change me and my business. It is good to be direct, and then let the relationship take its course before you bring in personal stories." It was advice that changed me. In fact, when she gave me feedback on our conversation, I apologized for taking the liberty to try to engage on a personal level. I was so eager to speak with another woman in technology that I jumped ahead of myself and assumed we'd be fast friends. She gave me another great lesson: "Never apologize for anything, everyone makes mistakes, you [as a woman] should never say sorry. Most men don't say that. That is how you will be able to make it in the playground." Since then, every time I want to say I am sorry, I pause and kick myself. I do chuckle from time to time as it is a Canadian thing to say sorry. The moral of this experience was that I will do things from time to time that may not be right, but your strength and confidence should always remain. Do not apologize for things you really don't mean to apologize for simply out of habit. To take the liberty and the strength to do anything, whether someone likes it or not, is not a cause for an apology. This is not intended to be an arrogant statement. It's really a realization that in life we just need to march forward. We are our own worst critics as most people would not recognize you had done something wrong or inappropriate. Apologizing will always put you in a unflattering limelight, so just don't do it, unless you really mean it.

Strength develops over time. I began to see myself change; my ability to hire and direct my company was changing. Every day more focus and priority was being created. This is how momentum builds within an organization, and then it becomes contagious. Everyone gains inspiration to keep the pendulum going and have it move faster and farther. Every day is a new day with new goals and a checkpoint to a long term strategy.

While it's important to have clear cut plans and milestones, one should never forget to dream. I am a dreamer, someone who has dreams and sees things if all goes well. I never forget to have these visions. It's easy to be a dreamer when you are in motion. It adds some excitement and uncertainty in your life. It also allows for further creativity and imagination. This also takes you away from applying too much pressure on yourself. I have learned something over the past decade as a young career-focused woman: Every time you set a goal and apply yourself, you will achieve it as long as the goal is truly attainable and in reach. As you dream and imagine new major milestones in your life, I learned that no matter what goal you set, new goals will always surface.

As my father always puts it "Enjoy the journey," as that is the most enjoyable part. It's true, you develop into someone you didn't know existed when you focus on the way you are defining your path. Your journey is what excites you no matter the day, good or bad. You will learn to adjust reality to your desired action. If you enjoy every minute of the journey and keep pushing yourself, your learning experience becomes priceless. The journey itself is worth more than the end result. When you think about how much you have learned and accomplished outside of just a simple goal, you realize there is nothing to lose. My biggest goals in life are health, family and joy. That is what I strive for everyday; everything else is bonus.

Enjoy the journey. Push yourself. Be resilient and patient. And don't forget to dream.

19 Dayna Shereck

Ligh heel boots have always been more my thing. A good pair of high heel boots allows a woman to reinvent herself over and over again.

I think I knew instinctively from a very young age that there were going to be times in my life where I was going to need to reinvent myself or start over and so my preparation started early. I always felt I was someone who would do many things—not just one. I would mix with many types of people, and my life would take many twists and turns, but I never quite knew what that would mean.

I had a lot of ideas in my head even as a child and many of those are still playing out for me in some ways now as an adult. I guess I could never quite let go of an idea, but that has proved to be a good thing for me as I don't give up easily.

Even though I was too young to know it, my life would be impacted forever when my father walked out on my mother when I was just 11 months old.

My mother, who was only 24 years old at the time, was left with a note and nothing more. Devastated, it was not till 24 years later that my mom would find the man that she would eventually marry.

I spent my childhood in the company of adults; my mother moved us in right away with my grandmother who was a widow already for many years and so began our eccentric and beautiful life all together.

We were three generations of women; my mother and I were without any support so although she was a free spirited artist, she sacrificed her own dreams and got a 9-5 office job to raise me. But still, money was tight.

The days were filled with stories from the old country from my Jewish grandmother, singing songs together, and as I got older, I enjoyed creating dreams with my mother. We decided one summer that we were going to get in shape and run, and so we downloaded Bruce Springsteen's "Born to Run", "Out on The Street", the "Flashdance" soundtrack, and many other great songs and we put on our head phones and went out to the track every night. At one point, we were running 2–3 miles a few times a week. We went through other times that we went out to fitness classes and aquafit and came home on snowy evenings by bus. I'm sure my mother was exhausted after a long day at work, but still, she 'schlepped' me out as we were always in the process of re-inventing and bettering ourselves.

My mom gave me the feeling that we could do and be anything we wanted to be together. I am quite sure that my feeling of not being afraid to take risks in life came directly from her, as she was the most empowering person anyone could have as a parent. My grandmother gave us a feeling of security to go out in the world and take chances and she would love to hear a great story at the end of the day.

There were nights my grandmother and I spent hours talking almost all night together about life. I will treasure those moments forever and they are very special to me. She always would tell me, "Dayna, you are different, you are able to do things other people wouldn't dream of doing, and you are never afraid". In truth I was very afraid, but my fears were different than what people would expect them to be.

We had a close extended family as my mother had two brothers that were very close and one who lived with us too for a period of time. I felt very insulated and I felt very protected.

As the years went on, my father re-appeared, though our contact was never consistent. I heard about his life through other people but was never part of it.

I remember him once dropping off for many months after we had established contact and later blaming me for that, saying I had not showed enough interest.

As a young child or pre-teen I was not ready to handle or negotiate an adult relationship. Sadly, this taught me that people leave and that it was my fault.

Growing up I knew that with little money and a fairly conservative family, with the exception of my mother, anything I wanted to do I would need to find a way to do myself. And that's how I preferred it anyway.

Somewhere in my early teen years, probably around age 13-14, I discovered the band U2. Their music resonated with me on every level, and being a fan of their music became part of my identity. The lyrics made sense to me and somehow comforted me. I not only learned everything there was to learn about the music, but I was also interested in how music could bring about social change.

I had remembered watching Live Aid as a kid and wanting to be part of that in some way. Years later, my uncle took me to the Human Rights Now concert for Amnesty International's Conspiracy of Hope tour and my love of music for the cause was further confirmed. This was another seed that was planted when I was quite young that would stay with me through my adult years and continued to inspire me for years to come.

School had been low on my priority list growing up. It bothered me on some level that people were required to spend almost twenty years of their lives in a confined environment adhering to a schedule that might not suit them. I was lucky enough to spend my last year or so of high school out of the physical school environment as much as I could. I got an internship at a teen magazine, and I would go to my placement along with a team of other people my age and I would write content all day. We worked out of a house and the woman who was hired to mind us, turned out to be one of my early mentors. I felt ready for grown up life and I had a lot to say and contribute. I was much happier going to a place where I could be myself and where I didn't feel confined.

When high school was officially over, I decided to travel. The thought of being trapped in another school for a series of years seemed like torture, so I left for Israel and spent the next couple of years volunteering, attending an Ulpan (a program where you work on a kibbutz for half the day, and learned Hebrew the other half) and exploring. I was in one of the most beautiful parts of Israel, near Eilat, on a kibbutz that was full of flowers, greenery with a swimming pool and the ocean not far away. Despite the long days of hard work, it was a paradise.

I met one of my first boyfriends on the kibbutz and we left the kibbutz together, heading for Manchester, England, where he lived. I set up a new life in Manchester, I got a job, made friends and got to know my way around the city very well.

For at least a year of my life it became home. Fish and chips, trivia nights at the pub, Saturday's spent in Manchester Town Center, shopping and getting a loaded baked potato with chili, this is what I remember of Manchester. Eventually, I got my own apartment there, as I needed a little independence. It was a small bachelor with a coin heater. I remember my boyfriend bringing over coins and fish and chips in the evenings. I was enjoying Manchester's music scene as some of the UK's great bands like Oasis were coming out of Manchester at the time. The city also had a long history of breeding great bands, such as Joy Division, New Order, Happy Mondays, Simply Red, The Verve and the list goes on. At the time, I had a job around the corner from the famous or infamous Hacienda. Though I never fully got into the grunge scene, it was alive and well in Manchester and leading the music scene around the world at that time. Before coming back to live in Toronto, my boyfriend and I drove to Wales and caught the ferry to Dublin and spent Christmas Eve and my birthday that year in Dublin. He knew how much U2 meant to me and so we took

photos at the hotel where U2's Bono and his wife Ali were married. We
sat in pubs and drank pints. I thoroughly enjoyed Ireland and found even
the ferry ride over full of characters was worth the journey. We later came
back to Toronto and tried living here for a few months, but we were still
young and hadn't yet found ourselves to be starting a life together in a new
country. He went back to Manchester.

I would say these were the years of finding myself, trying new things,
living in new places, not sure where I would end up or what I would end
up doing.

I still had no idea what I wanted to do.

Some time in the months after returning from Manchester, I met
someone who would turn out to be very significant to me. He was an
artist, a mime-like automaton that had just come back from living in Paris
for the last 10 years. Having always been a romantic and sometimes
even a tragic romantic, our beginnings were perfect. Meeting on the
train to catch a foreign film, walking through the city all night, cooking
together and drinking lots of wine, it was perfectly unconventional and
exactly what I wanted. We moved in together quickly and spent the years
being each other's cheerleaders. He brought me out of my shell, and
encouraged me to dream. He showed me that he was always proud of
me and wanted the world to know that. I was good at bringing some
of his dreams to reality and being able to cultivate our life together. We
eventually got married.

Our life together was colourful; I worked a million jobs to keep things
afloat, and he was the artist.

I would get up early to waitress in expensive hotels, and took jobs in
banks. I eventually became a flight attendant and we were able to travel
together. He later introduced me to working in film and our schedules
were always all over the place.

I got my ACTRA membership after getting a short role in an American
commercial, and ended up landing a billboard for Toyota's Rav 4.

There was nothing dull about our life. We were always hustling to make
our next dollar, and to do the next thing. This life was much more suited
to me than having a 9–5 guy. In those years, I worked so many jobs that I
learned about many industries.

I became good at getting jobs; I enjoyed interviews and testing my
abilities.

My husband and I had been brought together for a reason, as we had a
wonderful friendship and we were able to give one another the solid base
we both needed.

We were slowly building ourselves up, I had given birth to a wonderful daughter and we had just purchased a condo and were now looking at houses.

Life seemed very hopeful, though there were still some pockets and gaps, but I resolved it by thinking that is the case with everyone.

During my 9th month of pregnancy with my son, our second child, my then husband was diagnosed with Acute Myeloid Leukemia.

I was told 2 weeks before giving birth that he only had a 20% chance of survival.

We had just moved into a new house and 3 weeks after moving in, he got a cough that would not go away. In my gut I felt something was very wrong and I even remember thinking that I knew what it was. I can't explain how I knew but I somehow did. After many doctors kept saying it was nothing, we finally went to our family doctor. I remember going into the office with him and just knowing. She called me in first and told me that this was going to be bad, and all of my built up fears and anxiety boiled over. I felt I was going to pass out. She also told me that I needed to be the rock right now, because otherwise none of us would get through this. And that's what I did. By the same afternoon he was an inpatient at Princess Margaret Hospital, and the nightmare began. I could not believe what was happening, I was so afraid that he was scared, and I didn't know how to make that better, because there was a reason to be scared. Intensive treatment began immediately. I gave birth a couple of weeks later on New Years day at Mount Sinai Hospital and his nurses brought him through the hospital tunnel on a stretcher to be there for the birth. He was so sick and weak, and here I was giving birth, it felt like life and death were happening at the same time and it made everything feel so intense and fragile.

While I was in overdrive, trying to balance a newborn baby, a toddler, and no income, he never lost his faith. I spent even more time with my mother and my grandmother around this time, as now we were 4 generations of women plus one little baby boy.

We gave our son the Hebrew middle name "Avichai" meaning life, and it was the most fitting and wonderful name.

My days were spent with the kids at home, and working with social workers who were trying to give us whatever support was available to us during this time. The evenings were spent visiting the hospital and sometimes I could only be there for a short visit after long days with the kids. It was the most depressing and horrible time ever.

I was very lucky to have a wonderful family, and so fortunate to be part of our Jewish community, which not only made sure we had delivered food at our door, but provided an abundance of faith. We wrote on his hospital room wall, "This Too Shall Pass" and almost two years and 1 relapse later, it finally did.

The doctor came in the room and casually said that an unrelated bone marrow donor match had been found. Given my husband's mixed Moroccan and European background a match was very unlikely, yet somehow it came and we felt so blessed that this had been turned around. We had a sheer miracle on our hands.

We had spent the majority of two years spending so much time apart, with him in hospital a lot of the time and me with the kids. I eventually started a small flower business out of my home. I had always been drawn to flowers but somehow during this time, I felt flowers actually made me feel better, especially tulips, which are my favorite. I got some orders and had a small booth in a community center, but I gave a lot of my surplus away. Truthfully, just working and smelling the flowers, putting them together and cutting the stems somehow made me feel grounded.

After my husband came home, it seemed that life was very different. Although we were still the best of friends, we had realized our relationship was a friendship and we had been struggling to climb this ladder as a family, but after this happened we realized that we have been focusing on the wrong things.

Having at this point lost our house, all of our money and having been through emotional trauma, we felt like "what now"? Although I had held strong during the entire time he had been sick, now that he was getting better, my cracks were starting to show. I began suffering with panic attacks that would come on at any time. I became afraid of all the things I had used to do so easily.

Travelling, a traffic jam, being in a stopped subway, all created horrible panic for me, as well as a number of other things. Trying to overcome something I barely understood was extremely difficult. The overall trauma and fear of losing all that I considered secure, took a toll on me emotionally. I came out of this a very different person and my own fragility was now exposing itself.

When I was a little girl and things upset me, I was in the nurse's office with a stomach ache; the doctors said that it was all stress. My emotions and stress directly showed themselves in my body, and my overall health.

The panic attacks were much more difficult for me, because they were emotional and they stopped me in my tracks. It was like seeing the world through a lens of fear and terror for a short amount of time and then it would go back to normal.

They began to lift and be less frequent when life got a little calmer for me. Though I knew that this was now part of my make up and that I would have to accept it.

Eventually, my husband and I made the decision to separate, but it was a gradual one and we knew that no matter what, we were going to still be there for one another. In truth, we ended up moving into apartments next door to one another and still took care of each other and our children but were just no longer married. In my mind, he continued to be part of my family and we made up our own rules of how we were going to get through all of this.

I enrolled in a mature student program at UofT as I had become interested in the kind of work that the social workers in the hospital did. I had become a bit of an expert at filling out disability forms, learning about community resources and all the things families needed when they were in crises. I thought maybe I could help other people. I actually needed to help other people. I realized that although my previous work experience had included lots of unique times, all I had ever really taken away from any of them was a paycheck and now I had nothing. I had worked hard for 10 years, but with all of our money now gone, I realized, I had done nothing rewarding or fulfilling with my life. It was time to turn over a new page.

I had heard about a program where I could become a job developer. I could help people who were struggling to find meaningful work, do just that. In turn, I would get to do something meaningful too and earn a salary. I was thrilled.

The woman, who taught our program, became a very important mentor in my life who has since provided numerous opportunities for me. She was a person, who made me feel that there was light at the end of the tunnel and that I could do this.

I got an internship at an AIDS organization where I could help people that were in the return to work program. As I listened to their stories—and some were very sad—I slowly healed myself. I often cried along with my clients. I took them out to look for jobs, and would stop and have a coffee with them at the end to talk about life. There was no great division for me, from where their lives ended and mine began. I threw myself into my new role with everything I had.

I needed them as much as they needed me. I was successful at helping them get jobs, and my placement rate was high. I joined an umbrella organization for job developers and received a certificate of excellence for my work in the field.

I got into a bit of trouble at times for not having the greatest boundaries, talking to them about their passions when that was someone else's job, visiting a client in the hospital when she was no longer part of the program, but I knew that this job was about heart. Four years working within the AIDS movement, even in a small way and attending the International AIDS Conferences in Toronto and Mexico City, was the most fulfilling work I have ever done. I treasure the unique and poignant opportunity I was given to be part of a wonderful organization and movement.

During this time, I felt two major themes were starting to take over my life. The first was that post-divorce dating was proving more difficult than I could have ever imagined. If I had subconsciously tried to avoid heartache by getting into a serious relationship in my early twenties, it was coming back for me with a vengeance in my thirties.

No escaping it.

My new relationships provided me with intensity, but little comfort or security.

The second theme that was emerging was that I was aching to create. I was seeking a freedom of expression that I was unable to fulfill in my personal life. Feeling boxed in was starting to affect the way my brain functioned. I began to see in my work life that administrative tasks were becoming more of a struggle for me, yet my ideas were constantly flowing. I came into work meetings full of inspiration and enthusiasm but writing an e-mail was sometimes a struggle.

I could feel with each passing day that the creative side of my brain was slowly taking over the linear side. Though I had played no instruments, I had just purchased a guitar and had a very good friend showing me the basics, and by basics I mean I know how to play 4-5 easy chords, with very poor strumming.

I had eventually left my job for another one, and this new place was just not the right place for me. I came to their HR department one day and I was just struggling.

I walked into the director's office in tears. I was frustrated by everything.

I didn't feel my feelings were being considered in a relationship I was in, and it was dragging me down. I was working out of a cubicle which was physically making me sick, as I am someone that needs human contact. Nothing was going well.

This felt like rock bottom.

My HR director saw something in me at the moment and granted me a lay off, with a month of benefits to get my health in order. She saw at that moment how much I was struggling just to keep it together and it was her kindness and empathy that made a world of difference in my life.

I said to myself when I left her office that if someone was going to be kind enough to help me out of this, I was going to use my time wisely; I was going to get in touch with who I am, get help I needed to make better choices and throw myself into creativity and healing.

When I left the job, I spent at least 4-5 hours a day writing music; after a month I was also writing my songs on the piano. I have no idea how I was able to play, as it would be very hard for me to replicate anything I have played, but luckily, I would use my iPhone and record everything. During that intense period of songwriting and focusing on myself, I had written about 12 songs. I eventually found a student to produce them, and I recorded them slowly as it was still an expensive enterprise.

I had no idea what I would even do with the songs, but I felt that if they were coming out of me, then they needed to be recorded.

I used this time to focus on parenting and giving more attention to my children. I got involved in their play dates and spent evenings playing trivia with them and doing homework.

I remembered how much I like to cook and entertain. I stopped running all over for everyone and tried to stay centered and focused on what I needed to do.

I started to treat myself with more importance than I had previously.

I used this time for self-discovery. The feeling of accomplishment after writing a song and hearing it recorded was worth every penny, more than any shopping spree I could ever go on, or any high heel boots I could buy.

I was re-inventing myself from the inside out, instead of from the other way around.

At the same time, I was exploring my roots. I was trying to figure out who I was, and I thought a lot about the music that had made me the happiest and the messages that I felt so aligned with; it always came back to U2.

I coincidentally met a friend, Tami Falus, for lunch around this time in the late spring of 2011. She and I had gone to see U2 together in 2009. As we were catching up and talking about life, I just said to her "Can we make a documentary together about general admission", U2 is coming back in 6 weeks, and I needed to do something meaningful. Tami seriously thought about it, and came back to me two days later and said "I'm in". Her saying yes and the weeks and months that followed provided so much happiness and sense of purpose that it literally turned my life around.

We had no idea how we were going to do it, but it didn't matter, we would figure it out. The most important thing to me was that I was now going to throw myself into something that I could feel good about and a project that was close to who I am.

As we got started, momentum was all around us; in the spiritual sense and in the amount of drive that I felt.

Positive feedback was everywhere and I had a gut feeling that we were on to something good, even if it meant it would just be good for us to do for ourselves.

As the film was coming to completion, I didn't know what would come of it, but I knew I was changed by it and I had found my voice.

My grandmother passed away during the time this chapter was being edited. Life is forever changed by her no longer being with us. She was a strong life force, and her voice and message is in my head daily.

I don't know what the future will hold. Those lessons and tough times happened for a reason, and I hope I can use my experiences to help other people that are stuck.

I do know that now that I have found my creativity and my voice, I don't want to ever let go of it.

I still buy myself tulips every chance I get, I am planning a trip to Nashville this fall for my songwriting and I am once again reinventing myself.

20 Barbara Adhiya

There are three words I live by. They have been ingrained since before I can remember. All my life has been driven forward because of them, whether consciously or not. Those three words are: Never Give Up.

I come from a very large family; at a cost of two. I lost my mother and then my father when I was six years old. My mother died when I was six, and my father, although after visiting on weekends for a year, then disappeared from our lives. The reason was of a cultural difference. My mother's family is Indian and it is with them that I lived and was raised after my mom died. My father is Dutch and the family was not going to even consider letting one young man of another culture raise three young children all by himself. My father with no education could not raise three small children alone, my brother being only 2 and my sister 2 months old. As my grandparents' relationship broke down with my father, then, too did any contact I got to have with him.

And so I was raised with my mother's family in one house, a family of six adults and eight children. I was the eldest. My grandfather ruled over the family, setting values, rules, and my grandmother was in charge of running the house. They went on to become my adoptive parents when I was 14. Between my cousins and their parents I could see a special bond—one that I didn't have and couldn't feel. I could physically see that spiritual bond between parent and child and it was so glaring to me, because I didn't have it. I became an Adhiya, and have a strong bond with each adult and child, but I am missing my parental bond. You grow up faster when you don't have parents.

As I grew older, the cultural differences between what I felt life should be and what my grandparents did, began to differ. I had lived with my parents in their apartments and lives before my mom passed. Unlike the Indian home, it was more Canadian. We used to eat meat. But once with my grandparents, who were strict vegetarians, I took to sneaking meals that had some meat. I would hide cans of tuna in my school bag and come home and make a mayo and cucumber sandwich, go up to my room having stashed the can opener on my body and close the door to watch TV, whereupon I would open my can and had a great tuna sandwich. There was always Indian food ready to eat at home but I still craved meat and in this household it was a sin to even say the word. I would save up my allowance and when at the mall at lunch would have burgers and fries and of course say I had only fries when asked at home what I ate for lunch.

My grandparents didn't like me to have non-Indians as friends. They felt they would be a bad influence on me and get me into trouble. I attended Gujarati reading and writing classes on Sundays and also participated in Indian Dance competitions from when I was 12 to 15. I had made friends there and they thought that was plenty. But I went to a Canadian school and made friends from other cultures. As I grew older, conflicts and friction began over going out to play badminton, or seeing a movie or hanging with friends in the evening. School dances were out of the question as were most overnight school trips. They were lucky I wasn't a bad kid, but just wanted to be a normal teen. More and more I knew I had to eventually get my own life and hoped to go away to University. I felt I wasn't Indian but I also didn't know what a Canadian life was like. I just knew I had to live to figure it out.

The arguments and fights became worse as I pushed for my independence and being the eldest girl they held on as tight as they could. Many times I went to look at basement apartments and thought about leaving when I was in my last years of high school. I had a friend who wanted to leave her family home too and we could share it. But each time it came close to leaving, I backed down. I was worried about leaving my brother behind. I wanted to take him with me but I knew no one would let me just take him. I wasn't old enough to be his guardian. I had a secret boyfriend also and hoped to escape with him too. But I eventually caved to my grandparents' bribe of a car and went to the University of Toronto Mississauga campus so I could live at home. I had been accepted at Western in London Ontario, and McGill in Montreal, but didn't take the chance to leave the city. I still couldn't completely leave.

In my first year of University, I became News Director of the campus radio station. My grandfather had wanted me to go to Ryerson for journalism as he was a former lawyer and journalist and I had appeared on his radio and TV programs since I was 7. But Ryerson was a Polytechnic Institute and I wanted to go to a University. So I took first level Canadian Political Science and Canadian History (both mandatory) and second year Political Philosophy, European History, and French. Unfortunately, I didn't find University any more challenging than high school. I fast-traced through high school to get my degree and OACs for University in four years instead of five. I felt meeting teacher's expectations for good grades was about writing papers in their perspective and answering exams by regurgitation. I had hoped University would be more challenging to my mind. I was wrong. I had more lecture classes with hundreds of students listening, taking notes and then every six weeks handing in a paper. If anything, it was worse. I ended up visiting the radio station, and through hanging out there became their News Director. I also had a reggae show and would fill in for DJs if they didn't show up for their slot time. Needless to say I wasn't in class much and after the first year had a 56 percent average in all classes except my second year Political Philosophy course—the same class in which my Professor could turn on the room speaker and hear me perform my afternoon reggae show. They were on at the same time. I guess I can write a good Philosophy paper.

It was tough living at home, fighting for freedom, having a part-time job at a bank and being News Director and having classes. I decided to apply for the Broadcast Journalism program at Ryerson for the next year. A news announcer I directed also was applying so I wrote her referral letter for her application to the same program. Thought it was odd that I'd be writing the referral for someone else to the same program I was applying to, but I also thought it couldn't hurt. Might even be an advantage for me! My marks from U of T weren't great but I had the radio experience and had my family's program which was on actual TV to show for experience. Out of 20,000 applicants they chose 275, and I was in, as was the girl for whom I had written the letter. Most of those accepted came right from high school. I was only 17 but had a year of post secondary under my belt. People thought I was older. Even though it was my second year at university I still couldn't drink. Not legally anyways.

Things at home became more and more stressed. I had learned to live a secret life and the constant maneuvering was making me tired. Every time there was a block to what I wanted to do, I had always found a way around it. I would lie of course but not because I wanted to and after a while it was exhausting keeping your story straight. I would sneak out after they were asleep to go to parties, and sometimes just to meet friends. I was coming home late when they expected me home before dark. I know it would have been easier if I just became the good Indian girl they wanted but it just wasn't me. I didn't know what 'me' was yet but I was very eager to get out there and find out. I respected their culture and understood it was mine too, but it wasn't all of me. I knew they couldn't see me any other way, but I knew who I was inside, and it wasn't what they imagined. I never gave up on who I was from the beginning. I just knew I had to go around things. Giving up and stopping and becoming something I wasn't, was not an option; never once in my mind. So this force stayed the undercurrent of my spirit. Never letting me rest no matter how strenuous or difficult a situation became, there was a way around it and I just had to find it. It's how I left home, threw myself out into the world and changed from a naive protected girl to a wiser more worldly awakening of myself.

It was a weekday evening and I wanted to go out and meet my boyfriend's family at a local restaurant for dinner. I told my grandfather I was going to go just hang out with some friends and he was against it. I wasn't going to be out late especially on a weeknight, but after breaking that rule many times before he didn't believe it this time. After arguing 'til we were screaming at each other, I grabbed my jacket and ran taking a pathway away from the street. My grandfather being mad called my uncle who was at home and told him to go get me. My uncle must've been having a bad day and had a temper, so now he started out for me. The path ends at a street and I'd have to walk it a while to get to the restaurant. Before I knew it my uncle was in his car, came down the middle of the street behind me and stopped right beside me. He came rushing out, grabbing me by the arms saying "let's go" I pushed against him and struggled to get free. "I'm just going to go eat with friends and will be back!" I screamed, but he was not letting go. Pushing and shoving me he dragged me across the street to put me in the car. Opening the front door he grabbed my hair and tried shoving me inside. I had my hands on the frame and braced not to fall in. At that moment, another car pulled over on the street, my uncle's car was still right in the middle. The man came over stopping my uncle and asking what was going on. My uncle just said he was taking me home and I was misbehaving. The guy asked how old I was. I answered 17. He turns to my uncle and says he can't do that to me. I'm over 16, and can go where I want, being tough wasn't okay. My uncle tried to yah-yah him saying he knows, he gets angry but he's taking me home. Luckily the guy goes on to explain how he's got to let me be and try to guide me more but that he can't use violence. As they are talking I make a run for it and headed off again through the pathway. Running with tears I followed paths behind the neighborhood and got to a phone booth calling my boyfriend to tell him the story. He said to come meet them at the restaurant; they'd be there in ten minutes. I met them there and through dinner it's decided I'd be going with them that night. After that, I never went back home.

I stayed with my boyfriend's family on the couch for almost a week. I couldn't stay longer as they were Turkish and me being a girlfriend they didn't want overnight stays forever. At Ryerson, most of my friends knew I had left home and offered places to crash. So I went friend to friend staying on their couches for weeks. It was difficult being in school, first year of the

Journalism program, and having to get a full time job to start earning some money to survive. Going home was not an option and some days were filled with tears as I called home often to let them know I was okay, and my grandmother would be crying for me to come home. It was always difficult to hear her cry but I didn't give in. I knew I had to keep going forward. I wasn't scared as they were for me, a 17-year-old girl living in downtown Toronto by herself. I wanted the mystery of each day and wanted to figure out life. I went back after a week to collect my things in a suitcase. I went in the daytime so my grandfather would be at work, and I wouldn't have to talk to him. It was stressful enough.

After a while you do run out of friends. You can't stay with people forever, so I ended up in a shelter in downtown Toronto for homeless women and children. It was a large basement of a place with rows upon rows of cots and another room with a kitchen and tables, a few chairs and a small TV. There was a shared bathroom and shower area. It had strict rules of breakfast and dinner time; you had to be out by 10am, and doors opened again at 6pm but closed at 9pm. No exceptions. If you weren't inside you were left out. Most people were young women and their kids, some were mentally unstable older women, and some were just runaway kids. For me it was a bed, food, bathroom, and closet. Every Friday, the Salvation Army would drop by a pile of clothes from which you could take what you needed. I was applying for full time work, and got a job at a retail shop in the Eaton Centre. I had to start making money for somewhere to go, as the shelter only allowed you to stay for three months, then you had to leave. Most guests just moved on to another shelter. The ones who needed the most help, were mentally incapable and spent years going from shelter to shelter. I wrote articles for my class of the experience and realized that I was lucky I had the chance of moving forward. I knew that it was only the beginning and I was starting out at the bottom. But I knew I had a chance. My family still loved me and wouldn't turn me away. But I felt all the choices had to be mine. I had to step forward with my own foot and create my life, whatever that might be.

I stayed at the shelter for two months, missing a few curfews crashing with friends after a night out, but saving up first and last month's rent to move into a condo with two other people. It was a two bedroom. I was renting the solarium at $400.00. It was right downtown at Yonge and Dundas above the World's biggest bookstore, and two blocks from Ryerson. I was keeping up with classes by borrowing friends' notes and reading the texts. When test time came, my friends would give me a heads up and I'd take the day off and go write it. At the same time I had taken the position of Promotions Director at U of T's radio station. I had sometimes just spent the night there sleeping on the floor. I also had a Top Ten show and sent a copy to be played on CIUT, the downtown U of T radio station. All this along with my boyfriend, a relationship that was consistent only in being on and then off, I was kept busy. My room was small but life was full and I was on my way, creating my life.

After a while, my family realized I wasn't coming home and were supportive of me by helping with cash sometimes and loaning me cars. It was easier going out to the radio station with one rather than using two city's public transportation systems to get there. I also kept watch over my siblings. I carried the guilt of having left my brother behind. I knew it was a difficult house to live in. My sister was spoiled by my grandparents so she would get pretty much what she wanted. My brother was more a responsible one who carried a lot of burden too. So I would take them and my cousins out when I could and as they got older into teenage years I was meeting up with them when they sneaked out. I was still the one who gave guidance to them all, who kept them when they fought with their parents and who was always there for them as they grew up with advice.

As time went by, I kept part-time jobs after getting OSAP grants (a past program from the government of Ontario- Ontario Student Assistance Program) in my second year, and continued to graduation. From working retail I went into restaurants and bars as the tips meant more money and the hours were more flexible. I had an adventurous young life, travelling, going out with friends and working. There were many times I could have gotten into serious trouble but for the most part I kept my distance. I was more of a watcher. A habit from my young years of wanting to fit in but not knowing how, so I would just watch how people lived and imitate. I wasn't a big drinker, or smoker, and didn't do any hard drugs. I experimented and had fun but because of my responsibilities I never got too out of control. If anything, I was the one people turned to for help or guidance when their lives were spinning from errors in choices, from being too reckless and young. I learned a lot and I learned fast. I was fighting for my future and I wasn't going to fall completely off the road ahead.

After working in the bar scene for years I began to worry I'd never get out of the field. I had been working for Rogers Television and had been making segments for York Region Community program. I would take out the truck with camera equipment, shoot my segment, shoot and conduct my interviews and shoot some more b-roll then drive back to the station, edit and cut the piece together to air later in the week. I was also working once a week producing on Niteline, a nightly entertainment wrap up show running five minutes before Letterman on OMNI. Trying to get more experience and break out of the 'we can't hire you because you have no experience yet but how do I get experience if you don't hire me' circle, I continued to apply for jobs, while working in the bar scene, having a contemptuous relationship with the boyfriend, and caring for my siblings. But I wasn't getting anywhere and after some time I was getting tired and frustrated; worried I'd be working in restaurants with no other future.

My boyfriend suggested a trip to Turkey with his family. I bought a manual 35mm camera and decided to experiment with shooting. I love black and whites and thought Turkey would have great scenes to photograph. I had a camera eye from my broadcasting experience and was confident in my picture taking abilities. It was a trip with much to see and photograph and I came back with hundreds of pictures. A friend suggested I try to sell them to a stock photo agency. A stock photo agency is one that sells pictures of everything for people to use in ads, or for editorial purposes. I saw that they were looking for a Photo Researcher in their library so I applied, but as that position got filled they offered me one in Business Development. And with that, I took a step out of the restaurant business and went into the first phase of my career.

Business Development involved searching for new business and keeping up relations with the advertising agencies who were our clients. It was a real office job with cubicles and meetings and gave me the chance to learn about the business environment. From speaking to being involved in meetings, to dress and office etiquette, I soaked it up. After three months, another position opened in the library for a researcher so I reapplied, and was moved to that department. Now, I spent my days looking for photographs to meet clients' requests for their textbook, catalogues or ad campaigns. I could see my photo selections out in the world, on billboards, and subway ads. It was a great feeling to feel a part of something, to feel like I had successfully accomplished moving to the next stage of life. I was in my mid-twenties. I was outgrowing my friends who still partied like there was nothing else and as my boyfriend still lived by this lifestyle I had no choice but to end that relationship. I had held on to him for my support and growth for 11 years. He wasn't ready to move on to the next and more serious stage of life and I couldn't remain in the stage behind. I left most of our friends after the break-up and moved across town. I started anew, again. Many people who knew us couldn't believe that I could just leave after so much time. They said it was a brave thing to do. I was sad but at the same time had that same undercurrent of push for a different type of life and I didn't want to give up on it. I loved him, but a vision of being a mother with children with a man who believed the word 'party' to still be a meaningful verb, was unnerving to me. And I couldn't do it.

I went on to another relationship with a photographer. I'm a serial monogamy person believing in building relationships over time. And now, I believe you pick your partners for reasons and they are in your life for a purpose. There is always much to learn. He was more a jealous type who let his insecurities get in the way of our growth as a couple. Of course, I didn't know this at first. I fell in love with him because of his adventurous artsy ways and his lifestyle. He lived in a loft above his photo studio and did commercial work for ads for clients. I would help him on shoots and would be a subject in many projects. I had my job as researcher at a stock photo agency, but it didn't pay very much. So I began taking night shifts at the restaurant again to supplement my income. It was very different to have a full time office job and work some weeknights and weekends in the bar scene. It's a tiring life and I knew I couldn't keep it up for long.

I had gotten a couple of small raises and promoted to the title of supervisor in the library but the pay was still minimal. I had to look for the next new change. I had learned a lot about photography and was learning more photoshop skills through my boyfriend. I wanted to be an editor but wasn't selected when the position came up. One day I saw an ad for a national media company. This news service was looking for a photo editor. It was a great usage of all my skills. I had a journalism degree, I was still a news junkie reading the papers whenever I could, and I was editing through thousands of photos a day in my selections for clients. I couldn't think of a better job for me. My old friend from Ryerson had worked there since graduation. He filled me in on the position and the two managers that would be interviewing me. I went in filled with excitement and confidence that I was a perfect fit for the job.

But I didn't get it. During the part of the interview where they showed me pictures and wanted me to correct the photos for tone, I knew it was my weak point. I didn't know how to do it. I could tell them what was wrong with the pic but I wasn't sure how to correct it. They were impressed with my journalism background, with my skills in organization, my semi-fluent French and being well versed in the news of the day. They told me someone was retiring in a few months and if I reapplied I'd be at the top of their list. I would have to have my photoshop skills down by then. And that I did. My photographer boyfriend allowed me to learn and experiment on his computer and in three months time I was the new photo editor at a national media company.

The relationship with that boyfriend fizzled out and once again I was on my own, leaving the life and friends we had made and starting fresh. It didn't bother me to start alone again. I relished it really, as I got to rebuild, learn from my mistakes before and live as I wished. Stress and boyfriend free, I learned to be more self reliant and learned to be by myself. I was still a mom to my brother and watched over my sister. I was guiding my cousins who were starting out in their worlds now, making their ways. I visited my grandparents often still declining offers to move back home. I was 31 now. I was free. I was me.

Working for a national media company was fun and educational. I saw events around the world through photos from a global news service, for which we were the Canadian distributer. There was always something new. I worked shift work, which can be difficult but can also give you the free time off when others are working. After breaking up with my photographer boyfriend, I had some family difficulties as well and decided it was time to break away from everything and everyone. I needed to stop being a caregiver for everyone and take care of myself and my own psyche which was exhausted at this point. I sold everything I owned, and bought a one-way-ticket to Thailand departing on Christmas morning 2003. I would just buy the next one-way-ticket to the next country I felt like visiting when I wished. They gave me a year leave even though I had gone in to quit, so I had the real freedom of just being. I traveled to Thailand, India, Turkey, Greece, France, Egypt, and Amsterdam visiting friends but spending many days by myself trying to figure out what I wanted in life and who I wanted to be. The couch surfing trip, as I call it, was the best thing I did in my life. People thought I was crazy at first, selling everything giving up my rental house, and just throwing myself out to the universe. But sometimes you have to have faith and you have to throw yourself into the unknown. You will be surprised by what life has to show you.

Eventually running out of savings, I returned to my job at the same company and gave Toronto another try. I set a timeline of a year. I preferred the more social life of Europe and didn't like how closed TO could feel sometimes. In that year I met a man online. I was dating on Lavalife and was getting tired of all the non-possibilities discovered in the first few minutes of many coffee dates. But I thought I'd give it one more try. A man had e-mailed me and seemed to have all my requirements. He travelled, cooked, and liked food from all cultures. We began by talking on the phone and in an unusual step for me I allowed Louis to take me out to dinner. On that dinner we discovered we had grown up across the street from each other, and knew some of the same people in the old neighborhood. He had worked at the ad agency in the north tower when I worked for a stock photo agency in the south tower and I had been sending photo searches to him. We had lunch at the Italian place in the lobby many times but had never met. When I moved to the media company, he changed jobs to an ad agency two blocks from my office. We realized we had crossed paths many times in life but had never met. I suppose the universe had its own timing in mind.

I met Louis a month after my grandfather died. I had already booked a four week trip to Thailand and Amsterdam (I had found my dad two years previously and took trips to see him when I could in Amsterdam. That story is one for another time). So after four weeks of dating I had to leave on this trip. Louis surprised me by calling me when I was still in the waiting room at the airport to tell me he'd bought a ticket and was meeting me in Amsterdam. He met my dad and my aunt and asked me to buy a house with him. I said yes and seven months from our first date, we closed on our house. Four years later we flew with friends and family to Italy and got married. He was a surprise from the universe. He'd been there all the time but I wasn't ready to meet him before. Timing is everything.

Eleven years of photo editing at the media company, I hit a point again of stagnant growth. I had the least seniority with nowhere to move up or laterally. I felt I had learned what I could and was not agreeing with the way things were going. The industry was changing with digital cameras and social media having its influence on every person. I wanted to make a change and move forward. I was growing again and it is always a painful process. Work became frustrating. So I knew it was time to take another leap of faith and quit. I had applied at many jobs, but hadn't even been offered an interview. I decided I would quit and go unemployed. I need to find my way again. Life is like that. You have to decide when to change roads even if you have to go off road for a while to get to where you want to be. I knew I would leave at the end of 2012. Before I could give notice, I got a call from another global media company. I interviewed with them on that one phone call. And on the day I had my resignation letter in hand to give in, was the day I was offered the job on their new North American Pictures Desk in Toronto. I had to close one door for another to open.

This is my career. This is my life. It was built step by step by moving each foot forward, building level upon level of experiences to become who I am today. Life is full of choices, scary ones, safe ones, and ones that require patience and careful consideration. Some will even be mistakes. But to make a choice is to move forward. Without choice there is no movement, there is no future and there is no chance of success or failure. Standing still and refusing to make a choice leaves you stuck in that one spot. THAT is being unsuccessful. Making a choice, even if it turns out to be a mistake, is still something to learn from, something that will shape your character for the next challenge life has to give you. The choice of life is always yours. Are you going to soldier on, through ups and downs, or are you going to just sit down and give up forever? You have to accept and more importantly, believe the paths are there, through choice. They never end. Be prepared to walk forward. And never give up.

21

Jennifer Love and Alyssa Fraser

While working together at another Toronto PR firm, we both found ourselves thinking, *if this were our business, we would do things differently.* These thoughts became a conversation that took place over several post-work dinners we couldn't afford; weeks later we met for coffee, bought our domain name and ordered 600 business cards adorning a logo we created ourselves—Duet Public Relations was born. We had a wishy-washy business plan, but we had a concrete and mutual sense of what we would offer and how we were going to offer it.

Today, we have a steady roster of clients, a solid track record and a slew of mantras we firmly believe in (some we wish we knew sooner). Here they are:

FAKE IT 'TIL YOU MAKE IT
Perception isn't everything, but it counts for a lot. People often ask us how we got started without a coveted list of industry contacts or relationships with media bigwigs. This is what we did: we conducted ourselves as though we had been doing this for years. Yes, we proofread each e-mail we sent 100 times and rehearsed every phone call we made, but we *never* made a point of saying, "Hi, we're a brand new company that you've never heard of, but we hope you'll take us seriously."

We attended networking events, wore nice outfits and when asked, we simply said that we "worked for Duet Public Relations"—not that we were a startup or that we owned the company (we looked too young for that). As we flew under the radar, never broadcasting our inexperience, we steadily built relationships and credibility.

Don't be a phoney, but be confident in what you know and what you're good at until others recognize your success.

IT'S OK TO SAY NO

Delving into many projects at once is part of the young-and-hungry career journey, but it's up to you to assess opportunities, agree to do the tasks you can do well, and be okay with turning some down. There are only 24 hours in the day and you do need to sleep. If you can't handle something on your own and can't find help to get it done, say no.

We're not suggesting that you become your office's resident Debbie Downer and refuse to lend a hand or take on new projects, but you don't have to say yes every time either. Your peers and your boss will quickly learn that when you do commit to something, you will follow through and do it well.

Saying no can still be a challenge for us, but we have felt liberated as of late, saying no when we just can't help and focusing completely on the clients we've said yes to. Everyone ends up happier that way.

SET UNREALISTIC GOALS

There is inarguable validity to the school of thought that relies on carefully calculated equations to achieve realistic goals, namely financial ones. (i.e. save X per month in order to pay off student loan by year X, spend X more hours at the office in order to justify asking for a raise by month X, and so on.) In fact, we both know it would do us good to spend more time mapping out our workload and payoff in Excel spreadsheets. But we have adopted a somewhat unorthodox goal-setting method, cementing what seem to be pipe-dream goals.

Like many entrepreneurial adventures, the financial fruits of our first year in business were scant, but we sat down and dreamed up these major goals for year two anyway: *we will both become homeowners, double our client load and double our company's worth.* They seemed incomprehensible tasks at the time, but we achieved them.

It might be rooted in some sort of law-of-attraction philosophy, but to us it's simple: setting unrealistic goals gives us a vision that motivates us to work our butts off, manage our time more efficiently, be more creative in order to get better results for our clients, and seek and nourish relationships that lead to long-term payoff. It is a method for dreamers that should be supplemented by the careful work of a reliable accountant, but if you're like us, it will push you to achieve more than seems reasonable when looking at an Excel spreadsheet.

YOU'RE NOT TOO YOUNG TO BE GREAT

At 22 and 25 years old, we started our own business. Our parents and friends, who maintained a more traditional, work-through-the-ranks philosophy, wondered why we didn't keep working under someone more experienced and slowly work our way to the top. But we knew we had creative ideas, a good understanding of the journalist-publicist relationship, a natural ease with clients and our own beliefs about how a business should be run. So, why wait?

Now that we've succeeded in a more traditional sense (and others see what we're doing as "real jobs") we can confidently impart this little piece of wisdom:

You're not too young to be great. Experience is important, but it isn't the only thing that's important. There is something to be said about bringing fresh ideas and a new perspective to a job. If you know you're good at what you do, believe in it. If you feel like you can go out on your own (or with a brilliant friend), go for it.

www.duetpublicrelations.com

22 Shay Lowe

A small town girl, a city girl at heart; and I am making it happen in high heels every day. I'm making life happen, and hopefully, in a great pair of designer heels.

I grew up in the city of Timmins, Ontario. It was such a beautiful place to grow up in. Hazy summers, playing outdoors, and exposed to nature everywhere I turned; incredibly cold winters and I remember counting the stars as I made snow angels by myself dreaming of my future. I loved doing that. I learned such a sense of community growing up there, and forged long-standing relationships, many of which I still have today. As much as I loved growing up there, I always knew I wouldn't build my life there. What I knew from a very young age, was that I was going to see the world. I had such a strong sense of knowing, a drive and energy within me, and somehow that whatever I did in this world would involve going to the big city and making it. Being a Piscean, I am naturally dreamy, but this was different, I had a sense of my fate.

What does it really mean to 'make it' anyway? And why?

What I am about to share with you, is a summary of my journey that brought me to being an entrepreneur, my struggles, lessons learned, and tips for success in life and starting your own business. I hope by sharing my story, it will inspire someone out there. Someone in a small town or even the city, who, even when faced with adversity and the worst of circumstances, can make it—or what 'making it' means to you.

I think back on my days of high school and what I wanted to do. I excelled in Math and Science. I had such a keen interest in it and for the longest time I thought about forensics; even law. But somehow, I could not stay focused on this goal. I wanted to leave and travel, spread my wings. I always had a million things going on and socializing was huge for me even back then. I loved being around people and having so many different types of friends in my life. I watched, I learned, and took inspiration from those around me. It was this love of friendships and making connections that would help me later in my journey.

I didn't go to University right away. I needed time to think about what

I wanted to do. I wasn't ready. I had my own mind and always had a bit of an aversion to convention. Why should I go to University right away? Why can't I live life, explore my goals, but in a structured way. What I couldn't get out of my mind was that I wanted to travel to a big city and experience that energy. I wanted to venture to New York City—the city of all big cities. My cousins were studying the Arts there, and my aunt was going to be making a trip. I thought—this is the time to do it. I worked at a local restaurant, I saved, and next thing I knew we were going on the trip together. I just wanted to be there, and see what it was like. I remember the excitement and also the pride in saving for something I just had to do.

I fell in love! I instantly felt at home. The buzz, the energy; it was larger than life. It wasn't my last time there. Since then, I have travelled and worked there numerous times over the years.

It was in New York that I started to wonder and gain a curiosity about fashion. Fashion wasn't very important where I came from, but I started having an interest in it when reading Vogue and all the big magazines. The fashion industry is so huge in New York. Somehow, I was drawn to the idea of fashion, but as to the specifics, I was not sure. The city invigorated me. I explored, I gained such a sense of independence and I felt brave going to what was perceived by me as a scary city. When I got home, this began my journey and I moved away not long after.

I eventually left Timmins and moved to Oakville to live with my best friend going to school there with a goal of working in restaurants and saving to move to Toronto. This was my number one goal. Would I go to school there right way? Eventually. I just didn't know exactly when and I was okay with that, but I had to get there. I would figure it out as long as I had a paying job and a place to live.

Interestingly, my curiosity about fashion led to temporary modelling work in Toronto and New York for a short time. It wasn't totally for me, but I made money and it was exciting. And again, it further exposed me to the fashion industry.

Growing up, our family did well, but we were not affluent by any means. My father instilled in both my brother and I to work for what we wanted, to set a goal and make it happen.

My parents always encouraged me from as far back as I remember that I could do anything. Looking back on books my mother kept that had items from each year of school, there was a section I could write what I wanted to be and where I wanted to travel to. My lists were always a mile long.

I watched my mother excel in academics and her nursing career. She was so beautiful, loved fashion, loved music, loved learning and reading.

My father was successful in government and also had a love for music. He would often travel for business, but also play in a band sometime on weekends. So I witnessed the intellectual and the creative ways of living. Both of my parents were creative in their own way and cerebral too. In terms of character, I looked up to my mother for her kindness. She did not have a mean bone in her body. She showed me how to be happy, she was always bubbly and friendly and loved to laugh. My father was also very personable and outgoing, but so strong, didn't take nonsense from anyone and nothing could faze him. Even later in life, my father taught me so much about negotiating and going after what I wanted. I often wonder who I am more alike but it's definitely a blend of both. And it is these qualities that became instilled in me, that anchored me then, and more so now.

Sadly, both of my parents have passed; both from heart-related issues and both of them were sudden. I suffered these losses throughout my journey that I am sharing with you here. My father passed during my mid– 20s and my mother in recent years. I cannot tell you how difficult this was, and still is for me. But I picked myself up and continued on; I had to, for me, and for them. I know this is what they would want. They were both so strong in their own way and it is what I learned from them. My whole foundation of what I thought my world was, was shaken to the core. But somehow, it also set me free. I made a choice. I could choose to suffer, or not to suffer. I chose not to suffer. Thankfully, I have a strong relationship with my brother, and many aunts and uncles and cousins who stepped in and are always there for me. We all lose our parents and loved ones eventually. Just for me, it happened sooner. And I know there are many people out there, who have had it much worse than I. It is from these losses that I learned self-love, compassion, courage, and strength and fortitude.

If this has happened to you and you've suffered the loss of a loved one, I know sometimes you think your world is over. I can tell you without a doubt it is not. Life is not fair. It can be cruel. But life can be so beautiful. Hang on, and fight, stay positive. It will get better. You can create your own life. And you are never alone.

Life is so interesting and where it takes you. You think you have a plan and if you are open, things can go in a different direction. I did reach my goal of moving to Toronto. I went to College and University and paid my own way and worked at the same time. Let me tell you, it was tough. I still had thoughts of maybe going into law, but the timing didn't feel right. Later, I would learn it wasn't the timing, it was a realization and embracing my authentic self. In the moment, I just loved learning. It taught me so many skills like time management, dealing with a heavy workload, and critical thinking.

My first job was at a company that specialized in a program for highly successful entrepreneurs. I wanted to make money. I was hired as a receptionist and was quickly promoted into managing events and conferences. This company was amazing. I travelled for my work, had 6 weeks of vacation a year, I made amazing friends, but most importantly, this company had wonderful energy and was highly creative. The philosophies taught in the program permeated my life in every way. The culture of the company fostered positivity, goal setting and learning how to strategize around obstacles. I learned office politics and how to conduct myself in a business, how to embrace my unique abilities and how to delegate things I was not excellent at. Everything you could imagine! I worked there for many years and cherished every moment. At the time, I treated it as a wonderful learning experience and a great place to work.

I appreciate and value it that much more now that I have become an entrepreneur myself. Who knew that working there would help and inspire me so many years later? I am so grateful for my experience there. Everything has a purpose.

After I left this company, I was ready to pursue the idea of law. But I didn't jump into school; I had a strategy to be sure this is what I wanted.

After much perseverance and with management skills behind me, I landed a fantastic job in a major law firm managing their professional development program and associates. Was a career in law what I really wanted? I decided to give myself time while making good money and learning as much as I could about law in the real world. I built programs, managed a huge workload, saw how a large firm really works. Seeing the business (because law is a business) from the inside gave me incredible insight and it paid off. Eventually, I moved on.

After many years at the firm, I had a burning desire to leave the country and travel again. I didn't want it to be for vacation. I wanted some time away. I was feeling stifled, had just suffered a failed engagement and wanted out of the country. Be careful what you ask for!

Through a mutual friend, I was asked to be considered for a job working as a personal assistant for one of Canada's most prominent families. It was never a goal of mine, but somehow, the universe heard my request and it happened. The job involved travel. To London, England for long periods of time, and the U.S. I decided to take it and see what would happen. It interested me and in many ways and it was an honour to be considered. I felt with the business skills I had learned along the way, I could handle it.

I lived and worked in the U.K. off and on over the course of a year and spent time in the U.S. I learned so much about the etiquette side of international business, running a job independently and being the liaison for many other staff, being a strong woman, living alone and away from home. I worked for a woman who was such an inspiration. To me, she is the epitome of grace and so intelligent and just being in her presence affected me.

Eventually, I needed to get back to the real world. One of the lawyers I was working with before I left, had gone off and started his own practice. He said if you are still interested in law and working for me until you go to law school, I suggest you do it. We had an amazing working relationship and I knew I would learn a tremendous amount from working with him and at the firm.

I spent a few years at the firm learning as much as I could and with many laughs along the way. It was such a great group to work with. I learned heavy research, detail, working under pressure, teamwork; you name it. You have to have a strong personality to work in law, whether you are a lawyer or not. But I loved every moment. My boss was incredibly brilliant and not only did he teach me pretty much everything I know about the legal world, he also taught me about life and with a great sense of humour. He was the best mentor I've ever had. I was very lucky to work there.

What I learned as well was how much of an independent thinker I was. I was always trying to implement something new, and do things differently. In law, you have to follow convention and rules, and this I also loved as I am really organized and love detail. But it was something else, things started feeling negative. Not with who I was working for or the work, it was something stirring inside of me. It was showing up in ways that were not always positive and later, I learned why.

When I was little, I was always doing something creative. Whether it was drawing, dance, making miniatures for my Barbies, getting into my mom's spice rack and making mystery "concoctions" (she was furious), I was always expressing talents and abilities involving creativity and exploration in some way. As I grew older, these qualities still showed up in different ways, and I always resigned them to just being hobbies.

Looking back, I also always expressed thinking outside the box. Always curious, always full of ideas and telling people how they could do something differently, I found ways for them to make money doing it. So weird when I think back on that, but I couldn't help it. I still do it.

In any job I've ever had, I always wanted to be in charge and was always thinking of ways to grow the business and add value.

While I worked in my last paying job at the firm, in the last two years prior, I began designing jewellery on the side. Initially, it was a creative outlet for me with the intensity of the work I was doing. I needed a break. This creative outlet led to my career today running my own business.

When I first designed jewellery (self-taught by the way), I didn't care if it made money. I just loved creating. I was so drawn to crystal, beauty, and statement pieces. Being so involved in the arts community on the side as well as committee work, I would put pieces in silent auctions for charity. I would wear my pieces everywhere; and proudly so.

What happened along this journey I could have never imagined. I don't recall ever having a goal of wanting to run my own business for one, or become a jewellery designer. But eventually, I realized this and it truly was as Oprah would say, an "ah ha" moment.

Everyone constantly asked me where they could buy my jewellery, more requests for silent auction items came in, and eventually, my first editorial shoot.

I had built up my network so well over the years while working and attending galas and charities in my free time and it naturally assisted later in building my business.

So eventually, after my jewellery gained so much exposure and after building my network, I started to see and feel that maybe I was on to something here. While I loved my job and still had an interest in law, I realized it did not bring out the best in me. When I created, I was happy and networking made me happy. Thinking big and outside convention, made me happy. I thought back on my years of experience in business and working with entrepreneurs. Through experience, time and getting to know myself and having confidence in that, I realized that I was born an entrepreneur. I felt it. I wanted to take risks, I wanted to venture out.

I didn't have a plan or a ton of capital saved up, but being the risk-taker I am, I knew it was time to leave and give this a shot. So eventually, I left the firm. It wasn't easy, but I had faith in myself. I believed in what I had and just knew I could do it. All of my experiences led me to this moment.

Luckily, right before I left I had partnered up with a wonderful Canadian designer, Nada Shepherd, on her runway collection for L'Oreal Fashion Week in Toronto. It was a side project I was working on in my free time and on many late nights while I was still working at the firm. The show was in mid-October. I left my job October 31st and at the worst time economically. But somehow, that did not factor into my decision.

Designing for fashion week propelled me into the fashion world. Nada was an amazing mentor to me. She helped open me up creatively and taught me about the design process. She taught me the ins and outs of the business, how to build a collection, how to be a strong business woman. The fashion industry moves quickly and you need to be ready.

And the rest is history as they say. I have been officially running my jewellery design business full-time the past several years. And I haven't looked back.

What have I learned about the journey that led me here? What can I share with you?

You must without a doubt, despite all adversity believe in yourself. Have hope when things are so bad and you think it will never get better.

Explore, don't stay stagnant. If something is not working, change it. Keep moving. Have faith. Have confidence. Learn everything you can. Take initiative and work hard.

I learned to trust my own instincts, and never let anyone bring me down. Be strong but also be kind. Get a thick skin, because it can be a very tough world out there.

I learned to always maintain a positive outlook on life and how I engage with others. If you are sincere, genuine and happy, others will connect with you and be drawn to that. You can't fake it, you have to really feel good energy and exude it.

I learned that you have to ask questions, network, ask for help when you need it. Some of the most amazing opportunities I have had were through asking questions, putting it out there to people on what I wanted and how I could make it happen. More often than not, people want to help others succeed.

I learned that what you put out there, comes right back at you. Give back. Get involved and your business should always be about your customer, not you.

Treat people well and always remember to be thankful. Never forget where you came from or those who helped and supported you along the way.

Despite my struggles along the way of family tragedy and supporting myself, I never gave up. Never. There were extremely difficult times in starting my business, a very poignant moment when I thought I would give up, but I hung on. I made it through.

And I expect more struggles. That's just the way life is. It's how you handle it that counts.

If I were to give any advice about making the jump and starting your own business, I say with extreme caution, know what you are getting yourself into. It is not for everyone.

But I truly believe entrepreneurs are a special breed. There are certain qualities that an entrepreneur has that cannot be taught.

Running a business involves incredible sacrifice, dealing with the unknown, no security, and it can consume your life. I personally have sacrificed so much, but thankfully I have a supportive family who understands.

Take care of your health and manage your stress. Nothing is more important. Without it, you are no good to your business, or anyone.

It's risky and it's tough out there and you have to really know what you are doing.

But with a strong vision, confidence and thick skin you can have the makings of it. Do your research about what it takes, study it if you can, and learn everything you need to know about running a business. Critical— have a business plan and involve others.

The reason why I love being an entrepreneur is because I am myself. I LOVE creating and being a visionary. I am setting my own destiny. I answer to no one but me. I meet wonderful people. I have amazing clients. I have tremendous freedom. The world really is at your fingertips. There is financial success, and just a great sense of achievement and making a name for yourself. There is always something new around the corner. It's exciting.

But there is a price to pay for that, and you will work your tail off. You will fail at times. You will learn that you can't please everyone so stick to your vision and what feels right. Focus on opportunities that are right for you and your business, not others' expectations.

Know that you can't be good at everything. Surround yourself with great people. Focus on your unique abilities. For me, this is creating, collaborating, and growing my business. I love getting out there and making things happen and meeting people, the bigger-picture stuff.

Have fun in life and your business. It should not feel like traditional work. You have to love it.

You have to be hungry, and very passionate. You have to really want to run a business and be totally fearless.

So if this is what you are feeling too, go out there and get it. Dream big. Believe in yourself completely. Have faith. You can make it. And in high heels!

With hard work, I went from designing pieces for silent auctions, fashion week, major campaigns and this year, designing an exhibit piece for Swarovski in Austria. Swarovski, in my opinion, is the epitome of the designer jewellery world. I was selected amongst designers around the globe to design a piece. My statement necklace travelled from Hong Kong, to Paris, to New York. It was a dream come true.

One day, I hope to pen a book on more details of my journey and my tips for success in running a business. My goal is to mentor women who want to go into business and I also hope to establish a fund one day and more resources for budding entrepreneurs. For now, I hope I have inspired you. You can come from a small town with very little means and make it.

You can suffer incredible loss and still make it. Just when you think you are alone in this world, you are more blessed than you could ever dream of and excited about the world and what's next. I count my blessings every day and take nothing and no one for granted.

The key is YOU make it; no one else does it for you. It is your own version of success.

So I made it in high heels. And you can too.

About Shay Lowe

The Designer

As a passionate designer and entrepreneur, Shay Lowe creates stunning jewellery that makes a statement.

Based in Toronto, Shay is a dedicated supporter of the arts community and was a founding Co-Chair of *Turnout*, The National Ballet of Canada's young professionals group. She has sat on numerous committees, including Rethink Breast Cancer's annual *Boobyball*, The Ontario Science Centre's LG Innovators' Ball, and Operanation for The Canadian Opera Company. She is currently a committee member of Artbound, The Design Exchange Black and White Gala, an outreach alumni member of the Toronto Fashion Incubator, and a Mentor in the Passion for Fashion program.

Noted as a 'Designer on the Rise', she was chosen as one of the Top 15 Designers across Canada for the Cashmere 2010 campaign featured at The Bay, Shay's ambitious and striking designs have also earned her a coveted position as one of Toronto's Most Creative Women, featured in Pierre Maraval's exhibit during Luminato, *Toronto Mille Femmes*.

Shay's work is featured in a coffee table book by Swarovski, just released this year.

The Brand—Shay Lowe Jewellery Design

Bold, alluring, and statement-making, Shay Lowe Jewellery Design's philosophy is, "Be Extraordinary". We are a designer jewellery lifestyle brand focused on luxury, glamour, and beauty within. The Collections are inspired by art, culture, travel, love, society, and old world glamour, and each piece has a signature sparkle and bold design. Shay Lowe's designs have been featured on the cover of FLARE magazine, LG Fashion Week, Fashion magazine, Entertainment Tonight Canada and ETalk Daily, The Emmy Awards, the Gemini Awards, and Breakfast Television.

In 2011, Shay Lowe Jewellery Design was selected by Swarovski Austria to create a piece for their international exhibit showcasing top and emerging talent worldwide. The exhibit piece travelled to New York, Paris, and Hong Kong.

Shay Lowe Jewellery was chosen to design a tutu for The National Ballet's Tutu Project, commemorating its 60th Anniversary.

With a focus on philanthropy, Shay Lowe's designs have been featured in countless silent auctions, and launched a special project with Toronto's Sheena's Place, the Heart 2 Heart Campaign, to raise $25,000 for its support programs.

Every design is custom made-to-order in Toronto and New York.

23

Lindsay Ann

If you would have asked me just a few years ago where I would be right now, never in my wildest dreams would I have imagined I would be a successful, young entrepreneur, recognized by millions as the winner of a nationally televised baking competition.

It took me years to realize my talents and find something I felt really passionate about. Growing up I struggled trying to find my place, trying to figure out what I was good at and what it was that I was going to contribute to this world. Nothing in school had really grabbed my attention so outside of class I got involved with various extracurricular activities trying to find my niche. It took years of exploring different avenues before I found something I wanted to do, and once I did, it didn't come easy. I quickly discovered I was going to have to push myself to overcome my fears and work harder than I had ever worked before. I was going to have to learn to really believe in myself if I wanted to be able to do what I love.

It all began with an afternoon visit to the local arts and crafts store as a young girl. Arts and crafts was something I had always loved to occupy my weekends with as a kid. As I browsed the aisles, I eventually stumbled upon a section of the store I had never noticed before. A whole section dedicated to cake decorating and candy making that I never even knew existed. It immediately drew me in. I was intrigued and felt an excitement to learn more. I must have sat on the floor in that aisle for hours with baking magazines on my lap. I was transfixed, flipping through the pictures of incredibly decorated cakes adorned with fondant sculptures, diamonds and pearls made of sugar, tiers of billowy frosting as pink as a cotton candy sky. I walked down the aisle looking at all of the dazzling displays of colorful sprinkles, 3D cake pans and wildly shaped tools on the shelves. My imagination was racing. I could almost smell the sweet buttery cake layers and taste the fluffy vanilla icing right out of the magazine. I was so inspired. I fantasized about all of the incredible cakes and candies I could create. I wanted to take the entire aisle of products home with me. I begged my mom to buy me some tubes of icing with fancy decorating tips, spatulas and decorating tools so I could go home and create the cake I saw on the front cover of the magazine. It was a beautiful cake covered with swirls of intricate frosting designs, fancy borders and gorgeous icing flowers. I got home and raced to the kitchen. I couldn't wait to try all of my new things. I laid all of my brand new tools out in front of me, making sure to read all of the instructions so I wouldn't miss a thing. My cake was going to be perfect. I whipped up a box of yellow cake mix from the cupboard. I could hardly wait for the "canvas" of my creation to bake and cool. With a smile from ear to ear, I began to frost and decorate my cake as if I was already a pro, piping on swirls of frosting decorations and flowers. But my smile quickly began to fade. My flowers didn't look like the flowers on the front of the magazine. I had no idea how to pipe fancy frosting borders and intricate icing roses. I looked at my novice attempt at replicating a professionally decorated cake and was crushed. The fantasy in my head of creating stunningly artistic cakes and confections from my kitchen disappeared just as fast as it came. Frustrated and let down, I put my new cake decorating tools in a bag and placed them on the top shelf of the cupboards where they would not be re-visited until years later. I had felt a spark, a passion deep down, that this could be something that would bring me great joy. Yet, because my first attempt didn't come easy to me and it wasn't perfect, I told myself I would never be good enough and just gave up on it all together.

I was re-introduced to art in a different way a few years later in a drawing class I took in high school. With a few quick attempts, a lot of erasers, and a little patience, I discovered I was a natural. I was one of the best artists in the school. I had found something I was really good at and was recognized for. During our graduation ceremony, everyone looked at me smiling, nudging me as they announced the art award. Yet, my name was not called. I was not given the award. I sunk so low in my seat I almost disappeared. I was shocked and devastated. I thought I deserved it. Art class was the one subject in school I had a real interest in. It was the one class I had found the perseverance to stick with and excel at. Not getting that award made me feel like I was being told I was not good enough, that my talents were nothing special, that there were a million other people out there better than me. Even though everyone else saw my talent, without a formal award and recognition, I wouldn't see it. After high school, I didn't create another piece of art until years later. And once again, just like with my cake decorating, I would give up on myself and my creative talent that would one day bring me to great places, because I refused to believe in myself.

Every year, for my birthday I would get all different kinds of brightly colored pastels, professional grade pencils, thick textured drawing pads and various art supplies. And every year, I would neatly put away my new art supplies in the closet, just as I did with my cake decorating supplies. I wanted to wait until I was really, really good, then I would use them. For years I sketched on plain printer paper with cheap dull pencils and smudgy erasers. My new supplies slowly accumulated dust, the pile got larger as the years went on, still untouched. It wasn't until the end of college that I really got back into my passion for arts and crafts and started drawing again. I had begun to use my professional art supplies that I had put away years ago. I used my erasers until my fingertips hit the paper. I used my pencils until they were too small to work with. I had scribbled out, ripped up, and crumpled up page after page, but I kept on creating because I enjoyed it, and eventually it led me somewhere. My art ended up winning local contests. My original drawings and designs were selected among many by a clothing company to be printed on a new line of T-shirts. It felt good to be recognized. I felt that maybe I *was* good enough. Yet, my talent was simply a hobby, I had never dreamed it could actually lead to something more.

I was about to graduate college and the pressures of finding a steady career path made it too scary to commit to the uncertainty of where my art could take me. I watched my friends on their way to the careers they had dreamed of since they were kids. I felt like I was aimlessly drifting down a road without a direction towards a clear goal. Although I got my Bachelors degree, I didn't know what the next step was. I knew I wasn't going to be a doctor and save lives. I knew I wasn't going to be a chemist and find a cure for diseases, or go out and save the world. But knowing what I didn't want to do didn't help me figure out what I *did* want to do. I explored a variety of career paths after college trying to settle on a job I was content with, from trying to break into the corporate world, to working in an office, and even becoming a teacher. Yet nothing made me as happy, or got me as excited as that day in the arts and crafts store years ago. It wasn't until I eventually gave my passion, something I dubbed a "hobby", a real chance, that I led myself to a path that would really take me somewhere.

I knew that if I were not going to pursue my drawing, I would have to find a way to use my creative talents in a different way to be truly happy. I had to push myself to get over the thoughts that I wasn't good enough and put myself out there. I had done it when I took my art supplies out of the closet and started drawing again and I knew I needed to do it again and unpack my baking and cake decorating supplies I had abandoned long ago. If I was able to overcome my fear of failure and actually succeed as an artist using paper and pencil, there was no reason I couldn't do the same in a different medium and succeed as an artist using cake and frosting. I made the decision to try my hand at cake decorating one more time. After days of planning and browsing the internet for tips, tricks and inspiration, I instantly felt that spark of excitement, just as I had felt while browsing the cake decorating and candy making aisle at the arts and crafts store as a child. I told myself that no matter what went wrong, I was not going to give up this time, but boy did things go wrong.

That weekend was my friend's birthday, a perfect opportunity to hone my skills. I planned out every detail of the cake I was going to make to assure it would come out perfect. That Friday night after work, I baked and frosted a perfect chocolate layer cake and was ready to get started on the decorating. As I slid the spatula under the cake to transport it to my decorating area, I helplessly watched in terror as the top layer of the cake slid off on to the kitchen counter while the bottom layer tore apart beneath it. Practically in tears, I anxiously drove to the grocery store to buy a chocolate cake mix. It was getting late and time was running out, I didn't have time for any more mishaps. When I returned home, I was horrified to find that my dog had devoured the slab of chocolate cake crumbled across the counter. I frantically rushed her to the 24-hour emergency vet before she got sick from the lethal amount of chocolate she consumed. By the time we got back home it was after midnight. I was exhausted, but knew I could not show up empty handed. It took me all night but I finally finished the cake. I brought it to the party and everyone loved it. Yet, even with all of the compliments, I had lost all enthusiasm for my new craft. I never wanted to bake again.

Yet, even after another let down, I knew I couldn't let myself give up again. I believed in myself and persevered. Instead of tackling a whole cake, I decided to start small. When Halloween rolled around I created miniature desserts to give to my friends and family. I was able to use my art background to draw with melted chocolate, sculpt with cake and craft with candy. I had found the perfect medium for my art and creativity. My tiny treats were a success and I had never loved doing anything as much as I loved creating my little pieces of edible art. My imagination was saturated with the endless possibilities of themed desserts I could create. I made over 100 bite-sized treats the next month for Thanksgiving. They were perfect. I placed them on baking sheets on top of the stove, up high and out of reach. A few hours later I walked back into the kitchen to find nearly half of my little chocolate covered creations melted from the heat of the oven underneath them that had been preheated for dinner. My jaw dropped as I stood there in shock, staring at yet another disaster. But I was determined not to let any obstacle get in my way. The next morning I re-made each and every one, boxed them up with fancy ribbon and festive tissue paper. I gave them to all of my co-workers, friends and family. They ended up being a huge hit. Word quickly spread and I actually started receiving my first "orders" from people outside my close-knit support system. The thought of turning a hobby I had such enthusiasm for into a real small business, encouraged me to make this possibility a reality.

I decided that if I was really going to do this, I had to ditch the store—bought boxed mixes and learn to bake from scratch, to create an edible canvas for my art that would taste as good as it looked. I packed a year of formal training into a few months, all on my own. I taught myself everything there is to know about the science of baking to compliment my art for decorating. I read books, I did research online and I talked to professionals. I had my family and friends over for taste tests, comparing my recipes to local bakeries, published recipes and store bought mixes, making sure my cupcakes were the best. I went days without sleep trying to fit it all in. I was up around the clock, trying to balance my day job with my new business endeavor. I was so incredibly intrigued and enthused about all I had to learn. I enrolled in a cake decorating class at the same arts and crafts store I had went to as a kid, where I first walked down that cake decorating and candy making aisle. I eventually mastered my new art and had compiled a list of my best original recipes. My focus on small batch desserts and miniature treats led me to a fitting business name, and just like that, "Dollhouse Bake Shoppe" was born. I got the word out any way I could and slowly started selling my treats locally and catering small events with my baked goods on weekends.

Just months after getting my new business up and running, I saw a casting call online for a new show on the Food Network called "Cupcake Wars". On a whim I sent in some photos of my work and filled out an application. I got a call back, completed the interview process, and a few weeks later, after a nationwide search for the country's top bakers, I was chosen to compete on the series premiere, in June 2010! I was almost there; I was on my way to success.

Leading up to the show, there were a few nights when I wanted to back out, when I was scared of failing, when I thought I couldn't do it, and that I wasn't good enough, but I pushed myself to keep my head up. I had to. I had come this far and something inside me wouldn't let myself give up this time. It was a roller coaster ride full of ups and downs, but I was moving forward and I was almost there. To have national recognition at something I was good at meant the world to me. To be able to impress the judges and the world, and receive an award I had worked so hard for, in just a matter of months was a once in a lifetime opportunity that meant more than any high school art award.

The day of filming I was terrified and excited. I was up against industry professionals who went to culinary school, talented pastry chefs and bakery owners. And there I was, little old me, competing with the best of the best on national television. I felt like I was in a dream. I wanted this so badly. I had never worked so hard for anything in my life. With my heart racing and my hands shaking, I put everything I had into those cupcakes, and every round, I watched as the contestants standing next to me were eliminated. I had made it. My talent, creativity, and will to not give up led me to victory. I ended up winning first place in the series premiere. I was even asked to come back for another episode, making my second Food Network television appearance shortly after in January 2011 as a featured "Cupcake Wars Champion".

My talents were increasingly recognized on a nationwide level as I accrued a loyal fan base across the country. It was all so surreal. I started receiving tons of e-mails from people telling me what an inspiration I was, asking me for recipes, baking tips and advice. Being able to be a resource people could come to was something I took great pride in. I slowly began to change the direction of my business and shift my focus towards creating a brand where I could share my passion on a broader scale. I did this by creating Dollhousebakeshoppe.com, a website featuring my award winning dessert recipes, baking tips, decorating tutorials, videos and more, giving people all across the world the chance to bake like a pro right in their own kitchen. Most importantly for me, was my goal to provide the opportunity for girls and women of any age to be able to have fun and gain confidence through baking and cake decorating. I wanted to develop a product in which young girls could proudly create *their* first tiered cake with the fancy borders and perfect icing rose, without the feeling of failure I had experienced as a girl. This led me to the launch of my first product, The *Dollhouse Bake Shoppe Deluxe Cake Kit*, which includes everything to bake, frost, design and decorate a fun and professional looking cake right from home, with no experience needed. To think that I could possibly play a small part in bringing a smile to a young girl's face when she looks at her beautiful creation means more to me than anything.

Dollhousebakeshoppe.com became my pride and joy. I loved being able to teach the tricks of my trade and share my creativity with the world. My work slowly started getting more attention. I was winning more and more contests, receiving opportunities to have my work published in popular magazines and chances to work with some nationally recognized brands. I had never been so excited and passionate about anything. I had created a life I never knew was even an option for me, and the momentum pushed me to keep going and see where I could really take this.

I put an endless amount of non-stop hard work and dedication into my brand, and although at times it gets grueling, at the end of the day it is worth every minute. I am so incredibly lucky to be able to do what I love and be recognized for it. It is still sometimes hard to believe that people really like what I do and follow my work. The encouragement and fan mail I receive everyday is what keeps me going, even on the toughest days. The touching thank you letters from mothers inspired by my advice to start their own cupcake catering business, girls who had used my recipes to donate goodies to local senior homes for the holidays, women who had made my treats to bring to their family during tough hospital visits, is what makes it all worth it. I never imagined I could have the power to touch so many lives and inspire so many. I never thought that without being a doctor, saving lives, or out saving the world, I could still impact the lives of others, and bring joy to so many in such a unique way.

If you would have asked me just a few years ago, where I would be right now, never in my wildest dreams would I have imagined I would be where I am today, sharing my story with you. My story is not that unusual. There are hundreds of thousands of girls around the world who haven't found their passion in life yet, what they can be recognized for, what makes them special or what they can contribute to this world. But I made it where I am today, because I pushed myself to overcome my fears. I gave myself a real chance and found something I loved to do. I worked hard, put myself out there and kept moving forward; and most importantly, I learned to believe in myself, and that made all the difference.

24 Alexandra Orlando

Many years ago when I was just a little girl with the whole world at my fingertips, I told my family that one day I was going to go to the Olympic Games. My parents brought up my older sister and I believing that we could be anything that we wanted to be. If we worked hard and wanted it bad enough the sky wasn't even the limit. I am forever grateful for their love, as they have and always will support every one of our dreams. They might have laughed a little when I went through princess envy or my serious astronaut phase, I even have the many science books to prove it, but not once did they put me down. I have to admit, I am relieved they watched me let go of the NASA plan because my younger self would've been greatly disappointed at my inability to grasp quantum physics.

Unlike any other of my future aspirations, the Olympics never faded in and out like a one hit wonder. It was a chart topper. I started rhythmic gymnastics when I was five years old, fell in love and never looked back. I was a natural athlete and as I got older I played it all: soccer, volleyball, softball, and even ran track, but there was something about gymnastics that made me give them all up. It was the most challenging, unique sport I had ever tried. My younger persona, always wanting to be center of attention, had to be different and stray from the pack. Rhythmic gymnastics is an eastern European dominated sport combining gymnastics with dance, acrobatics, flexibility and extreme coordination into five events: rope, hoop, ball, clubs and ribbon. There are probably only a few readers who actually know what I'm talking about, that's how unknown it is in North America. The figure skating of the summer Olympics, rhythmic gymnastics is a performance sport based as much on technical difficulty and mind boggling tricks as personal expression and artistry. Not only do we have to perform some of the most physically demanding skills, but we have to make it look beautiful and effortless at the same time. Think performing three somersaults underneath an unforgiving rotating set of hard plastic clubs, catching them bent in half upside down on the floor, perfectly on point with every beat of a piece of music. Don't try it at home. We have to be lean, but muscular; extremely flexible, but strong enough to control it. We have to have incredible hand eye coordination and spatial awareness, but grace and rhythm as well. We have to have no fear of pushing the boundaries of our sport and testing our body's limits. Whoever said rhythmic gymnastics was easy, I beg to differ.

Ever since I became serious about becoming a Canadian rhythmic gymnast I faced the taunting and teasing that coincides with performance sports and anything else that's not hockey here in my hometown, Toronto. Meanwhile, I have been training six days, 30 hours a week since I was 10 years old and in my prime I could squat 200 lbs with ease. The reaction of men in the gym would be priceless. If I had a dollar for every time someone asked me if I was sure I wanted that much weight on the bar I would be a very rich woman by now. I faced adversity, even from a very young age as the school boys loved to continuously reassure me that I wasn't a real athlete. As the tough little girl that I was, I defended my sport as best as I could, followed by challenging them to do the splits. That never ended well.

At eleven years old, I competed for Canada for the first time and any doubts I had, if there were any, about my sport disappeared. It was that moment of wearing the Canadian flag on my back and being a part of something bigger than any of my peers could imagine when I knew I had found what I had been looking for. I so desperately wanted to be an Olympian and this was how I was going to do it. From then on, I ate, slept and breathed gymnastics. All other sports fell to the wayside as I had my head and my heart set on the 2004 Olympic Games.

However, for a typically known 'pretty' sport, my career has been anything but. My Olympic journey is one full of heartbreak, disappointment, struggle and fight, but it made me the woman I am today and the Olympian that I have become. I learnt the hard way that we don't always get what we want, even if we think we deserve it. Looking back now that I'm retired from competitive sport, I wouldn't have wanted it any other way. When I was fifteen years old, I had already sacrificed nights at the mall and weekends at the cottage for years to see where my sport could take me and there I was on the eve of qualifying for my first Olympics. My biggest fear has always been quitting before I truly saw how far I could push myself as an athlete. People always ask me now if I regret not being a normal teenager or University student and I say the same thing to each and every one of them: Not a chance. I knew that I would have my whole life to do 'normal' things, but one shot to be one of the best rhythmic gymnasts in the world. The training was grueling, the travelling was exhausting and my diets were harsh, but the feeling of honing your body and performance to perfection is immeasurable. I remember tossing and turning the night before the 2004

Olympic Games Qualification Tournament, knowing that every minute in the gym for the last 10 years came down to this moment. The top 20 gymnasts out of 150 that compete at World Championships qualify for the Games and then it's all over. All you get is one chance. As two-time Canadian national champion, I was still one of the youngest competitors and the underdog, but could feel the Olympic berth just in my grasp. My parents had flown to Budapest, Hungary to cheer me on and wave the Canadian flag up high for me to see it from the stands. Knowing that they were there with me gave me that extra strength I needed to stop my legs from shaking.

Even with putting in the best performance of my career to date, I missed qualifying for the Olympics by one tenth of a point that day. I can still remember the very moment I saw my name get knocked out of contention up on the giant score board in the stadium. It was as if from then on everything turned to slow motion. My heavy heart sank and everything around me started to blur. I don't remember any sounds, just the pounding of my racing heart echoing in my ears. My world had come crashing down. The mixture of shock, sadness, anger and frustration clashed inside of me. I had just let my Olympic dream slip through my fingers. One of my most vivid memories from that day is ducking out of the gymnasium before seeing my family or teammates and heading back to the hotel without telling anyone. I ran the entire way back hoping the burning in my legs would take my mind off the ache in my chest. The sun was setting in Budapest after a long day and I stood shivering on the balcony gazing off into the distance; emotionless. My best friend and teammate, Yana Tsikardze, had quietly come in and found me standing there for who knows how long. Her heart was broken along with mine; she wanted this for me just as badly as I did. Without a word, she came on to the balcony and put her arm around me. With her shoulder to lean on, I let go of my silent tears and we stood there until the little warmth of the dying sun that was left was gone.

There are no real words to describe the significance of that moment in my life and the crushing devastation that it put me through. Without the love and support of my family, friends and coaches that put up with me afterwards, I don't know if I would've ever gotten over it. Once I got home and everyone had found out what had happened, I wanted to hide under a rock. Facing the constant looks of pity and the standard "don't worry, it's going to be alright" comments; all of a sudden I wanted to hate everything for this happening to me. I became that awful, unpredictable moody teenager that I never wanted to be. I took out my frustration on my family, especially my mom, who to this day still doesn't know how sorry I am for putting her through that. I can't imagine what it's like to see your child in so much pain and not be able to help them. You are stronger than I could ever be and I am a better person because of you. I, unfortunately, had to figure out what I was feeling and how I could fix it for myself. Deep down I knew that the love that I had for my sport had made me who I was and nothing compared to how it felt to represent my country. I always believed that I could be whatever I wanted and that was an Olympian. It dawned on me then that I couldn't give up on my dream that easily. I had my first epiphany. I had never let anyone tell me what I could or couldn't do before so why would I start now? If these Games weren't meant to be mine then the 2008 Beijing Olympic Games would be.

Coming back to the gym after my life had been turned upside down, I was a different person. I needed to get my confidence back and prove to myself that I deserved to be in that top 20 and I was going to go above and beyond to get there. I began training more hours with my coach, taking private ballet lessons, using a personal trainer and travelling and competing more than I had ever before. Let's just say, I stepped up my game in a big way. This newfound determination and focus came from never wanting to feel that kind of disappointment ever again. Every day empowered me a little bit more as I took one step closer to the Olympics. I wish I could tell you that it was as easy as that, but in 2005 I tore three ligaments in my left ankle and missed half a season on my couch completely helpless.

I was 17 years old and the second I stopped training my body completely changed. I grew, gained some curves and became a young woman. You could imagine how thrilled my sport federation and coaches were. Once I was back in the gym injuryfree I was 5'7" and 130 pounds. It was then that I was asked to consider signing up for Jenny Craig because I was too heavy to compete. The hurt and disgust I felt triggered something inside of me. They were telling me I wouldn't make it to the Olympics if I looked the way I did. I have seen so many young girls battle eating disorders and have witnessed up close the mental and physical breakdown of a person. I always promised myself I would be stronger than that. I am a fighter and I refused to accept that if I was just as good out there on the mat I deserved the same scores regardless of my weight. But the constant obsession with my appearance weighed me down as it became harder and harder to ignore. Every day was a battle to not let it get to me and keep training as hard as I was before. Dieting became my new best friend as over the next year my weight would fluctuate 5 lbs. daily. I needed to prove to myself and my country that I was still one of the best rhythmic gymnasts in the world and show all the young girls out there that you didn't have to be a size 0 to compete and make a difference on the gymnastics world stage. We are all beautiful and unique in our own ways.

I finally had my opportunity in 2006 at the Commonwealth Games in Melbourne, Australia. With all the criticism and doubts, I broke a world record for my sport and tied the Games' record for most gold medals ever won by a single athlete. Winning all 6 of the possible gold medals in rhythmic gymnastics, I had done the impossible. Standing on top of the podium in front of 20,000 screaming fans, I heard my national anthem over and over and over. It was electrifying. I can still close my eyes now and hear my name being called, see that beautiful flag being raised and feel the excitement in the air. As the most decorated Canadian athlete at the Games, I was given the honor of carrying the flag at closing ceremonies. Walking into that stadium was a precious few minutes I will hold with me forever. I looked around me at the sparkling stands and realized against all odds that I had made it. From then on, I knew deep down in my heart that no one or nothing could stop me. We are all so much stronger than we think we are; it just took me a little while to realize it.

The next two years were the most incredible years of my life. I was unstoppable. I was in the best mindset and shape I had ever been in. Not compromising my values and beliefs, I watched my diet, but never hurt myself for the perfect figure. I loved being muscular and athletic and I made it work for me. I stood out in my sport for being expressive, but powerful, fast and strong. I didn't look like a ballerina out there is all I'm saying. My last competition before Olympic qualifiers was the 2007 Pan American Games in Rio de Janeiro, Brazil. Winning three more gold medals and carrying the Canadian flag at closing ceremonies for the second time gave me the extra confidence and motivation I needed to walk into qualifiers with a smile on my face. I wasn't even nervous, because I had given my whole self to my Olympic dream and done everything I could have done to be prepared.

I lost a lot of friends and relationships along the way, but they never understood how important this was to me. You know who your real friends are when they stick around when things get tough. This time I left my whole heart out there on the floor and walked away with no regrets. I anxiously watched each athlete finish competing and saw their total scores flash up on the scoreboard, but my name was still there. As the last competitor finished I was 9th in the World easily clinching a spot to the 2008 Olympic Games, as the only North or South American gymnast. A top ten result no other Canadian rhythmic gymnast had achieved in over 20 years. My coach, Mimi Masleva, who had been by my side through it all, broke down in tears. This was my time, this was my moment.

I waited my whole life to compete at the Olympic Games and a day doesn't go by when I don't remember what it felt like to be there. My time in Beijing was indescribable. It took me 16 years to get there, but those two weeks made all the blood, sweat and tears worth it. I was a part of inspiring a nation and a celebration of sport that brings the world together in unity and peace. It didn't matter where you were from, what your background, religion or race was. We all stood as one. The Olympics is so much more than just sport. It is the pursuit of excellence and the ideals of respect, teamwork, leadership and dedication that touch billions of people worldwide. The Games truly bring out the best in all of us. The experience changed me as an athlete and a person. I knew that even though this would be the last time I competed and I was hanging up my gloves for good, I wanted to remain a part of this Olympic spirit and energy forever. As a newly retired athlete, it can sometimes be difficult to find your place in the world not quite like all your peers or your teammates anymore. I refused to be 'normal', as my friends called it, and even though I went back to school and began working a 'normal' job, I threw myself into the sporting arena; this time with a briefcase in hand, not a gym bag.

Currently, I call myself an athlete advocate, sitting on the Canadian Olympic Committee Athlete Commission and President of the Pan American Sport Organization Athlete Council. I helped bring the Toronto 2015 Pan and Parapan American Games to my hometown, Toronto, and work for the TO2015 Organizing Committee. I am an active rhythmic gymnastics coach, choreographer and international judge, but still find time to mentor athletes and work on their mental skills on the side. I tell all my friends and family that no fancy degree or years of schooling could ever pull me away from what I love; although I will be graduating in a few months with a Political Science specialist and Economics minor from the University of Toronto. Clearly, I love sports and want to represent our athletes and support them the way they should be treated for them to reach their true potential. I also use what I've gone through to help motivate and empower young women to find their strength within and fight the constant negative body image pressures they face on a daily basis. I made a difference in people's lives as an Olympian and an athlete, now I want to make a difference as a woman. Sport is a typically male dominated field and I want to change that. If I've learned anything from my athletic career it is keep your head up and never take no for an answer. You can't rely on others to take you to the top, but you can do everything in your power to get there. Where there's a will, there's a way.

My father once quoted Muhammad Ali when I was a little girl and it stuck with me: "Champions aren't made in the gyms. They are made from something deep inside of them, a desire, a dream, a vision". I have a desire, a dream and a vision. Nothing can stop me now.

25

Jennifer Leigh

his isn't a cookie cutter story where I tell you that all my life I worked hard and excelled at everything I did. I am a professional poker player and have had quite an interesting journey finding my way into this profession. To use a poker metaphor—I promise this is the first and only one—my life has had a lot of swings. When I take a step back and look at it all, I can see that I got dealt a great hand (ok, two). I am very fortunate.

In high school, I didn't really apply myself, because I didn't really care. I'm not sure why I didn't care and I wish I could say with some sort of pretend retro-active plan that "I just *knew* my path wasn't through school." If I did say that, it'd be total B.S. Like most kids, I hated school and I didn't want to go. I considered quitting altogether, but instead, I did whatever I could to excuse myself from class.

I did however, become a part of a club in high school called the Technology Student's Association. The TSA was a club with competitions like anything else, and while some kids were rehearsing their rebuttals for speech and debate, I won awards for being the quickest to assemble and disassemble a computer, or to diagnose problems with one. Now which is a more valuable life skill? Being able to fix your own computer or being able to argue both sides of the debate on the subject of euthanasia in less than 90 seconds?

In my early teens, I realized the computer was a way for me to communicate with other people like myself. People who also felt they were somewhat outcasts, because of their interests in computers and video games. It's a bit of a cliché now, but I was a pioneer for the generation that found it easier to express itself through keyboards and a mouse than vocal cords and a mouth.

This was where I created my nickname, "jennicide." The name kind of stuck, and it became my moniker for most video games and computer forums. At the time, girls my age in school were chasing boys, talking about school dances or playing sports. I was teaching myself all I could about the ways of the Internet and became a part of the computer hacker world. Though, if Twilight were around, I probably would have been *totally* into that.

Before we go any further, I think I should make it clear what a "hacker" is. It's a scary word, and some people can get confused by its definition. To assume that a hacker is someone, who is automatically bad, is like assuming a poker player is automatically dishonest. Maybe that's not the best metaphor since both of those apply to me. Assuming a hacker is a bad person is like assuming a spider wants to bite you. They might look creepy, but the vast majority will go completely unnoticed by you; and it's just a few bad apples that spoil it for the bunch. Whoa! That's a lot of metaphors in one paragraph. To this day, I still maintain relationships with some of the people I "grew up" with online.

In college, applying myself was a different story. College *mattered*. I worked my ass off in college, because I wanted to become an attorney. But no matter how hard I worked, I never felt it was my "dream" job. To steal an overused expression from my generation: I loved it, but I wasn't *in* love with it. Turns out, I wanted to be an attorney, because I felt like it was the most socially acceptable thing to do. It was a profession I could be proud to tell others about.

"I'm going to be a lawyer," had a nice ring to it. I was going to go to college, get a degree, and have a high-paying, "respectable" career. I was essentially basing my decisions on the opinions of others. This all changed when I played my first hand of poker.

A friend of mine I had known online for years insisted I give online poker a try. At first, I was pretty hesitant. I had never been the gambling type. It didn't matter. I immediately knew poker would be something I loved. Oh, and would be *in* love with.

My first game of poker was a $5.00 sit and go, which is a small tournament that takes a short amount of time to complete, because it's usually limited to just a few tables (usually one). Lo and behold, I caught a bit of what the fogies call "beginner's luck." Also, due to my video game background, I was also pretty aggressive. There is probably no more profitable combination in poker than lucky and aggressive. Lucky and just about anything else is good, but lucky and aggressive is better.

Soon enough, within my first year of playing, I became the highest ranked female in online tournaments. I was so good at poker that most people didn't even believe I was female. Most of the guys playing online poker rarely spoke to females other than their moms, let alone get so regularly beaten by one. At that time, there were only a handful of successful female poker players, who were frequenting live tournaments and poker rooms. Online, it was almost unheard of.

In 2003, when I was 21, a man named Chris Moneymaker won a $3.00 satellite into the $10,000.00 World Series of Poker main event and ended up winning $2.5 million dollars on ESPN. This is the event that started the "poker boom," as it gave the general public the idea that anyone could win. It was the rebirth of the American dream: you could win something from nothing. Personally, I had not heard of poker even being televised, but the more involved I got with the industry, the more television I became exposed to.

The competition. The adrenaline. The gratification of winning. They all drew me into the game. As I spent more time learning the game of poker, I started spending less and less time focusing on my classes. And because of my late night online poker sessions, I rarely woke up in time to attend them. I was cheating on college with poker!

If you were to chart my poker earnings with my grades, you'd notice the graphs are inversely proportional. In case there are any other (spoiler alert) college dropouts out there, "inversely proportional" means they move like a see-saw. One goes up, and the other goes down. The more money I made, the less I cared about a dumb-ol' law degree! I was soon placed on academic dismissal. In case I hadn't mentioned, I'm a "glass is half-full" kind of gal and rather than get upset over basically getting expelled, I took it as a sign that I should continue playing poker.

In 2005, I was asked to be a part of a television show called "Poker Royale: Battle of the Ages" on GSN. It featured young professional poker players from ages 21–28 playing against seasoned pros 50 and over. There was real money on the line, and I was fortunate enough to walk away from the show with $16,000, after beating two of the world's most respected veteran poker players. And that was the first time I had ever even touched an actual poker chip!

Although I lucked out to find a career that doesn't require a college degree, I wish I had completed college just to have that added achievement, and maybe even that whole "something to fall back on," thing. I eventually ended up "falling back" on getting naked for a Playboy shoot. I won't say whether or not I regret that choice, but I will say that when your fallback is as a paralegal, no one ever comes up to you on the street and tells you about having seen you in such a private way.

Sometimes, I'd throw all my effort in the other direction. When I entered into relationships with men, I often times played the fool, putting the relationship ahead of my own goals and aspirations. The back burner is a dangerous place to keep your dreams. Now, having learned from those mistakes, I have a better ability to balance my social life and my career. Sure, some of that has come with age as well, but it's a mistake I'll never make again. I know never to put my own dreams aside in hopes of winning some one's affection or friendship. Those who are truly worth that sort of sacrifice would never ask it of you.

Although to many, I have already achieved a great amount of success in my career, there are still so many things I want to accomplish. In the spring of 2010, I won an online championship title and it only gave me a taste of winning major tournaments. Now, I am on the quest to earn more titles and victories.

I always have to remember to stay grounded, even when things seem to be going favorably. When we're complacent, we put our guards down. It's pretty easy for trouble to sneak up on you if you're not paying any attention. Do not lose sight of who you are. You'll also lose sight of trouble ahead.

Hard work, devotion, and dedication are not the end-all, be-all. Some people don't reach their dreams through hard work alone. Much like poker, you still have to make the right decisions at the right times, and luck can sometimes make or break you. In general, if there were some sort of formula that could be applied where hard work plus time equals end goal, it wouldn't be worth it. For example, if you knew the ending of every book, before even opening it, what would be the reason to read it? Life carries many surprises, twists, and turns. Remember: sometimes the "how" matters more than the "what." In poker, we're always trying to maximize the value of our winning hands. Learning to maximize your life's value, while at the same time avoiding being affected by negativity, were the keys to achieving my dreams.

Male-dominated industries are difficult to excel in, because of some of the flack you'll receive and negative attention from chauvinistic mentalities. Sometimes, women are quickly judged based on their looks and often, their success is discredited as being inferior, because of their gender. When I first entered the poker world, any accomplishments I had were quickly passed off to the idea that I had some *guy* helping me. This was not true. Although, I have many male friends, I am a self-taught poker player. My father always told me, "One's attitude greatly determines the outcome of any difficult task." Allowing yourself to rise above negative stereotypes will give you the strength you need to conquer anything.

In conclusion, not only is my story *not* cookie-cutter, but there are many choices I made that I cannot advocate in any way, shape, or form. I won't tell you which ones. I'll leave that up to you to decide. You might wonder why I might choose to be so honest. I just want it to be known that there are many paths that lead to success, and not all of them require you live your life in fear of making mistakes.

Sometimes, as a poker player, I make a bad call or play. Although that particular tournament might be lost, learning from those mistakes has shaped me into a better player, and a better person. Mistakes and failures build character. They make you who you are. Trial and error pave the way to success.

Reach for your dreams and—most of all—do not be afraid to take calculated risks when making that reach. You don't have to have the cookie-cutter story either.

26 Angelica Di Castro

The Early Years

I was born to middle-class Italian immigrants in 1978. I am the youngest of three sisters.

My parents come from a very small town in Italy and decided to move to Canada for a better life.

I remember that from a young age, music was something that brought me a lot of happiness.

I would sit in my room for hours listening to singers on the radio and try to impersonate their sound. My parents could see that I had a raw talent and that I had a passion for singing.

I was a shy girl in school, but when it came time to sing, I transformed into a performer.

I recall one day at school recess, I was with my friends and decided to belt out singing on the soccer field. It seemed that for a few seconds, everyone around me stopped what they were doing to listen to my voice. Children would begin walking towards me asking for my autograph.

It was in that moment I knew my destiny was to be a singer and performer.

When I was 10 years old, I asked my parents to sign me up for singing lessons. They did not hesitate and were very supportive of my passion and dedication. I never missed a class. Whether it was a heavy storm or bad weather, I could be sure that my parents would get me to my lesson.

They sacrificed their time and money to make me happy and I am forever grateful for this.

I was guided by my vision and motivated by my convictions. I was ready to take on the tough world of the music industry.

At 15, I was discovered at a summer music festival by two record producers, who were looking to put together a single. I was excited at the idea of recording songs in the studio and having the chance to have a record. I thought it would be easy at first: record two songs in one shot and that was it. It was a big shock when I discovered that the art of recording a song takes time and practice.

When I first arrived in the studio, I was given advice on how the song should be sung. Being a teenager, I found myself to be a bit rebellious and not wanting to take the experts' advice. I realized that if I wanted to be the best at my craft, I would need to practice, focus and work hard. I thought that it would be a short process to record the songs, but to my surprise, it actually took a week.

The vocal quality, arrangement and production all took time to perfect and I realized that performing live and recording in the studio are two separate things. When you're in the studio, you don't have an audience so you are really focused on listening to the sound of your own voice, as well as the dynamics and emotion. Sometimes, there is more pressure when you're in the studio, because on the other side of the room music experts are listening to your every phrase, every word and so you know that they will be listening closely for pitch, tonality, diction, emotion and accuracy.

At first, I felt nervous about having to sing in a studio where music experts would be listening and judging my recording performance, but as time went on, I looked up to these people, because I knew they were looking out for my best interests and wanted to bring out the best in my voice.

The whole process of putting together a CD was a lot of work. Once the songs were ready to be put on the final master CD, it was time for my first photo shoot with a photographer and stylist.

It was fun trying on different clothes and looking at the different images I could portray.

The photo shoot took place outdoors in Orangeville and I remember that I didn't know the first thing about how to pose for the camera; I was quite shy and nervous. I could tell that the photographer was a bit annoyed with me, but I really had no idea what to do. After a few hours, I began to feel more comfortable and had a few photos that I could choose from for the album.

I felt proud of myself that I was able to experience the professional world of music and I was thankful for the opportunity to record songs and present them to the world.

I found the first taste of success at the age of 15 with my first acclaimed single "I Can See It In Your Eyes".

My career gained a significant boost when the single received positive reviews in Billboard Magazine, The Chart and The Record. When my manager at the time came to me with the Billboard Magazine, I was thrilled, because I knew that he had good news to share with me.

I saw a single review write-up on my CD and I remember crying, because I couldn't believe that just a few months before, I was a regular girl going to school, singing in church and suddenly, my world was changing and I was experiencing success on a bigger scale than I ever imagined for myself.

The success of the first single motivated me to release a full album to show my fans that I was a serious artist and I was here to stay.

The album was called "A World Of Love". It was a mix of ballads, rock and dance songs. Reviews for that album have described my music as "powerful and stylish", "stunning vocals", "distinctive and powerful" (*Billboard Magazine*, *The Chart* and *The Record*). I was honoured to be featured on magazines and playlists in Europe such as Vision (Italy), Primo Piano Molise (Italy), M&M Magazine (U.K.) and Radio Elbag FM (Poland).

While continuing to record and perform, I decided that I wanted to continue with my vocal studies. I always had a great respect for classical singers, because I knew the amount of discipline and dedication it took for them to achieve such great voices. In my private lessons with opera coaches, I was able to learn beautiful operatic pieces and listen to a different colour of my voice. They say that if you can master the art of classical singing, you can sing anything. My training in classical singing was used as a platform for me to utilize it for all other styles of singing.

I knew that I wanted to study classical voice and so I enrolled at York University and graduated with Honours in the classical voice program. I would travel on the weekends singing and promoting the album and then return to school and study for exams and prepare for music recitals. It was hard work, but I was willing to put 100% of my time to performing and studying. Throughout the years, I have recorded 5 albums independently.

I kept my options open when choosing the material for my albums. I recorded songs written by David Foster, Jud Friedman and Joel Feeney, who have written for Celine Dion, Whitney Houston and LeAnn Rimes.

The Challenging and Dark Moments in my Career

The most challenging moment in my career was when I had written to a well-known record producer. I had a well-produced CD and I was ready to work with a Manager/Record Producer, who could help advance my career.

I never expected for the producer to write back, but surprisingly, he did. I had received an e-mail back a few weeks later from him saying how he wanted to work with me and could help my career reach greater heights. I had spent money travelling back and forth to meet with this producer, thinking it was my break, but out of nowhere, he stopped e-mailing back and told me he no longer had time to work on songs.

It was disappointing to think that I had finally gotten an opportunity as a professional singer and suddenly, it was gone. Although I was sad and disappointed, it only made me stronger and allowed me to gain a "tougher skin". There had been times when I would send my CD to managers and they would say that it is impossible for me to make it in the business, because it was just too difficult. At times, it became a lot of talk and no action. False promises was all I would get from a few music industry people.

My Advice for Aspiring Singers
The starting point has to be the recording of a demo that is sent to record companies. It is imperative that your music captures attention. A great sounding demo is number one.

With an indie artist having to bear all the finances in setting up a career, be prepared to spend the money on your music career. Remember it's a business just like any other; you have to invest in it in order to hopefully make money back.

Recording a demo is one aspect, trying to find an audience is another. It takes hard work and perseverance. Get out there and sing at as many places you can find. Exposure is key to any successful artist; create the buzz. Know who you are as an artist and try to find something that sets you apart from the rest.

You have to know who you are. There will be plenty of advice and it is good to take it, but you have to be knowledgeable and choose what is best for you.

Don't hesitate to ask for feedback on your music or to take advice from a music veteran. There are a lot of knowledgeable people who know the ins and outs of the business, listen to what they have to say.

One has to be cautious. Don't sign any music contracts without having it looked at by an entertainment lawyer first. Read about the business to get a better idea of what it really takes.

Money is not the key component. It's all about spreading the word. Play for free if you have to and build up a fan base. And with the impact of the Internet growing, bring your attention to the importance of sites like Facebook, MySpace and YouTube.

Apart from performing, the artist has other things to take care of. The venue has to be selected, the musicians have to be paid and the concert publicized. Handling all these tasks takes careful planning. Staging a successful concert calls for a reputable publicist. The word has to get out, people have to come in. If necessary, a singer has to take on the many hats of promoter and manager as well.

Success does not come easily. There is the pain and the hurt of rejection; what matters is who's going to be the last one standing and who is going to make it to the finish line.

Remember, no one wants your dreams to come true more than you. You have to be willing to work hard every day. There will be plenty of No's, but keep after your goals.

All it takes is one Yes. The last and most important thing I learned is "It's not whether you get knocked down; it's whether you get up."—Vince Lombardi

27 Simone Ciafardini

I never set out to work in the beauty industry. In fact, as a child I just always assumed I would be a famous. For what, it remained to be seen. It was through my failure to achieve fame that I stumbled on my career. My story is not unique, but it's mine; bunions and all.

I grew up in circumstances of sheer unadulterated boredom. Living in the average family and attending average schools. My family was, in my mind, dull as dishwater. Kind, decent, hard working and honest, but at the time it felt as if I was stuck with a painfully ordinary family. It would take decades before I realized how unique and special they are. Unfortunately, at the time they did not inspire me to achieve anything more than what we already had—comfort. I didn't want to live a "Hush Puppy" existence. I craved heights.

I was adopted at 6 months old, aware of this fact from the age of 5. I was certain that my birth parents were people of stature and eccentric character. My imaginary parents often took on real identities. Jack Nicolson and Angelica Houston were my predominant fantasy. How else could I explain an incendiary desire to be more than a sum of my surroundings?

On my 16th birthday, I found myself employed and enjoying a stiletto-induced growth spurt.

Thom McAn hot pink, 5-inch high, plastic, with a bow in the back: my very first shoe purchase. My mother was mortified. I was elated and in agony. I loved these shoes more than anything I owned up to that point in my life. They were so shiny; the kind of illumination that eludes real leather. I just knew I had to work in that shoe store and I learned a lot there. For example, plastic stilettos are a certain path to blisters and bunions, children's shoes pay far less commission than Timberlands and never open a shoe box in front of a client before checking the contents. (My introduction to off-colored office humour)

With these lessons under my belt, I moved onto the beauty industry at a small department store, Steinbecks. I was the beauty consultant for Germaine Monteil and Ultima II. My passion was so great that I came to work hours early and left well after my schedule dictated. It wasn't that the position demanded such dedication, mind you. We had maybe 4-10 clients a day. I just loved being around the stuff. I could spend hours rearranging the case lines, practicing my application skills on cleaning staff, counting and re-counting my merchandise. When the store manager approached me and said she wasn't going to pay me over-time, I was dumbfounded. It had never occurred to me that I would get paid any more than my regular weekly salary. She was dumbfounded that I was truly that earnest. With an attitude like that, she quickly gave me more responsibility, a more impressive title and the same salary. I was positively thrilled.

Soon, the inevitable boredom of working at a place called "Steinbecks" seeped in. It was a year into my new position as Cosmetic Department Manager that we received an invitation to a Chanel fragrance seminar in New York City. Holding that training invitation in my hand left more of an indelible impression on me than the countless courses at community college. I had been to New York City only once, even though it was just 45 minutes from my home. Funnily, for all of my desire to see the world, to break out of my small town, New York City seemed unreachable, until I made my first trip.

I was 18 at the time. I didn't end up working for Chanel as it turned out, but I was fortunate enough to find a company that embodied everything I wanted my life to be associated with: style, integrity, composure, compassion and products that I use to this day—Clinique. I had never used their skin care formulations before my interview, but slowly, fell in love with them.

I moved into the city 3 months later. It never occurred to me that I had taken a step back in my career, going from Department Manager to beauty consultant. I also took a base salary drop without consideration. I knew that the commission would make up the difference and more.

At the time, the Clinique counter at Macy's Herald Square was the largest in size, sales volume and staff in the world. It became my universe. I became the Counter Manager. I got there early and left late. I unloaded thousands of cases of Facial Soap, Clarifying Lotion, Dramatically Different Moisturizing Lotion. I cleaned and re-merchandised hundreds of display cases and backdrops. I suffered uncountable bruises from drawers left open and a fractured nose from a customer who came across, quite by accident, her husband's pregnant lover whilst I was serving her. I was assisting the pregnant woman with a foundation shade selection when all of a sudden the wife jumped her from behind. I jumped over the counter and began pulling off the aggressor. In the heat of the moment, I became the target. In my crisp white Clinique lab coat now splattered with blood, I resembled a nurse in one of those 1970's horror flicks. At the time I was angry, but it taught me one important lesson in business. Know when to duck.

Shortly after that incident I was invited to a special Clinique training. It was to be conducted by the grand dame of all trainers, Iris Model. Iris was one of the original four employees when Clinique began in 1968. A tough as nails German woman, she didn't suffer fools or foes. In the room was another Clinique grand dame, Deborah Rebellido, my first fairy godmother. Deborah was the impossibly glamorous Vice President of Clinique International Training. Deborah and I clicked instantly. I confided that I had always wanted to live abroad. It was company lore that no one, absolutely no one, went from the US market to International. My first taste of corporate politics. Thankfully, I was somewhat oblivious to the turmoil that ensued. I had no idea the flack that she took for helping me achieve my goals. She took the heat and I took a job in London. I am forever grateful. I asked her years later why she took a risk on a kid she barely knew. She said she had never met anyone who loved their job more. She admired my "authenticity."

I arrived in the UK eager to start my job as Clinique trainer. My salary was half of what I was making in New York but I didn't care. I was living in London! I was a trainer! They bought me a one-way economy ticket and I brought with me whatever could fit into a suitcase.

Well into my second month in London, I invited my supervisor home. I was so proud until I saw her stunned expression. It was a very cold November. I remember the look on her kind, yet horrified face, when she realized that I had no blanket, a spoon and one frying pan.

The next week we were having a meeting with all of the trainers— or as we were called at Clinique, Education Managers—from around the United Kingdom. Debbie telephoned everyone about my meagre living conditions. On the first day of our meeting, eight beautifully coiffed Education Managers, eager to meet the crazy American with one spoon, came bearing duvets, waffle makers, pots and pans, and utensils. They also brought their friendship.

Over the next four years, those eight women taught me one of my most valuable lessons. Have a laugh and don't take it all so seriously; that is unless you really are curing cancer. I knew that I was going to be friends with these women for the rest of my life. I also knew I wanted to be British and to this day am a proud card-carrying anglophile.

I had it all. A wonderful job, wonderful friends, a wonderful life. But as everyone knows, with sugar come some lumps.

One night, at our company Christmas party, our Managing Director inquired how I was settling in. I was positively effusive going on and on about how I loved my job and my co-workers. I went on to say how I felt the UK surpassed its New York rival when it came to colleague camaraderie and communication. I walked right into what was to be my most painful lesson. Naively, I agreed to write a few bullet points summarizing my observations. I did so innocently only to have, unbeknownst to me, sentences added, points deleted and then the whole memo sent to the CEO in New York, with my name as author. I had no idea this had unfolded until a month later I telephoned to speak to some of my ex-colleagues in New York. It was too late. No explanation or apology ever repaired the relationships. My throat still swells to this day when this memory surfaces. I had been stabbed in the back with a blush brush. I knew then, I would never fully trust anyone in business unless, through time and deed, it was earned. I also knew I would never take advantage of anyone, no matter the windfall for me.

Outside of that fiasco, my other mishaps in the UK were charmingly quaint. With my American rah-rah spirit and frequent language mishaps, I was a great source of humor and, on occasion, motivation for our British Clinique Consultants. When I wasn't causing squeals with my misuse of words such as fanny, ride and getting pissed, I was dating completely inappropriate guys such as Jazz, the street performer. My roommate affectionately called him the street clown. That was short-lived when he picked me up from the office on a unicycle.

Living in the UK opened the world to me, literally. I had the opportunity to vacation in Spain, Germany, Malta. I fell in love with Paris and Milan and was no longer the girl from Long Island.

One very early morning, I was in our head office preparing my training room for a beginner's seminar later that day. It was then I met a man named Michel Grunberg, the Estee Lauder Corporate Europe/Middle East and Africa Managing Director for Travel Retailing (Duty Free). As Clinique was a part of the Estee Lauder corporate family, he had an office one floor above. It was 6:30 am and he was not accustomed to finding anyone in the office at this hour or the hour after. Watching me scrub the scuffs off the training room floor in my crisp white Clinique uniform entertained him greatly. Once I realized that I had an audience, I introduced myself. We hit it off right away. It turns out that he was looking for a trainer for Clinique Travel Retailing within his region and would I be interested. I knew I had to have this job.

I was still monolingual so many were skeptical, but it never dawned on me that I wouldn't get the job. Even when I found out that a multilingual colleague of mine was also vying for the position, I just knew I would get the job. I knew, because I wanted it more. I wanted it more than anything in the world. My love of the products, the Consultants, the company would transcend language. And it did.

I showed up to the interview in my gleaming white Clinique lab coat. All other applicants showed up in business suits. I suspect that because I had not even considered wearing anything but my uniform, worked in my favor. I was as authentically a devotee as you could find.

In this position, I travelled by air, ship, train and car to every major, and not so major, destination in Europe and the Middle East. I met sales people, princes, movie stars and mad men. I spoke English to the French about fragrance and English to the Germans about skincare.

A few years later it came to my attention that the trainer in the Asia/Pacific region for Clinique was leaving. I loved my job in Europe and couldn't believe my fortune up until now, but there it was, staring me in the face. Japan, China, Thailand, Singapore: far-off, exotic lands that I had only dreamed of. This career move only lasted just over a year as the 1997 Asian Financial Crisis loomed. With budgets frozen, it was time to make my next move.

Estee Lauder had recently acquired a company called Bobbi Brown Essentials. The woman who conducted the interview was an industry veteran, Maggie Ciafardini. Gorgeous, sharp and with little time on her hands, she hired me right away. Bobbi Brown needed a trainer in Europe.

I immediately moved back to London. Once set up there, I traveled to New York for the company orientation. On my first night, I was scheduled to have dinner with Maggie and her son, Dominic. I had met Dominic in Singapore a few years back. He was teaching tennis and had a girlfriend. I was teaching skincare and had a boyfriend. End of story. Well not quite the end.

Maggie canceled last minute and Dominic and I had one of the most memorable evenings of my life. He made me laugh so hard my stomach ached all throughout the next day. I fell in love with him that night and a few months later begged the powers-that-be for a transfer back to New York. We were married two years later. Maggie was my second fairy godmother.

Whilst working there, I met a man named Chris Salgardo who led me to one of the best career moves in my life—Kiehl's Since 1851.

Kiehl's was founded as an old-world apothecary in New York's Lower East Side. Chris was newly hired as Vice President and was looking to fill several newly created positions.

His boss, Michelle Taylor, was the president since L'Óreal purchased the brand from Jamie Morse Heidegger in April 2000. Another industry veteran, Michelle is one of the smartest, most inspirational and fiercely loyal women I have ever met. She hired me as Kiehl's first Assistant Vice President of Global Education. I called my mother and father and cried upon exiting the building. I had circled the globe and now I felt as if I owned it.

On September 11th, 2001, Michelle, myself and the Kiehl's management team were in Paris for the annual L'Óreal global management meeting. As soon as we arrived to the meeting site, we knew something dreadful had happened. Crowds gathered at every television screen to take in the horrific images. As soon as I saw the airplane crash into the North Tower, I knew Dominic's brother, Maggie's son, was gone.

I won't go into details as I don't believe I can add anything beneficial to this book to be gleaned from that truly tragic day. I will say that on that day, and for three days after, Michelle called every person she knew trying to get me home. She was a huge source of care and comfort. I arrived in New York on the very first flight given clearance to land at JFK. I knew that I would do anything for her and that she would be an important presence in my life, always.

Michelle eventually left Kiehl's to move back to her native California. In 2003, she contacted me to see if I would be interested in working with her and Guthy-Renker, the direct sales beauty behemoth. I would be partnering with the supermodel and television personality Heidi Klum to help create a truly visionary skin care line. She wanted the line to be affordable and accessible and understood that Guthy-Renker was one of the few companies that could make that happen.

That is where I came in. Michelle was aware that I had worked extensively for decades with numerous beloved brands, cutting edge laboratories and with some of the most prominent dermatologists, scientists and chemists in the world. I had first-hand experience with many of the world's most treasured skin care formulations and for decades had been in an on-going conversation with customers all over the globe talking about their needs and common skin frustrations. Michelle suspected that I would have not only a very clear idea of how to make the skin care line Heidi envisioned, but also have access to the labs that could see it to fruition.

As it turns out, Heidi and I had met once before during Fashion Week. I was one of the makeup artists at a show she was working at and inevitably we ended up talking about the products we loved. As one of the most sought-after models in the world, she has used more products than most women on the planet. What I love about Heidi is that she doesn't compromise and quite frankly can't see why any woman should have to. This is really the crux of her philosophy behind *In an Instant*, the skin care line that we co-created. I will never forget that it was my third fairy god mother, Michelle, who allowed me the opportunity to use the accumulation of my knowledge to help create what I truly believe to be one of the finest skin care lines in the world, and, at a cost that makes it accessible to so many women.

In many ways, success is very much like skin care. The perfect career can elude us like the perfect moisturizer. The trick is to know what you want, don't settle for less and never be fooled by a fancy jar or the endless shine of hot pink, 5-inch high, plastic stilettos with a bow in the back. Wrinkles and bunions are no fun.

I've spent 20 years in the beauty industry, training people all over the world. High school graduates to card-carrying MBA hot shots. The only people who became indispensable to the company were the employees who were already devotees to the product or service they represented. They were the employees who loved people and found fulfillment spreading the good word. You can't train people to have this passion, who don't have joy. It is innate.

Be a joy and find passion in your work. If the shoe fits, wear it with pride.

28 Lindsey Penrose

People often begin a speech or introduction with the sentiment "I want to thank my family, friends and loved ones". I guess there is good reason for that as family and friends partly shape who we are and I believe they have greatly contributed to my success thus far. I won't belabour this point about how much I love them and how they are such wonderful people but I will say "Thank you to the people that love me".

I believe that you should appreciate the people who love you and keep you grounded, because when you fall hard, the ones that love you will be there for you without reservation. No amount of fame, money or success can ever buy that degree of loyalty.

The Penrose chapter begins...
I knew from a young age that I wanted to be a leader, a role model, a CEO. I remember picturing myself standing in a board room, hair pulled back, wearing a sophisticated business suit, having the full attention of the room as I point at some complicated chart; ending the meeting with everyone in the room clapping and nodding their heads in approval. I soon understood life isn't always that glamorous...

I had just finished school and was working a full-time job. I knew at that point in time I really just wanted to be in business for myself. My entrepreneurial instincts were kicking in.

Then, somewhat unexpectedly, the Edmonton Chapter of my life began. I got the opportunity from an associate to move out to Edmonton and work for a finance company. I was very excited, although anxious, but I took the offer and began to move out West. At this point in time, Edmonton was experiencing a major economic 'boom'.

I worked hard at my position at the company, although I realized it wasn't where I wanted to be, I wanted to give Edmonton a try. I started a company with two partners involved in land assembly while living in Edmonton and concentrated on learning the business and structuring deals. I was pretty much broke and on my last dime hoping I could close a transaction.

I remember standing in line at a hole in the wall café waiting to pay for my egg salad sandwich. I sat down on a plastic chair to eat my boring sandwich. Hey, at least it was better than Mr. Noodles, which I feared I would have to eat for a very long time unless this deal closed.

That's when the call came in. Typing this actually brings tears to my eyes.

My partners and I had closed our first deal!!!

We continued to have success in land assembly for the next year and a half and had assembled over 2000 acres of land by then. I learned a lot about money and that with money came jealousy, greed, harsh decisions and betrayal. It's very important to stay humble and realize that money doesn't buy happiness.

I learned some very valuable lessons about money. Especially, when I found out someone I thought was a dear true friend and someone I trusted, stepped on me to get ahead. And all for what? Money? The major lesson, for me, is that I won't compromise my integrity and morality over money. I believe that it is always better to do the right thing, even if it means I damage my own personal "payday". I pride myself in being an honest, loyal, hard-working person. I have learned that in business there is a great deal of corruption and dishonesty. It's very important to keep your core values intact. I also think it's important to identify a mentor in your career. A mentor is very important; someone you can learn from, respect and admire. Sometimes, the lessons a true mentor provides may be harsh and may illuminate deficiencies we don't want to see in ourselves. However, a true mentor who sees you as a protégé can help distill all the confusing and sometimes complex factors which challenge us into the more important issues we must deal with as executives. Sometimes, the most convoluted situations can be broken down into a very simple decision.

I am truly grateful for the experiences I have had, for the people who have helped me become successful and for the hardships that have made me stronger.

The Penrose Group Today

We are now on the verge of expanding. We have recently closed several deals of varying types in the real estate, M&A and finance industry. I am proud of what my team and I have accomplished. I am privileged to be working with the companies and clients I am associated with today. The real message that I want to make sure I accurately portray to every girl or boy that has a dream or goal they are trying to pursue is to TRY AND DO IT! Have no fear. Take the necessary steps to fulfill your dreams, whatever they may be. Everything takes work but if you are truly passionate about something then get motivated and start doing it. Do you want to open a business? Ask yourself: "What are the first steps?" Do you want to learn a language? What are the first steps? Do you want to travel? What are the first steps? Then, figure out time lines. How much time in a day will it take you to get started. How much money do you need to save to pursue your goals? Who do you know in the area who can assist you or give you advice? Are there grants available to help you succeed?

Lack of motivation will kill any goals or dreams a person may have, and, we have all been victims of demotivation at one point or another.

What keeps me motivated is the 'Art of the Deal'. I love the problem solving, the negotiating, the rapport building and the emotion vs. logic psychology involved in most business dealings. I enjoy the new information I learn from different types of deals, and then figuring out how to apply that knowledge into other areas. The entire process of starting a project and taking it through to completion gives me a feeling of satisfaction that I have not been able to replicate. It's very rewarding to know that when a transaction you initiated actually closes, you've changed people's lives and the course of their business forever; and usually for the better. Of course, making money is also a great feeling, when it happens (and it doesn't every time), but as discussed, that's merely part of the game. The broader picture is more important. Having loosely touched on some of the areas I feel are most important for anyone, especially any woman, looking to embark into the world of business on their own, my hope is that my story will serve as both a source of motivation, and as a point of reference for budding entrepreneurs everywhere.

29 Joan Kelley

People define success in many different ways. To me, success is how you get to where you are going, not the final destination itself. The challenge in life is to be true to yourself, to be a good person, to support your community, to be honest and trustworthy, to be a loyal friend and to be able to look in the mirror and be happy about the way you conduct yourself. Many people use titles to define success. Titles are necessary but should not be the ultimate goal in life, because I have found that often, when you achieve one goal, you are ready to move on to the next one and no longer want to be defined by the original title. For example, over the course of my life, I have worked in many different jobs and many different careers. It is human nature for colleagues and people you don't know well to define you according to your job. Don't allow that to happen. You are much bigger than that. Never stop growing and changing and improving yourself. Try to have a career that inspires and stimulates you. If you are not in that position right now, try to make the best of it and be the best at what you are doing right now while setting yourself up for something better. Remember to think of work as a means to an end and stay focussed. You need to take responsibility for yourself. There is no one out there waiting to take you from a lousy job to make you a superstar. You need to create your own destiny. That is the way it works.

Time is the most valuable commodity in life. Be careful with it. No one can be critical of how you spend your time. Meet your responsibilities but always make time for yourself. You need to recharge yourself by doing things that focus on you.

I graduated high school with a very vague goal of what I wanted to do for a career. Under 'ambition' in my high school yearbook, I wrote 'to find one'. The truth is that I wanted to work in TV, radio, film, modelling, acting, broadcasting; anything to get me out of the small town life. I was embarrassed to admit that I wanted to do these things. I felt like people would think I was conceited or something. There was a lot of peer pressure to conform to local things to do after high school. None were in my radar. I didn't realize that the things I wanted were easily within my grasp and that there is nothing wrong with going out on your own and doing something that was way outside the norm of my classmates.

As I look back on it now, I realize how silly it was for me to think that way. After all, that is a valid career choice, in a valid industry. My mistake was that I didn't do my own researching and planning, that I didn't spend enough time trying to find how to get started. My advice if you are starting out is to get busy and do your research. Ask anyone who has worked in related fields about their experience. Read books about the industry, do life planning charts, volunteer in the field, ask questions. See if there is a course you can take and if you can find a mentor. Be willing to work hard, put in lots of time, show that you are a positive person and are serious about reaching your goal. Clearly define what that goal is. A huge obstacle for me was that in my small town I was met with a negative or neutral reaction when I expressed what I wanted to do. In career days at school there was no mention of the arts or broadcast as a career. In hind sight, I should have pushed harder to discover my options.

When I was 16, a model scout came to the closest city to my small town. I managed to meet with him. It got the ball rolling for me but I learned that things are often not as you expect them to be. It's a process and you have to be open to all options and be realistic about your expectations.

Another really important thing to always remember is to never compare yourself with others. There will always be people that have more and less than you. Being in the modelling world, I made a huge mistake of pressuring myself to always be skinnier or prettier. It all backfired and I ended up with huge weight gain and I felt horrible. Believe me it didn't do much to help my confidence! Food is not for comfort. Food is for fuel. Period. Be sensible about that. It's very simple. If you eat too much or the wrong kinds of food, you gain weight. You have to exercise. It's true what they say, diet and exercise really work. You not only look better, you feel better. Its embarrassing to have extra pounds so deal with it. I learned that I had to get off my lazy feeling-sorry-for-myself butt and get active.

Young girls are really hard on themselves and on each other. I did get the weight off, but to this day, I have to work hard to keep it off. That's nothing to be ashamed of. Weight can play a huge role in self-esteem. I had some low moments as the scale rose. And pretty happy moments as the scale dropped. It is not good to define your self-esteem on a scale, but I am definitely much happier if I am in the comfort zone of my weight and fitness level. What is important is to find balance in your life. Dieting and working out should make you feel great. They should not be a crutch or the way you define yourself.

Something I feel very strongly about is smoking cigarettes or taking drugs. There is nothing good about it. Watch your alcohol intake. I am all up for a good time but really, there's nothing less attractive than a sloppy drunk chick and there's nothing good about taking drugs.

Meanwhile, as I muddled my way along, I did manage to get a good agent, which was pretty easy after I had lost the weight. Affording good photographers to shoot my portfolio was another issue seeing as I was supporting myself entirely. I supplemented my income by working as a waitress, which was not my favourite thing to do, but I did manage to make some good friends and to finally get to know my way around Toronto. As a young girl, on my own, far from home this was already an accomplishment. Allow yourself to enjoy all accomplishments along the way, no matter how small.

As you are going through your life and trying to get your career going, be open to and seek out mentors. Do not have a 'know it all attitude', ask questions and be open to criticisms and advice. I've had a few mentors in my day. They have been invaluable in moving my career along. They believed in me even when I didn't. They had a vision for me and gave me opportunities I never would have come upon myself. Mentors are very important. If someone agrees to help you, take it seriously and appreciate what they are doing for you. Work hard and always have a good attitude. Don't be afraid or too proud to start at the bottom. Take it seriously, keep your eyes open and show your dedication.

I'd like to share with you one experience that I learned a great deal from. I got a job as a morning anchor on a show in Toronto. It was a new show and had lots of growing pains. I was to be on air from 5–9 am each day but I had to be there at 3 am to pre-record a couple of segments. So I had to get up at 2:20 am, which was a tough schedule indeed. I was given very little training.

There were all kinds of technical problems. Sometimes, I would throw to another person and due to technical problems, they wouldn't be there. I had to kill time on live TV. It was far from ideal. The energy in the studio was uncomfortable day after day. Needless to say, my confidence plummeted. I may have been giving a stellar performance but I FELT like I was really bad! Mostly, because I wanted to be so good and I felt like I had no tools. It was really embarrassing to be live on TV every morning and not feel like I was doing a good job. I felt very stifled. But here's the good part: I learned that it was wrong of me to not speak up for myself. I should have gone straight up to the top, to the owners of the company and explained how unprepared I felt and what a shamble the show was. I should have asked for more support and told them of all the behind-the-scene problems with the show. I did not do this, much to my regret today.

I also learned that if I don't feel right about it, it would show on camera so I have to be in the right mental state to do the best job. I have a high standard for my level of performance. I will not let incompetence by any company or person stand in my way any more. Of course, at the time, people who watched the show would tell me it was fine but I knew in my gut it wasn't a good fit for me. I was also trying to protect the people I was working with and didn't want to be the one to tattle on their deficiencies. But there is a difference between being a tattle tale and being realistic about a professional situation that could be a lot better. There is a time in life to stand up for yourself. This was one of those times for me and I wish I had handled it more aggressively.

After that ended, I came upon a friend of a friend, Mike Hogan, who worked at a radio station, The FAN 590. He mentioned they needed a traffic person and he set up a meeting for me. So the next thing I know I am working as a traffic announcer on the Fan 590 and for the sister station Easy Rock 97.3. At Easy Rock, I also did live remotes, put together special reports called 'the Heart Beat Report', which meant I was travelling around the city to events and calling them in live. I clearly remember the first time I went live with my report. I was sitting in the Easy Rock van. I had written my own script. My heart was pounding and I felt flush so much that it was distracting noticing my own physical reaction to my nerves and mostly my pounding heart! I got through it and the next live hit was a bit less nerve racking and the one after that even less so. Eventually, I really came to enjoy the thrill. I loved the performance element and because there was writing and researching involved, it was something I enjoyed. Over the next eight years, I continued to enjoy working in radio in Toronto.

Being me and never quite having enough on my plate, I started up my own production company 'HERO MEDIA'. Now, I hire other freelancers. I never hesitate to give a break to someone who shows promise, enthusiasm and drive, someone who is serious about doing a great job to prove themselves to me and to others.

For the past few years, I have hosted a show called Red Carpet Diary. Another great gig where I get to interview movie stars, like Ben Affleck, Colin Firth, Ryan Reynolds, Kevin Spacey, Eva Mendes and Jennifer Garner (I have a very long list but you get the point). Now, I am at the stage in my life and career where I am able to be selective of the jobs I choose to do. This one is great, because I am able to use a lot of my skills all at once. It is challenging and fun. I still love to be able to dabble in a few jobs at the same time. I love the interviewing. I love seeing a project from beginning to end, looking at it from all angles, wearing different hats, so to speak. I am happy that all these elements build on one another. To some people, my career may have seemed a bit disjointed, but now it has all come together to make sense. Therefore, another lesson is to hang in there, because things will become clear eventually. If your gut is telling you to stick with something and you are not quite sure of the direction, don't discount your instincts. They are powerful if you are true to yourself.

After re-reading my story, I realize how blessed I have been. There are a lot of people in this world, who have huge obstacles to overcome before they reach success. I am fortunate in that I come from an exceptionally great family. My parents have been married for over 51 years! It is good to celebrate all accomplishments in life like anniversaries, birthdays, babies, promotions—anything to support the people in our lives and our loved ones. I didn't come from a refugee camp or experienced abuse or anything extreme, but I did have my own hurdles as we all do. It's the way you approach things that will define you. The perfect example of this for me is my mom, whom I adore. She was diagnosed with multiple sclerosis when she was only twenty six years old. She went on to marry and have my sister and I. She has not been without her own very difficult challenges, but if you were to meet her and ask "how are you doing?" she would always say "fine, just fine!" Her attitude is to never inflict her pain on anyone, because it wouldn't help the situation. She would never want to be seen as the one who is the downer in the room, rather, someone who always does her best no matter what. And that is something I aspire to. That is something I want to teach my own children. My mom has taught me that it's not what you are given, it's how you handle it that shows your true colors. It would be very easy to wallow in the pain of the situation, but it is a choice you make. My advice to you is to make a positive choice like my mom. When you make a positive choice, it reinforces positive thoughts in your own brain. Thoughts are things. You are your thoughts. Choose to make them good, for your own benefit and for the benefit of those around you. It is like a ripple effect.

Another thing I want to mention is that we as Canadians are truly blessed to be in such a wonderful, free country. When you get a chance to travel the world, you realize how very fortunate we are. Don't take that for granted, you are privileged.

My husband has always been a huge supporter of World Vision. I ended up hosting a series of national infomercials for World Vision. I donated my fee back to World Vision. A great opportunity presented itself for me to travel to some far reaching places like Rwanda, Kenya, Costa Rica, Tanzania, Mozambique and South Africa with World Vision. I was able to meet several of the children we sponsor and to see how they live. It is a very concrete example of how privileged we are, but it also drove the point home to me that we are all very similar as people who inhabit the globe. Mothers all over the world, no matter what their circumstances, all want what is best for their children, a better life. They want to keep a good, safe home for their families. Young girls want to find a love, that is loyal and kind to them. People love their families and their friends. The people I met have been dealt a different hand from me. But I noticed that these people for the most part have made their own choices to be positive and happy and make the best of their situation even though many that I met were affected by or infected by HIV/AIDS and extreme poverty. I believe it is a social responsibility we all have to help support others whether it is in our own community or abroad. It can be done by volunteering your time in your community, through your church or school or by sponsoring a child. However you decide, it is a great feeling to help others.

My advice to my own kids, my daughter, my niece, and to you, is to hold firmly onto your integrity, be gentle with people and yourself. Don't be afraid to strive for your dreams, no matter how they are perceived by others. Keep trying. Be consistent. Be true to yourself. Someone told me once that life is not how it is supposed to be, it is how it is. Make the most of it. You are your own guardian.

30 Miranda Furtado

I have one of the coolest jobs around. I am a style/entertainment editor for one of Canada's largest newspaper companies and a regular face on one of Canada's largest news channels.

Sure, my title may seem glamorous and it is most of the time, but life hasn't always been easy. In fact, I've pushed rock and stone to get to where I am. From the outside, most people see me as a beautiful girl, who has her life in order and everything going for her, but truly, my life has been anything but.

I guess we should start at the beginning, right? Since day one, I've had my fair share of setbacks. I was born with a cleft palate. Within hours of my birth, I was rushed to Sick Kids Hospital, where they would learn that I would suffer for years to come. By the age of two, I had already undergone my first surgery to repair my condition, but that was only the beginning of a long road ahead of me.

While most kids spent their days in school, only missing class for the odd sickness, I spent mine through various check-ups and visits to the hospital where I would go through tests and training to correct my speech impediment and wonky smile. I would spend hours commuting downtown with my parents to sit at doctor's offices and dental waiting rooms to fix my problems. "Peter Piper picked a pack of pickled peppers" is what I remember saying over and over again until the air coming out of my nose was at the right consistency.

The kids at school never understood what I was going through—and how could they? I was so young; I barely knew what was going on myself. I was pretty lucky though, despite the circumstances. My parents were well off; we lived a comfortable life in the country. Living in such a rural area didn't make for the up-to-date gossip queen that I am now, but instead made me the black sheep at school. I was the weird girl with frizzy hair, braces and a mouse-voice who didn't know who New Kids on the Block were.

Instead of spending my days watching after-school specials, I was forced to make my own fun (I am proud to say that I was one of the first kids in my school that knew how to cook, build a fire, and find a mean tobogganing hill!) I was a guy's girl; always outside playing or, when I spent time with my mother, I learned arts and crafts and the skill of sewing. I never had the trendy clothing. I made due with what was available.

I was always left to earn things on my own. Everything I ever wanted, I had to earn. I hated it. All the time. If I wanted something, my parents always made me put some effort into getting it. If I broke my jump rope, I was out in the backyard picking up bee-covered crab apples the next day to earn the money for a new one.

Funny enough, this kind of molded me into who I am today. I ended up getting creative and really honing in on my sewing skills. (If they weren't going to buy something for me, damn it, I was still going to get it somehow!) I used to spend hours at thrift stores (you know, before vintage shopping was cool) and I would just buy things that either I could alter and make cool or buy it for the fabric and create something new altogether.

My parents are two *very* different people. My dad: business oriented, straight to the point and not very family-oriented (thankfully, he's a changed man now, though.) My mother: artsy, passionate and family first. While both sides have their pros and cons, I'm happy to say that I'm a healthy mix between the two. Unfortunately, this yin-yang relationship didn't end up lasting.

Life started its downward spiral when we moved out of the country and into town. I'm not entirely sure what happened, but it felt like we were playing 'Keeping up with the Jones.' We moved into a big house, had the cool cars and were always in the market for the next best thing. Just because you buy the big glamorous house doesn't mean that it's a home. When we moved in, we didn't even paint. We just left it, as it was— someone else's palace.

During my grade eight graduation, while I was out celebrating, my mom took the opportunity to tell my dad that she wanted a divorce. No one saw it coming. My parents never fought—ever. From the outside looking in, it looked like the perfect family set-up, but deep down inside, I knew it was inevitable.

My mom gained custody and had me—most of the time. That whole "every-other weekend" plan didn't really work out. I can count on one hand how many times my dad took me in a year and when he did, would often toss a handful of cash in my pocket and point me in the direction of the nearest mall. Needless to say, I started to rebel and that's a major understatement. I skipped class, dyed my hair every colour of the rainbow and decided that my mother was the worst human being on Earth. On top of it, I couldn't stand those four walls that they called high school. I despised it. I made my parents' lives a living hell.

In retrospect, I have to give my mom props. She's a smart woman and she has had my back, despite the situations that I got myself into. No one could understand why I was acting the way I was—and neither could I at the time—or I just didn't feel like telling anyone what was going on. My head was a mess, my emotions were all over the place and the only feeling of happiness that I ever felt was when I was skipping school and hanging out with the very few friends that I did have. Being inside of a classroom was the last place I wanted to be. Kids taunted me, made fun of me and tried anything to make my life worse. No one knew what I was dealing with and I didn't want them to. I was living my own personal nightmare, over and over again and felt like there was no way to wake up from it.

My high school horror stories weren't confined to the brick and mortar of the building, either. I received late night phone calls, death threats and was even chased around the school, numerous times, by a gang of girls who wanted to beat me up. It was the first time that my mom had realized what I had been going through for so many years. Things were never that bad for me and I needed out. I quickly learned that skipping class wasn't the answer; I landed myself in summer school. Funny enough, summer school ended up being a savior at this point. Through my time with a shrink, it was suggested that I may be suffering from ADD.

That summer was my first experience with Ritalin. I had no idea what to expect. I gave it a solid try for a week or so and hated it. It made me feel like someone I wasn't. It played with my mind, in fact, I physically felt different while I was on it. My diagnosis was still a very new concept for my mother. Instead of forcing me to take it, she gave me the choice and told me "If it doesn't feel right, you don't need to take it." I think it was that freedom that led me to give it another try. I tested out my soon-to-be best friend while killing time and making up credits at summer school. It was like night and day. I went from being the dummy at the back of the classroom, to the brainiac sitting in the front row getting 70's and 80's (this was a big step from my 32.5% average!) I felt like a whole new person! I was happier than I had ever been. For once in my life, I felt like I was normal and fitting in.

Sadly, summer school didn't last forever and I was faced with going back to high school where girls would be waiting to kick my ass. I had loved my new out-of-town summer school so much, I couldn't bear the thought of returning to the place that was a living hell and the root of so many problems for me. I needed a change—and change was what I was going to get—no matter what. I knew that if I didn't get out of that school, I wouldn't have survived and/or graduated. I was going nowhere fast. After a long talk with my mom, I finally convinced her that switching schools was the best option for me and if she agreed to help me with this, I would indeed go to all of my required classes (and hey, how was I supposed to skip if I didn't even live in that town anyways?) I'd like to let you believe that it was an easy change, but it wasn't. I was contractually obligated to go to every class, required to have every teacher sign a piece of paper each day saying that I attended their class or else I would be booted out, back to my old school.

Between my new love of learning (thanks to Ritalin), my new set of rules and fresh start—I was pumped. It wasn't long until I began to fit in and it was completely surreal. Here I was, this girl who went from having three friends in her previous high school to knowing almost everyone. It was crazy. It felt as if I fell down a rabbit hole like Alice in Wonderland. I loved it. I found myself actually enjoying school and participating. I was no longer at the bottom of the grade point average, but instead, was at the top. I found time to participate in stuff that I never thought I would. I was the VP of Student Council, I was on the soccer team, Sports Athletic Committee, Yearbook Committee and I was rewarded for all of my hard effort. I was nominated for a slew of awards.

When it came time to figure out what I wanted to do for college, I was lost. There were so many things that I was interested in, but I had no idea how to narrow it down. With a bit of soul searching and some guidance from my mom, I went back to the basics. I thought about what I enjoyed doing as a kid, what my passions were, what my skills were and combined them into the perfect solution—well almost perfect solution— fashion. I began interning downtown Toronto, full day co-op and making the most of what I wanted to become. Little did I know that there were so many avenues in this fascinating career choice. For a girl who once had an average of 32.5%, it was a huge surprise when I was accepted into all five of my program choices. I opted for the Fashion Arts program at Humber College's business campus. This was a fit for me with a two-year program, three semesters of short internships, I couldn't have asked for more. This was my calling. College, for me, was easy. For once, it felt like we were being treated like adults and had the freedom to make or break our opportunities.

Sadly, however, I was hit with another major blow. My grandmother was diagnosed with bone cancer. When I could, I would spend my nights at the hospital visiting and keeping her company. Despite such a crappy circumstance, I made it work. I knew that my grandma was proud to see me make it to college so I did the best that I could.

I've always said that things happen for a reason and sometimes, and whether you see it or not, bad thing happen, so then you can appreciate the good. Ironically, on the day of my grandma's funeral, I received a phone call from a company offering me the perfect internship position at Snowboard Canada (SBC Media). To this day, I still like to think that my grandma made it happen.

Remember when I told you earlier that I've worked for everything that I've gotten? Well, here's a perfect example. When I say that I loved this placement I mean it. I found myself going in on my days off, working extra hours; doing whatever I needed to do to make a name for myself. I guess that showed when I ended up doing 152 hours instead of the 50 required hours and I still maintain some of these working friendships to this day.

During one of my overtime shifts, when I was, yet again, going above and beyond the call of duty at a movie premiere, we ended up grabbing drinks. I ended up meeting the Director of Marketing for West 49. Who knew that one beer could open so many doors? Just a few weeks later, I found myself walking through the West 49 head office doors for my first, real, big girl job interview.

I was floored and, needless to say, I kicked ass in that interview (perhaps it was the years of making excuses to teachers, or coming up with thick plotlines of why I skipped yet another class, but thinking on my feet and pulling things out of my ass, has always been my thing.) With one week left in my first year of college, I found myself looking down at my first-ever job offer. It wasn't much, but to me, it felt like I had achieved something great. I stayed with the company for a few years. If it wasn't for this position, I'm not sure how successful I would be today. It wasn't my favorite job ever, but it taught me a lot and gave me good insight on what to look for in a job and what to avoid. It built up my character.

After serving nearly three years at the office, I was headed out west to Whistler, BC. Why Whistler you ask? Well, it had always been a dream of mine, and after spending a few years in the career world, I felt like it was time to move on. I took a step down in my career and ended up working at store level in a management position. Hey, it was a free pass, guaranteed hours and had kick-ass staff.

Housing in Whistler isn't always easy to come by, and sometimes it takes a horrible landlord for you to realize that it's time to make a move (seriously, he used to show up and sleep on my couch!) The Olympics were just around the corner and I ended up giving up my dog in order to find a place to live. Surprisingly, like another act of fate, the amazing lady who ended up taking him found me by accident. I chocked it up to another twist of fate, because, wouldn't you know it—that wasn't the last time I was going to see her.

After a few years in the work world, and a season in the mountains, I decided to move back to Ontario and complete my last year of college—I mean it was about damn time. Who takes five years to complete a two-year course?

One of my girlfriends, who also dropped out at the same time, decided to return at the same time. It seemed like a million years since we had last been there. Things had changed; we were the older students in class; older students with experience. We kicked that college course's ass, if I do say so myself. Sure, it was hard getting along with students who seemed like babies to us at the time, but we made it work. Again, I went above and beyond with class projects and assignments, but it was the fateful encounter of my Whistler days that turned my life upside down. The woman who took my dog would turn out to be the Director of Marketing for a large company in Whistler. And that large company happened to be looking for a new host to appear on camera for 10 days for the TELUS World Ski and Snowboard Festival.

In order to apply, I had to make a YouTube video, saying why I wanted to become the "Face of the Festival". Thankfully, from my media training from West 49, I was a natural. Combine that with my fashion background, living in Whistler and my knack to crack a good joke, I ended up becoming 1 of 5 finalists. I did everything to win this thing. I made the most ridiculous videos and submissions to get votes, but I guess something worked out, because I ended up securing 4000 of 8000 votes which were split between five people. Hosting was a blast. I partied like a rock star, interviewed world-class musicians and athletes and had the ability to do what came naturally to me—host. Somewhere along the lines, someone took notice. One of the main sponsors, and now my current employer Dose.ca/Postmedia Network, ended up contacting me and asked me to interview for a new position as style and social networking editor for their website. A few months and a couple of interviews later, I was hired. I still pinch myself once in a while. Who knew a girl who came from such a troubled beginning would be on-air and writing about celebrities, attending red carpet events and interviewing stars to make a living?!